The Landscape of
Leadership
Preparation

To George M. Murphy

The Landscape of
Leadership
Preparation

Reframing the Education of School Administrators

Joseph Murphy

CORWIN PRESS, INC.
P. O. Box 2526
Newbury Park, CA 91319-8526

For information address:

Corwin Press, Inc.
A Sage Publications Company
2455 Teller Road
Newbury Park, California 91320

SAGE Publications Ltd.
6 Bonhill Street
London EC2A 4PU
United Kingdom

SAGE Publications India Pvt. Ltd.
M-32 Market
Greater Kailash I
New Delhi 110 048 India

Printed in the United States of America

Library of Congress Cataloging-in-Publication Data

Murphy, Joseph, 1949-
  The landscape of leadership preparation : reframing the education of school administrators / Joseph Murphy.
       p. cm.
  Includes bibliographical references (p.   ) and index.
  ISBN 0-8039-6027-1 (cl).— ISBN 0-8039-6028-X (pb)
  1. School administrators—Training of —United States.
2. Educational leadership—United States. 3. School management and organization—United States. I. Title.
LB1738.5.M87   1992
370.7'60973—dc20   92-16959

The paper in this book meets the specifications for permanence of the American National Standards Institute and the National Association of State Textbook Administrators.

92 93 94 95   10 9 8 7 6 5 4 3 2 1

Corwin Press Production Editor: Tara S. Mead

Contents

Preface

This book is designed to help inform the debate on administrator preparation and to provide material for shaping new designs for the education of tomorrow's school leaders.

The book is directed first toward those who are directly involved in the preparation of school leaders: university professors; leadership center staff; and professional development personnel housed in state departments, regional offices, and school districts. It is also intended to be of interest to all of us who have been on the receiving end of certification and degree programs in departments of education administration, especially those seeking explanations for their less-than-helpful training experiences and those wishing to participate in the debate about better forms of preparation. Those interested in the development of teachers may find Chapters 3-6 especially helpful. Finally, those involved in educating men and women for governmental and corporate positions may be interested in the material on the historical evolution of administrative training and on the new vision of leadership preparation.

The design of the volume is based on the belief that three broad areas need to be addressed in order to reach tenable conclusions about appropriate preparation for tomorrow's school leaders: a deep understanding of the history of preparation; a thorough review of the strengths and weaknesses of current programs; and a vision about the future of good education, schooling, and leadership. The first chapter charts the path to be followed in the book. Particular attention is devoted to overviewing pressures for the reform of leadership and leadership preparation and to providing caveats to hold in mind as the analysis unfolds. The next two chapters furnish an historical context. Chapter 2 focuses on the ideological and prescriptive eras—all that transpired before 1945—while Chapter 3 attends to the behavioral science era (1946-1985) and the emerging dialectic era. Chapter 4 follows this analysis with an in-depth examination of the current state of affairs in preparation programs. A similar format is employed in Chapters 2 through 4 to help the reader see how particular preparation strands (e.g., program content, faculty) have evolved over time. The final two chapters look forward. Chapter 5 discusses the future of schooling and leadership while Chapter 6 provides the construction material—goals and principles—to develop preparation programs for tomorrow's school leaders.

Acknowledgments are in order. To begin with, I would like to extend special thanks to the two people who were responsible for the production aspects of this volume. Jane A. Hale, Associate Professor of French and Comparative Literature at Brandeis University, did a magnificent job of editing the original manuscript. Laraine Caldwell demonstrated unparalleled skills in the actual preparation of the volume. I am deeply grateful for both of their contributions.

In writing this volume, I was profoundly influenced by the work of a large number of scholars from divers areas of study. The reference section reveals the extent of my debt.

Support for this research was provided by the National Center for Educational Leadership (NCEL) under U.S. Department of Education Contract No. R 117C8005. The views in this report are those of the authors and do not necessarily represent those of the sponsoring institution nor the Universities in the NCEL Consortium—The University of Chicago, Harvard University, and Vanderbilt University.

Finally, I would like to thank Vanderbilt University and the National Center for Educational Leadership (NCEL) for their support for all aspects of the work that went into this volume.

Joseph Murphy
Vanderbilt University

About the Author

Joseph Murphy is Professor and Chair in the Department of Educational Leadership at Peabody College of Vanderbilt University. He is also a Senior Research Fellow with the National Center for Educational Leadership. His work focuses on the issue of school improvement, with particular interest in the role that school administrators play in that process. Recent books include: *Approaches to Administrative Training*, edited with Philip Hallinger (1987); *The Reform of American Public Education in the 1980s: Perspectives and Cases* (1990); and *Restructuring Schools: Capturing and Assessing the Phenomena* (1991). Forthcoming volumes include: *A Cognitive Perspective on Educational Administration*, edited with Philip Hallinger and Kenneth Leithwood; *Restructuring Schooling: Learning From Ongoing Experiences*, edited with Philip Hallinger; and *Understanding the Principalship: A Metaphorical Analysis From 1920-1990*, with Lynn Beck.

Epigraph

As professors of educational administration, we might start by taking ourselves and our students seriously. The research and development of administrative technology is not a trivial job. University programs in educational administration have a responsibility to develop those skills and to train administrators who have the ability to use them. Major problems in analysis remain to be solved for administrators; major techniques remain to be developed; major limitations remain to be discovered. The task is large enough to occupy our talents for a long time. The intellectual challenge is significant; the technical demands are impressive; success is not certain. The job needs a high order of imagination, technical knowledge, and self-confidence. (March, 1974, p. 43)

We have the wherewithal within our ranks to use our collective energies to consider and develop a systematic response to the future that is all encompassing—a response that enables us to consider not only what we know at present, but what the long-range implications are in terms of our expectations for the future. (Scribner, 1991, p. 5)

One

Charting the Path

> There is, then, pressure either to get rid of administrators as we now know them, or to take people untarnished by departments of educational administration. While this is the rumbling, the criticisms of present-day administrators and their preparation are loud and clear and the demand for reform is heard on all sides. While some of the criticism is overstated, and certainly all does not apply to everyone, I find the central thrust to be accurate, and, in fact, to coincide with what so many in the profession have been saying in private for years. (Griffiths, 1988b, p. 8)

Prior to the mid-1980s, the reform movement that swept across the educational landscape left educational administration largely untouched. As late as 1985, Peterson and Finn were still able to report:

> at a time when the nation is deeply concerned about the performance of its schools, and near-to-obsessed with the credentials and careers of those who teach in them, scant attention has been paid to the preparation and qualifications of those who lead them. (1985, p. 42)

Since that time, however, considerably more attention has been devoted to the analysis of educational leadership in general and to training programs in particular. Two specific events seemed to galvanize interest in examining preparation for school leaders: the work of the National Commission on Excellence in Educational Administration (NCEEA), with its subsequent reports (Griffiths, Stout, & Forsyth, 1988a; National Commission on Excellence in Educational

1

Administration [NCEEA], 1987); and the report of the National Policy Board for Educational Administration (NPBEA) (National Policy Board for Educational Administration [NPBEA], 1989a). The products of these two groups, although subject to criticism from a variety of quarters,[1] captured much of the prevailing disenchantment with existing preparation programs and laid out some ideas about how the situation could be improved. The University Council for Educational Administration's (UCEA) report on the professoriate in educational administration (McCarthy, Kuh, Newell, & Iacona, 1988) and the National Society for the Study of Education's 1990 yearbook on school leadership (Mitchell & Cunningham, 1990) also helped fuel discussions about the actual and desired conditions of preparation programs in educational administration. Concurrently, reform efforts began to unfold throughout the country.[2] Assisted in large part by support from the Danforth Foundation,[3] a handful of individual programs and a few states[4] began the difficult process of overhauling the methods used to train prospective school leaders.

Suggestions for improvement in the profession and in the procedures used to prepare school leaders were not limited, however, to documents internal to the field. As the educational reform movement of the early 1980s began to mature, it became increasingly apparent that questions about the role of educational leadership in school improvement were too significant to be left unattended by the larger educational community. National reports and studies that had been relatively quiet on the issue of school administration five years earlier suddenly had a good deal to say (J. Murphy, 1990c). These more general reform documents uncovered many of the same problems in educational leadership and leadership preparation programs as did the more educational administration-specific reports noted above. Some, however, parted company from these administration-specific reports in the solutions they envisioned. Many of the general reform documents maintained that educational leaders were an important component of the larger reform movement, asserting that educational leaders were the gatekeepers of change and that, without their support, commitment, and assistance, lasting reform was unlikely to occur (see American Association of Colleges for Teacher Education [AACTE], 1988; National Governors' Association [NGA], 1986). However, other influential groups raised serious concerns about the reform of educational leadership itself. Noting the political vulnerability of administrators (Callahan, 1962; Campbell, Fleming,

Newell, & Bennion, 1987; Stout, 1973; Waller, 1932), their entrenched interest in the status quo (Chubb, 1988), and their perceived unwillingness to share the reins of power with teachers (Hallinger, Murphy, & Hausman, in press-a, in press-b; Holmes, 1986), these reformers tended to view administrators more as part of the problem than as part of the solution. Therefore, rather than promulgate suggestions that would enhance the gatekeeping role of principals and superintendents, these groups sought to neutralize or eliminate administrator influence. More recently, in order to garner greater support for their initiatives, some in this later group have begun to find room for school leadership in their reform agendas.[5] Their proposals include ideas on administrator preparation that parallel those of the NCEEA and the NPBEA.

What is clear from all this activity over the last six or seven years is that school administration and the preparation of educational leaders have been pushed to the center of the educational reform stage. Demands for improvement echo one another from nearly every area of the theater. There is a growing feeling among influential leaders both within[6] and outside of educational administration that training programs need to be improved—quickly and in fundamental ways—or be pushed off the stage altogether. The next section of this introductory chapter examines the forces behind the calls for the reform of preparation programs for school leaders. Its concluding section presents some cautions to consider as we move forward in our discussion of improvement strategies.

Pressures for Reform

Clearly, the immediate task of our nation is to make certain that principals are competent for the changing school; that the new conditions facing school leaders are connected to redesigned programs for their preparation and certification. Today, those connections are incidental, even misaligned. (National Commission for the Principalship, 1990, p. 9)

THE DECLINE OF THE EDUCATIONAL SYSTEM AND THE REFORM MOVEMENT OF THE 1980s AND 1990s

The nation's public schools are in trouble. By almost every measure—the commitment and competency of teachers, student test scores, truancy and dropout rates, crimes of violence—the performance of our schools falls far short of expectations. . . . Too many young people are leaving the schools without acquiring essential learning skills and without self-discipline or purpose. (Twentieth Century Fund, 1983, p. 3)

Public education consumes nearly 7% of our gross national product. Its expenditures have doubled or tripled in every postwar decade, even when enrollments declined. I can't think of any other single sector of American society that has absorbed more money by serving fewer people with steadily declining service. (Kearns, 1988, p. 566)

Unquestionably, a major catalyst for examining educational leadership training is the larger reform movement that is washing over education in general—or, as Miklos (in press) reported, "increased demands for fundamental improvements in administrator preparation programs are linked directly to pressures for educational reform" (p. 26). It is widely believed that school administrators are managing a failing enterprise and that better leadership is needed if the industry is to recover:

Modern criticisms of public school administrators stem from the current mood of dissatisfaction with public schooling in general. If public schools are not of sufficiently high quality (however defined), then perforce the blame must rest with the schools' administrators. Consequently, superintendents and principals are criticized for lack of leadership, lack of vision, lack of modern management skills, and lack of courage to do things that must be done in order to make schools more effective. (Griffiths, Stout, & Forsyth, 1988b, p. 285)

At the base of this belief is the perception that the United States is losing its economic competitiveness—that "America's ability to compete in world markets is eroding" (Carnegie Forum, 1986, p. 2) —and that our "once unchallenged preeminence in commerce, industry, science, and technological innovation" (National Commission on Excellence in Education [NCEE], 1983, p. 5) is quickly being overshadowed by gains made in other industrialized nations. Once this belief took root, reformers from all sectors of society, especially "leaders from business joined by political figures at all levels" (Cunningham, 1990, p. 6), quickly traced the cause of the problem to the educational system.[7] Initial investigations discovered that schooling leaves students largely unprepared for the needs of a postindustrial world. America's students were judged to be deficient on nearly every conceivable measure of academic (e.g., basic skills, functional literacy, preparation for employment, higher order skills, specialized subject area knowledge) and nonacademic (e.g., holding power, citizenship, responsibility) progress.[8]

Once the link was drawn between the poor economic health of the nation and the poor product of schooling, researchers began to examine the educational process in some detail. They undertook their task with a vengeance. It is hard to find a single component of schooling that escaped analysis and condemnation. Investigations revealed that teachers and administrators are drawn from the bottom of the intellectual barrel and then poorly trained for their roles. Conditions of employment for teachers are unprofessional and stifling. The basic operating structure of schools is inadequate. The management of the enterprise is wanting, especially in providing leadership. The curriculum is a mess, lacking both rigor and coherence. Instruction is poor, textbooks worse. Students are allowed to drift through school unchallenged and uneducated. And, as bad as schooling on the average is, it is even worse for less advantaged and minority pupils. Everywhere one finds intellectual softness, a lack of expectations and standards, and the absence of accountability.

School leadership suffers double condemnation in this dismal scenario. First, as just noted, it is judged to be one among many of the problems infecting the educational enterprise. Second, based on the view that "the more essential education becomes to society the more important its administration" (Gregg, 1969, p. 994) and following what March (1974) views as a well-entrenched, if somewhat unrealistic, belief that "the problems in education are the business of educational administration" and that "insofar as education is failing, the educational administrator is subject to indictment" (p. 17), school leadership is perceived to be a contributing factor to other problems in education. Equally important for our purposes here is the view that if educational administration as a profession is subject to indictment, then "schools of education are proper codefendants" (March, 1974, p. 17). In short, preparation programs for school administrators must be held accountable for the anemic state of leadership found in school systems throughout the nation. If administrators are to emerge to lead education out of the quagmire in which it finds itself and put the economy back on the road to health,[9] then fundamental reforms must take place.

DEMANDS OF A CHANGING WORLD

As we discuss more fully in Chapter 5, much of the improvement momentum in the field of leadership training stems from the larger environment in which schools operate and administrators manage.[10] On the one hand, administrators are being asked to restructure schooling in order to prepare students for a postindustrial society, one in which valued knowledge is considerably more complex than ever before. This shift will require dramatic changes in the core technology of education and in the ways in which schools are organized, governed, and managed. It will also necessitate a different type of leadership than that seen in many schools and a different model of leadership training than that found in most preparation programs. On the other hand, educational leaders are being asked to help devise educational systems that address the demands of a changing school-aged population—one that is becoming increasingly diverse. This change necessitates a "reconsideration of the appropriate role of the school" (Kirst, McLaughlin, & Massell, 1989, p. 7) and revisions in the ways administrators are prepared to work in schools.

PROBLEMS INTERNAL TO EDUCATIONAL LEADERSHIP

Dramatic changes are needed in programs to prepare school administrators if they are to lead their schools and faculties rather than just manage them. (AACTE, 1988, p. 1)

At a more micro level of analysis, it is difficult to overlook the fact that educational administration as a general field of study and preparation programs in particular are plagued by a series of troubling problems and deficiencies. Because these concerns are explored in detail in the following chapters, we touch on them only briefly here. To begin with, there are significant weaknesses in nearly every component of training programs used to prepare educational leaders—

from recruitment and selection of prospective administrators, to the model used to guide their learning experiences, to the content they receive. There is widespread dissatisfaction with the theory movement that has provided the foundations for preparation programs since the early 1950s as well as with the university-based arts and science model of training. Many insightful analysts have commented on the propensity of programs to prepare managers rather than leaders grounded in the "educational" aspects of schooling who have a deep understanding of and appreciation for the purposes of schooling and the values that inform purpose-defining activity. Others have shown that preparation programs as currently constituted have driven a wedge between the academic and the practice arms of the profession.

THE PRESENCE OF HOPEFUL SIGNPOSTS

The "restructuring" movement, a precursor to moving education and its reliance upon knowledge, values, morals and ethics to a higher plane in society, must influence not only public schools, but also the content, context and structure/delivery of preparation programs for education professionals. (Achilles, Brubaker, & Snyder, 1990, p. 11)

Demands for improvements in administrator preparation programs flow not only from an analysis of deficiencies and problems but also from the knowledge that promising alternatives exist. The first of these points educators in the direction of a growing body of literature that reveals that certain administrators make a real difference in the effectiveness of their schools and in the lives of the students and teachers who work there. More importantly, this literature directs reformers to the values, beliefs, cognitive processes, and behaviors of such leaders[11] and provides grist for those who wish to reshape training programs (J. Murphy & Hallinger, 1987). Concurrently, alternative organizational models that offer the promise of breaking the bureaucratic stranglehold on schooling are being spotlighted. As a number of authors in educational administration have pointed out over the last few years (Beare, 1989; Bredeson, 1989; J. Murphy, 1991b; M. J. Murphy & Hart, 1988; Rossmiller, 1985), embedded in these new or "restructured" organizational forms is the genetic material needed to guide the development of future educational leaders.

Caveats for the Voyage

Before entering more deeply into an analysis of patterns and possibilities in the field of administration preparation, a few flags of caution should be raised. It is rather commonly believed that there are clearly defined problems in the area of administrator training, that we can attack these problems, and, at least to some extent, solve them. In so doing, the logic holds, we should produce better leaders for tomorrow's schools and thereby improve education and in turn society. Although this perspective corresponds nicely with the Western view of the world, makes a good deal of intuitive sense, and complements the prevailing rational view of organizations and their managers, it has some inherent problems. First, according to March (1974):

> we need to be wary of the ideology of administration. It is an ideology that appears to be widely shared among modern administrators in business, public affairs, and education. It is linked to a rich collection of cultural and philosophical traditions that are important to us. It is seductive and often misleading.
> We can characterize that ideology by the following set of beliefs: If there is a problem there is a solution. If there is a solution it can be discovered by analysis, and implemented by skill in interpersonal relations or organizational design. The solution to a problem requires the identification of underlying causes, and the discovery and implementation of solutions are duties of the administrator. If a problem persists, it is due to inadequacy in an administrator's will, perception of problems, analysis, skill with people, or knowledge of organizations. Inadequacies in an administrator can be corrected through proper administrative training. (p. 18)

While March cautions us about all the connections embedded in the belief statements noted above, he draws special attention to the "conceit" (p. 21) that improving administration can dramatically improve education, which in turn will cure the "complex problems confronting society" (p. 20). He argues elsewhere that "there is little evidence in our experience to give credence to suggestions that administrative or organizational reform, however drastic, will produce large schooling effects" (March, 1978, p. 222). He concludes (1974):

> we should have only modest hope that a change in administrator training or behaviour will ameliorate the problems of modern education. Those problems respond to many factors; only a small proportion of them are amenable to administrative control. The argument suggests a style that is pessimistic about great drama, but ambitious about making marginal improvements that are perceptible. (pp. 18-19)

In a series of carefully controlled studies, Meindl, Ehrlich, and Dukerich (1985) raise similar concerns about the effects of leadership on organizational performance (see also McCall, 1976; J. Murphy, 1988; J. Murphy, Hallinger, Weil, & Mitman, 1983). In particular, they uncover problems with two links of the belief statement outlined above: that problems can be traced to leaders and that improvement should be attributed to them. Meindl and his colleagues remind us that although leadership is often viewed as the cause of organizational outcomes, it is just as likely to be an attributed effect of organizational performance. From this point of view, leadership is not a proactive state of activities, but, like other important organizational variables (e.g., goals; see M. Cohen, March, & Olson, 1972; March, 1978), it is constructed in a sort of postevents fashion to explain and give meaning to organizational activity. As Pfeffer (1978) notes:

> leadership is the outcome of an attributional process in which observers—in order to achieve a feeling of control over their environment—tend to attribute outcomes to persons rather than to context, and the identification of individuals with leadership positions facilitates this attribution process. (p. 31)

We noted earlier that momentum for the improvement of preparation programs draws support from two sets of conditions: the documented decline in the performance of our schools and the existence of highly effective schools and school leaders, both defined primarily in terms of student outcomes. Both sets of factors tend to exacerbate the "fundamental attribution error" (Donmoyer,

1985, p. 35) discussed above. Lieberson and O'Conner (1972) have shown that the overestimation of the amount of variance attributed to leadership is largest when performance measures are stressed. Moreover, the analysis of Meindl et al. (1985) confirms that in cases of extreme performance—when things are going either very well *or* very poorly for the organization—there is a tendency to overfocus on leadership as an explanatory factor. That is, "larger outcomes—whether they are positive or negative—are most likely to lead observers to make the inference that a leader was an important cause" (p. 92). This tendency to oversubscribe responsibility for the conditions of schooling to school administrators and their preparation programs should not be overlooked; and neither should March's (1974) "great drama" (p. 18) corollary: the danger of expecting more than we should from our efforts to improve training for the men and women who lead our schools.

Cuban (1990, 1991) focuses on other linkages in the belief system. He calls into question the traditional, rational view of problems: that they can be identified and isolated and, after a systematic search for appropriate options, solved. He finds serious flaws in the application of this scientific model of problem solving to the messy social issues confronting school administrators. Because for many of these issues he sees no clear criteria for assessment and no universal or permanent solution strategies, Cuban refers to them as "dilemmas" rather than as problems. Because dilemmas tend to get dealt with rather than solved, they have a tendency to reappear on a regular but unpredictable basis (see also Iannaccone, 1977). Even a casual reading of the history of our profession provides considerable support for Cuban's view that many of the issues in training programs look more like dilemmas than problems. Almost all the preparation program issues discussed in this volume (e.g., lack of quality students, poor subject matter, weak faculty) have been with us since the inception of educational administration. From time to time, one or more of these issues surfaces and is dealt with according to one set of criteria. The same issue may resurface at some future point when changing conditions dictating a more relevant set of criteria—one that usually highlights the inadequacies of the methods used to "solve" the issue previously—cause the old resolution to unravel.

Another reason that the logical belief pattern may be less viable than it might at first appear is that improvements in educational administration training programs, like those in a good deal of the general reform movement (J. Murphy, 1989a), may have less to do with addressing real needs than with establishing the appearance of change needed to legitimize programs in their larger environments (Meyer & Rowan, 1975)—especially with the university community, state agencies, and the practice arm of the profession. Ergo, a core tenet of the belief system that identified problems result in serious efforts at improvement is thrown into doubt.

All the authors cited in this section remind us that although preparation is "susceptible to improvement through the application of rational knowledge and conscientious effort" (Taylor, cited in Clifford & Guthrie, 1988, p. 41), we should also approach reform with a thorough understanding of the difficulties of the task and a sense of vision informed by the knowledge that the links between identified problems in society and education, leadership, and improved administrator preparation are weak. Critiques of the status quo in preparation programs and demands for change have been promulgated with regularity throughout the short history of educational administration. It is inevitable that they will continue as the profession matures and the environment in which it operates evolves.

Finally, it is important to acknowledge the fact that the frame of reference brought to the analysis of a phenomenon colors our perceptions of what we see. To a certain extent, therefore, "believing is seeing" (Lotto, 1983, p. 6). This point, as it relates to educational administration, has been nicely captured by Willower (1988):

> Patently, the assessments one makes of educational administration depend in great part on what one values and sees as important and whether one tends to be optimistic or pessimistic in looking at the world. (p. 729)

All these caveats do not, however, justify inaction. As the authors cited throughout this volume amply document, there is a serious crisis in our preparation programs that is a part of the "troubled times" (Miklos, 1987, p. 1) in which the field of educational administration finds itself as we head into the 21st century. There is much work to be done. Given the point we occupy in the history of preparation programs and some educated deductions about tomorrow's schools, it appears that much of the work will need to be of a transformative nature. As we set about that process, it is worth keeping in mind that significant change often results in conditions getting worse before they get better (J. T. Murphy, 1991). It is also important to understand the power of systemic change, of working with a sense of vision on many parts of the system simultaneously (Honig, 1990).

We return to these and related issues in Chapter 6 when we lay out the design of a preparation program for leaders of tomorrow's schools. Before undertaking that task, however, Chapters 2 and 3 examine the history of preparation programs to see what lessons are available to guide us in planning for the future. Chapter 4 follows this analysis with an in-depth examination of the current state of affairs in preparation programs. Because educational administration has been regularly shaped by changes in the larger social and political environment, Chapter 5 offers a look into the future of schooling and leadership to see if we can discern any important changes on the horizon. We turn now to the examination of the history of preparatory programs.

Part I

The Past

From the day of no educational administration to the present much has taken place. (Miller, 1957, p. 513)

Within the past two years Professor Strayer has declared that school administration is today less well equipped to cope with the problems of the next twenty years than was school administration of 1910 to cope with the two eventful decades that ensued. If such be the fact, a pronounced reorientation of the professional education of school executives is required. (Newlon, 1934, p. 258)

The professional preparation of school superintendents is badly in need of complete overhauling. (American Association of School Administrators [AASA], 1960, p. 84)

The time has come, I submit, for a fundamental, sweeping reassessment of our training programs. (Erikson, 1977, p. 137)

Seeing the seriousness of poorly prepared school executives, we are now experiencing the demands for a total overhaul of university preparation programs. (Spaedy, 1990, p. 156)

The societal context for which we are preparing educational administrators is changing constantly and, accordingly, our efforts to improve our preparatory programs must continue indefinitely. (Farquhar, 1977, p. 337)

Two

The Ideological and Prescriptive Eras

> Every person is an historian, using memory to make sense of the present . . . whether that past is consciously articulated and analyzed or simply taken for granted. (Tyack & Cummings, 1977, p. 46)

> The men who speak for administration and the men who train administrators need, and always have needed, a simple statement of what an administrator should be and do, and why. This has served as a justification of administrators and administration to the public and to the school staff, as well as a guide to administrators themselves. To be successful, the statement must be brief and simple, and it must have an appeal. Necessarily, it simplifies. It describes what should be and what is purported to be, and the good and the true, without distinguishing between them. If only an individual subscribed to it, we could call it a private credo, but the theme is shared. It is not simply the belief of an individual, but the generally shared statement of the public belief of spokesmen for school administration. (Button, 1966, p. 216)[1]

The next two chapters review the evolution of training programs over the last century to uncover guidance for the future, relying heavily upon the efforts of others who have already begun to fill in some of the pieces of this historical puzzle. For example, Table 2.1 and Table 2.2 provide skeletal pictures of stages in administrator preparation developed by some of the leading scholars in the field. Table 2.3 outlines additional groupings of periods in the evolution of educational administration as a general field of practice and scholarship; that is, although scholars represented in this portrait

15

include preparation in their stages of development, training is not the primary focus of their historical reviews. Table 2.4, which presents a synopsis of all of this work, guides the discussion in these two chapters.

For this discussion, the evolution of preparation programs has been divided into four broad eras[2]: the era of ideology (pre-1900); the prescriptive era (1900 to 1945); the era of professionalism/behavioral science (1946 to 1985); and the emerging, dialectic era (1985 to the present) (see Table 2.2 and Table 2.4). Within each period, some background information is provided and then the analysis is completed using a framework adopted from an earlier investigation of administrative training (J. Murphy, 1990e) and two studies conducted on the effects of the current educational reform movement on departments of educational leadership (J. Murphy, 1989b, 1991a).[3] The design is quite similar to one developed by Culbertson and his colleagues (Culbertson, Farquhar, Gaynor, & Shibles, 1969) and employed by Farquhar and Piele (1972) and Silver and Spuck (1978) in their influential studies.[4] It is comprised of six components: faculty, students, program structure, program content, instruction, and epistemology and philosophy.

At the outset, we should cite H. Moore's (1964) caution: "anyone who has tried his hand at writing history knows better than to claim that the beginning [or end] of a long-time, continuing trend can be dated with precision" (p. 11). Thus the specific dates employed here are somewhat arbitrary. Other analysts have developed slightly different groupings[5] (see Tables 2.1 and 2.3). Finally, it is important to acknowledge that these large aggregations of historical events may mask important phases of development within eras. Given these caveats, however, the groupings employed do furnish a useful rubric for tracking the development of preparation programs in educational administration.

Three additional reminders are needed. First, our historical review discusses primarily the formal preparation experiences offered in university-based programs—what Halpin (1960) calls "technical learning" (p. 10). Because "most of the preparation for administrative practice that educators experience is informal in nature and obtained at the school and district site" (Silver, 1982, p. 49), it is important to underscore this important limitation of the analysis. Second, the formal training of school administrators is a recent development (Cooper & Boyd, 1987), and one for which the information

(text continued on p. 21)

TABLE 2.1 Historical Eras in the Preparation of School Administrators

	Culbertson (1964)	Moore (1964)	Gregg (1969)	Farquar (1974)	Silver (1982)	Glass et al. (1986b)	Campbell et al. (1987)	Cooper-Boyd (1987)
1820						1820-1914 Ideology		1865-1900 Philosopher-Educator
1900	1900-1930 Era of Efficacy		Era of Scientific Management		1900-1925 Era of Scientific Management		1900-1945 Prescriptive Era	1900-1912 Educator-Capitalist
								1913-1915 Business Manager
						1915-1933 Conventional Wisdom		1915-1929 School Executive
	1930-1950 Era of Human Relations		Era of Human Relations		1926-1950 Era of Human Relations			1930-1950 Social Agent
						1934-1945 Concepts		
1946	1950-1963 Scientific Era	1947-1963 Era of Ferment	Era of Theory & Science	1946-1956 Era of Development	1950-1975 Era of Behavioral Science	1946-1955 Rhetoric	1945-1985 Era of Expansion	1950-1985 Behavioral Scientist
				1957-1967 Golden Era		1955-1985 Theory & Science		
				1968-1978 Era of Diversity & Adversity				
1985								

17

TABLE 2.2 Schematic of the Evolution of Periods (Doctrines) in the Preparation of School Leaders

1820-1900 Ideology Era
- 1820-1914 Ideology
- 1865-1900 Philosopher-Educator

1900-1945 Prescriptive Era
- 1900-1945 Prescriptive Era
  - 1900-1925 Era of Scientific Managment
    - 1900-1912 Educator-Capitalist
    - 1913-1915 Business Manager
    - 1915-1933 Conventional Wisdom
    - 1915-1929 School Executive
    - 1930-1950 Social Agent
    - 1934-1945 Concepts
  - 1925-1945 Era of Human Relations

1946-1985 Behavioral Science Era/Era of Professionalization
- 1945-1985 Era of Expansion
  - 1946-1955 Rhetoric
  - 1946-1956 Era of Development
    - 1947-1963 Era of Ferment
- 1950-1985 Behavioral Science
- 1950-1975 Era of Behavioral Sciences
  - 1955-1985 Theory & Science
    - 1957-1967 Golden Era
    - 1968-1978 Era of Diversity & Adversity
    - 1979-1990 Era of Turmoil

TABLE 2.3 Historical Eras in the Field of Educational Leadership (Non-Preparation Specific)

	Gregg (1960)	Callahan-Button (1964)	Button (1966)	Tyack & Hansot (1982)	Sergiovanni et al. (1987)	Kerchner (1988)
1820		1865-1900 Administrator as Philosopher-Educator	1870-1885 Administrator as Teacher of Teachers 1885-1905 Administrator as Applied Philosopher	1820-1890 Aristocracy of Character		Evangelical Period
1900	1910-1930 Administration as Management	1900-1930 Administrator as Business Executive 1900-1913 Transition Period 1913-1915 Administrator as Business Manager 1915-1929 Administrator as Executive	1905-1930 Administrator as Business Manager	1890-1954 Schooling by Design in a Corporate Society	1900-1934 Era of Efficacy	Progressive Period
	1930-1958 Human Relations	1930-1950 Search for New Concepts	1935-1950 Administrator as Technical Expert 1955- Administrator as Social Scientist		1930-1965 Era of the Person	
1946	1948-1958 Era of Theory			1954-1980 Dreams Defined	1946-1988 Era of Politics	Period of Discontent
1985					1985— Cultural Era	1985— Period of Choice

19

TABLE 2.4 A Composite Picture of Eras and Metaphors in School Administration Preparation Programs

Historical Eras	*Dominant Metaphors*
1820-1900 Era of Ideology	**Administrator as Philosopher-Educator**
1870-1885	Administrator as Teacher of Teachers
1885-1905	Administrator as Applied Philosopher
1900-1945 Prescriptive Era	**Administrator as Technical Expert**
1900-1930 Scientific Management Era	Administrator as Business Person
1900-1917	Administrator as Educator-Capitalist
1913-1915	Administrator as Business Manager
1915-1929	Administrator as School Executive
1930-1950 Human Relations Era	Administrator as Social Agent
1946-1985 Behavioral Science Era/Era of Professionalization	**Administrator as Social Scientist/Administrator as Professional**
1946-1957 Era of Development	
1956-1985 Theory Era	
1957-1967 Golden Era	
1958-1978 Era of Diversity & Adversity	
1979-1990 Era of Turmoil	
1986 Dialectic Era	

repository for the early decades is quite thin. Finally, readers of the scholarly literature in the field of educational administration may be troubled by what may at first look like rather late ending dates for our historical phases. One could argue, for example, that the termination of the behavioral science era might better be marked at 1974 than at 1985 (see Griffiths, 1988a). However, there has been historically, as Campbell and his colleagues (Campbell, Fleming, Newell, & Bennion, 1987) remind us, "a lag of a decade or more between the emergence of new ideas in educational administration and their general application in graduate study" (p. 193).[6]

The Era of Ideology

> Little had been written before 1900 on educational administration, and formal preparation programs for school administrators had not yet been developed. (Gregg, 1960, p. 20)

Although the administration of schools in the United States enjoys a relatively long history—one that "dates back at least a couple of hundred years" (Gregg, 1969, p. 993)—in its early days it "went largely unrecognized as an essential component of school operation" (Guba, 1960, p. 115), and the actual number of administrators was quite small until after the Civil War (Callahan & Button, 1964; Gregg, 1960). For example, the development of the school superintendency, the first administrative position in education, occurred during the latter part of the 19th century (Gregg, 1960). The Department of Superintendence, precursor of the American Association of School Administrators (AASA), was not organized until 1866 (Button, 1966). Moreover, because early schools were simple organizations, their administration was not an arduous task. As Gregg (1969) notes:

> under such circumstances, the administrator could learn his profession effectively on the job by trial-and-error processes. Little, if any, formal specialized preparation was needed, and none was provided. The minimal formal education which was designed for teachers was deemed sufficient for those who would become administrators. (pp. 993-994; see also Popper, 1987)

In 1875 William L. Payne, then a school superintendent in Michigan, wrote the first book dealing with school administration, *Chapters on School Supervision*. After receiving a faculty appointment in education at the University of Michigan in 1879, Payne also taught the first college-level course in school administration (Callahan & Button, 1964). Although other "departments of education" were also established in the 1870s, professors of educational leadership and programs specific to school administration "were unknown until the early 1900s" (Cooper & Boyd, 1987, p. 16). Thus the earliest

> formal training for administration included some basic pedagogy and a lifelong search for the "ideal" education, but not much self-consciousness or thought about their own roles as leaders, statesmen, or administrators. Hence, they attended no courses, received no credits, and applied for no licenses in educational administration. (Cooper & Boyd, 1987, p. 16)

What broad education departments such as that at Michigan did offer students were subject matter "relating to school management as well as to philosophy" (H. Moore, 1964, p. 11) and pedagogy. The "first teachings to prospective administrators were 'theories' about exemplary school leaders which were then rarefied into 'great man' and 'trait' theories" (Cooper & Boyd, 1987, p. 7).

As shown in Tables 2.3 and 2.4, Callahan and Button (1964) and Button (1966) have isolated two doctrines of school leadership before 1900 that, at least to some extent, exerted influence on thinking about the content to which administrators were exposed from 1870 to 1905 in these newly forming departments of education. Under the doctrine of administration as the teaching of teachers (1870 to 1885), "administration was very simple, really; administration was supervision" (Button, 1966, p. 218). Because the proper role of education was instruction, much of the limited education administrators did receive was in the areas of curriculum and instruction.

The doctrine of administration as applied philosophy (1885-1905)

> asserted that truth, concerning all things and all matters, was eternal and to be discovered. As in all other fields, this was necessary in education. It therefore followed that the learned administrator, who could discover relevant truths, was the best authority on all matters concerning education, and that the problem of administra-

tion was the application of philosophical knowledge to schools. (Button, 1966, p. 218)

This new doctrine, "with its emphasis on eternal wisdom and moral judgment, made the administrator into something like the clergyman and borrowed from him some of the clergyman's status"[7] (Button, 1966, p. 219). It also reinforced the emphasis on philosophy and theories about outstanding school leaders in the rudimentary subject matter being offered to students of school administration. (For a description of the content of textbooks from this era, see Mason, 1986.)

The Prescriptive Era

The period of sixty years, extending from the appearance of [Woodrow] Wilson's article [1887] to the beginning of recent ferment, saw many changes. Colleges of education employed professors of school administration, textbooks giving advice on management of schools filled many shelves, and administration became a foremost area of graduate study in education. Some university professors were known throughout the nation for their teaching and writing in school administration. (H. Moore, 1964, p. 12)

The prescriptive era witnessed the growth of administrative preparation programs from their infancy through early adolescence. As noted above, although there were some general departments of education, in 1900 there were no professors of educational management and no subdepartments of school administration. Specific formal preparation for the profession of school leadership was conspicuous by its absence. By the end of the Second World War, this situation had changed dramatically. Approximately 125 institutions offered programs to prepare school leaders (Silver, 1982).[8] A first generation of educational administration professors—men like Cubberley, Strayer, and Mort—had been actively engaged in laying the foundations of the field and in training a second generation of professors to take their place. Many states were requiring formal course work in educational leadership for administrative positions and were certifying graduates of preparation programs for employment (H. Moore, 1964).[9] As these elements of the profession began to find acceptance, more and more principals and superintendents embarked on their careers with university training in the practice of school administration.

SETTING THE STAGE

As has been true throughout their history, preparation programs during the prescriptive era were shaped to a significant extent by forces external to education and educational management; specifically, by social and political forces and historical trends in the larger society (Callahan, 1962; Campbell et al., 1987; Miller, 1957). Also, as has again always been the case, the fabric of preparation programs during the prescriptive era was woven and rewoven to mirror high-status professions in the larger society (Button, 1966; Callahan & Button, 1964). This meant preparing administrators to be business managers and school executives during the first quarter of the century and social agents during the second. In addition, as was to be true during transitions between future phases of administrator preparation, the shift from the era of ideology to the era of prescription was fueled by a formidable body of literature deploring the status quo and holding up loftier ideals to which the profession should aspire—as well as by one or two eloquent defenses of current arrangements by authors who were committed to the values of the existing order. Frank Spaulding's influential paper presented at the 1910 meeting of the National Society of College Teachers of Education provides a good example of the muckraking literature that accompanies periods of transition in educational administration training programs:

> Charging that the administration of public education was "grossly inefficient" and "the weakest phase of our great educational enterprise," he urged that the training of the administrator emphasize the practical aspects of the job and be based on "simple and sound business principles." (Callahan & Button, 1964, p. 81)

Finally, it is important to highlight a point richly developed by Callahan (1962) in his seminal work on educational administration during its formative years. The vulnerability of education as an institution in general and of its managers in particular made this muckraking literature all the more believable, the quest for status more important, and the need to respond to larger societal pressures more immediate.

Callahan and Button (1964) document that the seeds of demise for the ideological era were embedded in "the great material achievements of industrial capitalism in the late nineteenth century" (p. 77; see also Callahan, 1962). This movement resulted in a growing infatuation with issues of commerce, "the rise of the business and industrial group to a position of great prestige and influence[, and] the saturation of America with business-industrial values and practices" (p. 77). Given the conditions in education described above and the overwhelming power of the capitalist-industrial revolution—especially after "the spectacular entrance upon the American scene, in the autumn of 1910, of Frederick Taylor and his system of scientific management" (p. 79)—it was inevitable that these values would exert great influence over educational administration.

Other less obvious but nonetheless important reasons for the evolution of school administrators from philosophers to managers have been advanced by Button (1966):

> First, perhaps the school really was more like a business enterprise or factory than it was like a church, to push the clergyman analogy. It was a better "fit" once again. Second, the new doctrine justified administrative control over a wider variety of matters. In practice, the extent of administrator control had been increasing, and there were social advantages in a doctrine which would support the increase. Third, the new doctrine allied the administrator with a high status group, the businessmen. (p. 220)

The new doctrine also enhanced the status of administrators by cloaking their work in an aura of "scientific respectability" (Callahan & Button, 1964, p. 83):

> The new doctrine of school administration as management defined school administration as being like the management of a business or factory. . . . The appropriate basis for decision-making then was ideally a fiscal one. Like a business enterprise, the schools were to be operated at minimum cost. Like factories they were to be operated at maximum efficiency. The child was first the raw material and then the product; the teacher was the worker; and the school

was the factory. (Button, 1966, p. 219; see also Petrie, 1990; Schlechty, 1990, chap. 2)

The Depression, the New Deal that was undertaken to conquer it, and the Great War to free the world for democracy all brought an end to unbridled infatuation with the titans of business and with capitalist-industrial values (Beck & Murphy, in press-a, in press-b; Button, 1966). The "essential modes of thought which had given rise to" scientific management came under attack and the "captain of commerce" role lost a good deal of its luster (Belisle & Sargent, 1957, p. 106). Given these larger social forces, the tendency of educational administration as a field to gravitate toward high-status roles, and a body of literature that was increasingly critical of the status quo, "it is not surprising that the business-management doctrine was abandoned" by educational administration (Button, 1966, p. 221). The "social conscience" of administrators was awakened (Callahan & Button, 1964, p. 89). The purpose of schooling was now to promote democracy: "The role of administrators was to transmit democratic values to teachers, students, their parents, and community members" (Beck & Murphy, in press-b, Table 3).

THE PREPARATION PROGRAM

There is not an abundance of information about preparation programs during the prescriptive era. The data we do have are sketchy, uneven, and, in some cases, contradictory. Self-study and analysis were not a part of the culture of the formative years of educational administration preparation programs.

Faculty

We do know that "as late as 1900 no college or university offered courses designed specifically to prepare administrators" (Gregg, 1969, p. 994) and that there were no professors in this academic field (Campbell et al., 1987). Unlike those of the later behavioral science era, professors appointed during the first half of the 20th century were typically drawn from the world of practice, usually from the superintendency (Culbertson, 1965; Silver, 1982). In general, conditions in departments were less than ideal. Tyack and Cummings (1977) report that in 1921 three quarters of the leading graduate departments of education had fewer than 10 faculty members: "In half of these schools fewer than 50 percent of the professors had doctorates. Many did not even have master's degrees. Their normal teaching load exceeded 12 hours per week" (p. 60). Finally, we know that an influential cadre of well-known professors exerted considerable control over the evolution of the field and the development of preparation programs. These men and their students formed "webs [that] provided vital connections among scholars scattered across the continent—linking those who studied administration with those who practiced it" (Campbell et al., 1987, p. 180). They also trained the second generation of professors from which many of the leading lights in today's professoriate are only one generation removed.

Students

Students during the prescriptive era, like the faculty, were quite homogeneous. Almost all were white males.[10] Nearly all took course work while maintaining their full-time positions as teachers or, more likely, as administrators. For example, Tyack and Cummings (1977) discuss a 1923 survey that revealed "that only one-quarter of superintendents had pursued graduate study full time for a year or more" (p. 59). Part-time enrollment in turn meant that "master's and doctoral degrees were often received at or near mid-career" (Campbell, et al., 1987, p. 175). The range of leadership positions for which students prepared, especially during the scientific management era, was limited to the school superintendency and the professorship (Silver, 1982).

Program Structure

As noted earlier, the first college-level course in school administration was taught by William Payne at the University of Michigan in 1879. The first seminar in school administration was offered in 1898 at Teachers College by Nicholas Butler Murray (Callahan, 1962). In the 1900-1901 academic year, educational leadership was listed separately in the catalog for the first time at Teachers College, although only two courses were available. Between 1900 and 1910, only a few additional courses were added. With the advance of the scientific management movement, however, the rate of change began to quicken. By 1913, administrators were subjected to mounting displeasure over the ways schools were operated and, lacking training "in the managerial philosophy of Taylor, were falling like flies .... Administrators had no formal training, no preparation to be the new educational managers. . . . Teacher training was hardly enough" (Cooper & Boyd, 1987, pp. 7, 10). In response, "educators were forced to devote a great deal of attention to administration, and not only courses but whole programs were developed in that field in the universities" (Callahan & Button, 1964, p. 82).

Callahan and Button (1964) reported that "by 1915 a great change in educational administration was well underway, and in the next decade the basic patterns were extended and institutionalized through the development of graduate programs in administration" (pp. 84-85). The 1920s and 1930s were particularly active decades of program development in colleges and universities (H. Moore, 1964): "Before 1920 comparatively few superintendents or principals availed themselves of this formal preparation" (Campbell et al., 1987, p. 175), although after that date there was a gradual increase in the number of students attending preparation programs (Newlon, 1934). A 1937 study conducted by C. Moore found that 42 of 47 institutions of higher education offered either a "major in educational administration or a sufficient number of classes in educational administration to equal a major" (p. 630). As a basis of comparison for information provided later, it is worth noting that these new preparation programs were, collectively, graduating about 13 students with completed doctorates per year between 1911 and 1934 (Newlon, 1934). By 1937, 29 states were issuing administrative certificates for superintendents (C. Moore, 1937), although Campbell and his colleagues (1987, p. 175) have pointed out that "even where certificates were demanded, requirements were meager and work specifically in educational administration or supporting disciplines was minimal at best" (see also Grace, 1946). By 1950, the majority of school leaders acquired some graduate course work and 38 states "required a graduate degree in administration for superintendents and principals" (Cooper & Boyd, 1987, p. 11).

Program Content

Each of the four subphases of preparation during the prescriptive era discussed by Cooper and Boyd (1987; see Table 2.1) is characterized by distinctive, if not totally unique, program content. As discussed above, the first period—the educator-capitalist phase (1900-1912)—transpired before scientific management took over the educational landscape and before formal preparation was a reality for most school leaders. The program content during this era was largely undifferentiated from that received by teachers. Phases 2 and 3—the business manager (1913-1915) and school executive (1915-1929) eras —witnessed the first infusion of business and accounting techniques followed by materials and ideas from scientific management (Callahan, 1962; Beck & Murphy, in press-b): "Program content was consistent with prevailing emphases of science on fact gathering, inductive reasoning, and empirical generalizations" (Culbertson, 1988a, p. 9). During this time, "preservice education for school executives tended to stress: the technical and mechanical aspects of administration" (Gregg, 1969, p. 994); "specific and immediate tasks" (Callahan & Button, 1964, p. 87); and the practical aspects of the job (Newlon, 1934). The goal was to prepare students to understand the job of administration as it was and to perform successfully in the roles they undertook—as opposed to studying what might need to be done differently and preparing for roles as change agents.[11]

Operating under the premise that "one of the best criteria for judging the emphasis in the professional education of school administrators is . . . the problems in the field that have been chosen for research" (p. 260), Newlon (1934) completed a content analysis of dissertations[12] completed between 1910 and 1933. He concludes that departments of school administration were "principally" concerned with the "technical phases" of "the professional education of school executives" (p. 261). He reports an absence of attention "to the fundamental social and economic problems of school administration and to the social methods and techniques which their solution requires" (p. 262). Another analysis in Newlon's volume reviews the topics that professors and superintendents judged to be most important in the preparation of superintendents. This examination reveals a similar bias toward "the spheres of finance, business management, physical equipment, and the more mechanical aspects of administration, organization, personnel management, and the like" (p. 259). A third

> analysis of the contents of eighteen such textbooks published during the last fifty years . . . [reveals] that over four-fifths of the eight thousand pages are devoted to the purely executive,

organizational, and legal aspects of administration. Almost the
entire emphasis is on the "how" of administration. There is virtually no discussion of the "why," little critical examination of educational and social implications of the structures and procedures
discussed. (p. 93)

Finally, an investigation of actual courses in school administration
"shows clearly the emphasis on the technical and the factual, the
external. Most of the topics have to do with the mechanics of administration" (p. 99).

Using Teachers College as a model, Callahan and Button (1964)
conclude that the average preparatory program of this era

> was a fairly high-level service station which provided students
> with the practical skills (primarily in finance, business manage-
> ment, public relations, and "plant" management) which enabled
> them to acquire and keep jobs in a business society. (p. 86)

Callahan (1962) had similarly reported earlier:

> The courses which were developed in administration provided train-
> ing in the kinds of activity (records and reports, cost accounting,
> child accounting, and general business management) with which
> superintendents on the job were preoccupied. This, of course, was
> what Spaulding (and Strayer) advocated: dealing with the practi-
> cal problems. (p. 196)

It is instructive to note that the number of separate courses continued to expand throughout this period (H. Moore, 1964; Newlon, 1934).
For example, at Teachers College courses increased from 2 in 1900
to 29 in the 1924-1925 academic year and at the University of Chicago
from 2 in the 1912-1913 school year to 15 by the 1917-1918 academic
year. By the mid-1920s, in the leading preparation programs in the
country, "the pieces were all in place: the glow of 'science,' the language of 'management,' the goal of 'efficiency,' and finally the need
for central control and authority" (Cooper & Boyd, 1987, p. 10).

The "human relations" or "social agent" phase (1930 to 1950) of
the prescriptive era brought new purposes and goals to school administration, resulting in the infusion of new program content in
preparation programs. The Depression and the New Deal dramati-

cally altered the environment in which schools operated throughout the 1930s. Concurrently, the managerial-industrial worldview that had become so deeply ingrained in educational administration training programs came under heavy bombardment. The most visible and articulate critic of educational administration of the era was Jesse Newlon, whose seminal work has already been reviewed. Although not opposed to professional training per se, he was deeply troubled by what was absent in most training programs. He wrote in 1934, " 'expert business management,' very desirable in its place, palsies in the presence of such [profound social] issues" (p. 257). In response to analysts such as Newlon and Dewey and to a rapidly changing environment, social foundations were introduced into preparation programs (Miklos, in press): "human relations in cooperative educational activities" (Gregg, 1969, p. 994) were stressed; "the industrial engineer had to become a human engineer as well" (Guba, 1960, p. 117). According to Silver (1982), the human factor

> found its way into preparation programs in educational administration when readings by such leading authorities on management as McGregor, Argyris, and Maslow became incorporated into course content. Issues such as employee satisfaction and motivation, job enrichment, and personal growth and development were added to the curriculum of educational administration in the form of courses in "the human factor," sensitivity or leadership training experiences, and emphasis on the development of human relations skills. (p. 52)

All in all, however, at the end of World War II, "training was still highly practical, a blend of plant management, scheduling, and budgeting interspersed with courses on schools and the social order. Still missing were academic respectability and a sense of full professionalism" (Cooper & Boyd, 1987, p. 11), as well as the theoretical and conceptual scaffolding to hold the content of preparation programs together (Belisle & Sargent, 1957; Getzels, 1977; Griffiths, 1959, 1988a; H. Moore, 1964). Few scholars today would subscribe to Cubberley's belief that in the prescriptive era "training in educational administration had changed from guesswork to statistically based scholarship" (cited in Tyack & Cummings, 1977, p. 47).[13] The scholarship that informed course content throughout this era was little more than "naked empiricism" (Griffiths, 1965, p. 34; Halpin,

1957, p. 197) or "factualism" (Griffiths, 1959, p. 9), resulting in the development of: "fuzzy concepts" (Griffiths, 1988a, p. 29); "inadequately field-tested principles" (Crowson & McPherson, 1987, p. 47); and a mere "encyclopedia of facts" (Griffiths, 1959, p. 9) that lacked "the power of unifying interpretive theories" (Goldhammer, 1983; Tyack & Cummings, 1977, p. 62). The knowledge base was comprised of: "folklore, testimonials of reputedly successful administrators, . . . the speculation of college professors" (Griffiths, 1959, p. v); "personal success stories and lively anecdotes" (Marland, 1960, p. 25); "personal accounts or 'war stories,' and prescriptions offered by experienced practitioners" (Silver, 1982, p. 51); "experiences of practicing administrators as they managed the various problem areas of school administration" (Gregg, 1969, p. 996); "maxims, exhortations, and several innocuous variations on the theme of the Golden Rule" (Halpin, 1960, p. 4); and "preachments to administrators about ways in which they should perform" (Goldhammer, 1983, p. 250).[14]

The prescriptive era was a time in which "writers of texts on administration attempted to generalize from the experience of their acquaintances or to canonize the record of the happiest practices of their own personal experience" (Miller, 1957, p. 516) and to promulgate lists of principles derived from pseudo-scientific empirical studies (Glass, 1986b; Griffiths, 1965). The courses offered were "largely a summary of the concrete practical experience of some former successful school superintendent, now turned teacher in some newly established chair or department of education" (Cubberley, cited in Callahan, 1962, p. 188). It was an era of "status studies and collections of opinion" (Getzels, 1977, p. 9) rolled into "technique or 'prescription' courses" (Farquhar, 1968, p. 100). Program content was largely disconnected from the "larger streams of scholarship" (Campbell et al., 1987, p. 179) in the university (see also Grace, 1946). Furthermore, "empirical research on administration was slighted, and contributions from the behavioral sciences and personnel research in industry were zealously ignored" (Halpin, 1960, p. 4).

Epistemology and Philosophy

In concluding this analysis of the prescriptive period, two issues should be brought to the foreground; both issues are intertwined throughout our earlier discussion—the knowledge and values undergirding preparation programs of this era. The epistemological foundations of the prescriptive era are twofold: personal accounts of formerly practicing administrators and atheoretical empirical studies conducted under the banner of scientific management. In this latter area, in the search for greater efficiency, considerable effort was devoted to the "scientific" analysis of nearly every facet of schools. Students in preparation programs were often deeply involved in conducting these field studies and in "developing measuring instruments in order to obtain objective descriptions of the problem area being investigated" (Gregg, 1960, p. 21). These survey studies, described in great detail by Callahan (1962), "constituted the first descriptive research conducted on a large scale in the field of educational administration, thereby providing a large body of information to which graduate study might be anchored" (p. 174). During the latter part of the prescriptive era, descriptive studies were expanded by studies examining the human factor in schooling. Throughout this era, personal accounts from former practitioners-turned-professors continued to supplement information from the descriptive investigations. Taken together, this information caused the knowledge base of this period to be labeled "raw empiricism." It was "raw" in the sense that the findings from descriptive studies were untethered to larger explanatory frameworks and theoretical scaffolding. It was "raw" also because the practical wisdom of the era was largely nonreflective and uncritical in nature.

On the issue of values, it should be obvious by now that the training of school leaders of the era was, as always, strongly responsive to the values of the larger society (Beck & Murphy, in press-b). The dominant values of pre-World War II American society were shaped by the scientific management movement, a movement incorporating a

> system of values . . . built on four pillars. The first pillar was based on a *work-success ethic;* values of material achievement took precedence over values of human being. The second pillar, which was based on a *future time orientation,* affirmed that "time is money" and "a penny saved is a penny earned" and stressed that time should be used as frugally and efficiently as money itself. The third pillar emphasized *competitive individualism,* which epitomized the maxim "the race is to the swift" and stated that the primary responsibility was to oneself rather than to any collectivity. The fourth pillar, based on *Puritan morality,* marked respectability, thrift, self-restraint, and

cleanliness as the signs of common decency and sloth a sin second only to idolatry. (Getzels, 1977, p. 5)

According to Culbertson (1964), the idea that training would, in general, "mirror dominant social values is understandable," as is the fact "that the scientific values which were so influential in the larger society would have a strong impact on preparatory programs for administrators" (p. 309). The most thoughtful analysis of how this occurred has been provided by Callahan (1962):

It is clear in retrospect that part of the tragedy was in what proved to be the unfortunate timing and sequence of events. First, by 1910 a decade of concern with reform, stimulated by the muckraking journalists, had produced a public suspicious and ready to be critical of the management of all public institutions. Second, just at this time Taylor's system was brought dramatically before the nation, not with a mundane label such as "shop management" but with the appealing title of "scientific management." Very quickly the alleged mismanagement of the railroads was transferred to the management of other institutions, especially public institutions. By 1912 the full force of public criticism had hit the schools. Third, by 1912 the prestige of business and of businessmen was again in the ascendancy and Americans were urging that business methods be introduced into the operation of government and were electing businessmen to serve on their school boards. Fourth, and of basic importance, was the fact that the "profession" of school administration was in 1910 in its formative stage, just being developed. If America had had a tradition of graduate training in administration—genuinely educational, intellectual, and scholarly, if not scientific—such a tradition might have served as a brake or restraining force. As it was, all was in flux.

These facts must be coupled with an understanding of the great force of public opinion (especially opinion marshaled by the profit-motivated popular press) on the one hand, and, on the other, the almost pathetic vulnerability of public school administrators. The situation was one of a "profession" of school administration, vulnerable to the pressures of the community and with no solid tradition behind it to counteract these strong pressures, being criticized for inefficiency at the very time when the community's most influential group, the businessmen, were adopting a new panacea for this very problem, the panacea of scientific management. No wonder that schoolmen sought to emulate the efficiency of business and use whatever methods business had used to attain it. (p. 245)[15]

Later, as the values of society began to change, so did those in educational administration preparation programs: "The concepts of 'human relations' and 'democratic administration' made for a strong value orientation [in the work of many professors of administration and] in preparation programs" (Culbertson, 1964, p. 306)—one that was "isomorphic with the prevailing system of values and conceptions of human nature" (Getzels, 1977, p. 6). Commenting on the values of this era, Getzels (1977) concludes:

> The work-success ethic was giving way to an ethic of *sociability*; the American ethos shifted from Main Street to Madison Avenue, and the model for our young changed from the hard-working Horatio Alger hero to the affable young man in the grey flannel suit. Future time orientation was giving way to *present time orientation*; the former national slogan "a penny saved is a penny earned" was replaced by the new slogan "buy now, pay later." Competitive individualism was giving way to *adaptive conformity*; inner-direction was transformed to other-direction; self-made man became organization man. And Puritan morality was giving way to *moral relativism*; morality became a statistical rather than an ethical concept; virtue was whatever the group one belonged to thought was virtuous. (pp. 6-7)

Not surprisingly, according to Beck and Murphy (in press-b), the dominant values of this era for administrators were faith in humanity's ability to solve social problems, commitment to equality of educational opportunity, and belief in democracy.

Three

The Behavioral Science and Dialectic Eras

In 1946 and 1947, three events occurred to disturb the setting described in the preceding paragraphs: (a) The Kellogg Foundation received a recommendation from its education advisory committee that school administration was a field which deserved Foundation support; (b) the planning committee of the AASA included in its statement of goals for the association "the initiation of studies and programs looking toward further professionalization of the superintendency," and (c) the professors of educational administration formed an organization which was to focus on the scientific study of administration, the elements of leadership, and the dissemination of practices encountered in the preparation of school administrators. (H. Moore, 1964, p. 15)

The Behavioral Science Era

As we leave the age of educational alchemy we should note that we could never have left it had we not entered it. It would not have been possible to improve the work of our predecessors had they not done that work. (Griffiths, 1957, p. 389)

To parody Wordsworth on the French Revolution, it was great to be an administrator and scholar of educational administration in the decade of the 1950s, but to be young and have a part in the rebuilding of a professional orientation "was very heaven." The field was permeated with a new enthusiasm and hope that out of the new research and analysis would come the true foundations for a sound professional approach to educational administration. (Goldhammer, 1983, p. 249)

The era of professionalization witnessed the growth of educational administration preparation programs from their adolescence to their early adulthood (see Table 2.3 and Figure 2.1). It was a period of great excitement, programmatic support, influential leadership (Crowson & McPherson, 1987), unparalleled activity, and considerable growth (Willower, 1983)—a period of considerable ferment in educational administration (H. Moore, 1964) and of "the development of educational administration as a self-conscious field of professional preparation" (Farquhar, 1977, p. 329). As Griffiths concluded in 1959, "the study of administration is now in its most fruitful period to date, and this is particularly true in educational administration" (p. 4). Goals were ambitious and hopes were high:

> Not only would a solid knowledge base be generated but out of it would come verified standards of practice that would lift the field to its rightful professional status. The spirit of inquiry permeated the field and led even the most prosaic of professors to believe that a sophisticated profession would emerge and take its place among those that had achieved such status in the past. (Goldhammer, 1983, p. 250)

As a consequence, "the purposes, content, and processes of graduate education in school administration [were] undergoing rapid change" (Wynn, 1957, p. 472). There was no evidence at the time that the landscape over which this new era of training would travel would be so tortuous nor that a scant 30 years later the wheels would come off the behavioral science engine that was driving the new movement.

SETTING THE STAGE

By 1950, relevant concepts from the behavioral sciences were more plentifully available, and additional ones would appear soon. The scientist, physical and behavioral, was rising in esteem. In part, the new doctrine was an honest attempt to restore the prestige of administrators. Briefly and approximately, the logic went like this: If the status of administration was to be repaired and improved, it was necessary to "professionalize" it. The first step in professionalization was to improve the preparation of those entering the field and to incorporate "basic" knowledge; knowledge of the behavorial sciences was the best choice. (Button, 1966, p. 222)

After the Second World War, the fabric of American society and thus the issues confronting its school leaders began to change (see Hencley, 1962; J. Norton, 1957; Watson, 1977) and, as had happened in the past, preparation programs in school administration responded in turn. Scientists, not businesspeople, now held center stage (Halpin, 1960). The quest for a science of administration in general and of school administration in particular began (see Culbertson, 1965, and Griffiths, 1988a, for reviews). According to T. Greenfield (1988), Halpin's "New Movement" in educational administration, as well as the "modern organizational theory" movement in general, may both

> be seen as movements reflecting Simon's pioneering attempt to establish the study of organizations and administration on an objective scientific basis. Both began with a conscious break from previous studies that were viewed as mired in "social philosophy" (Halpin, 1958, p. xii). Both advocated that science, cast in an objective, positivistic mould, could save the field from the philosophers, moralists, and other subjectivists. Together they represented the deliberate founding of a new science of organization which aimed to establish the experimental verification of "hypoytheticodeductive theory"—abstract, mathematically expressed theory that was held by its proponents to be the highest form of scientific knowledge. . . . Such theory, it was held, would produce control over organizations in the same way that it permitted control over the physical world. The aim of the New Movement in educational administration was to generate such theory about schools, to place it in the hands of administrators, and to train them in its use. And so began the effort to train educational administrators in the science of organizations. (p. 142)

As discussed earlier, significant alterations in the content of preparation programs are neither simply a response to changes in the larger environment nor simply attempts to enhance the status of program graduates. Some of the impetus for the periodic eras of ferment in educational administration can be traced to disgruntlement with methods and procedures employed in training programs, especially with the cognitive base undergirding the programs and with the values that they espouse. In the transition from the prescriptive to the behavioral science era there was increasing dissatisfaction with "the economic view of administration and organization" (Culbertson, 1965, p. 5) that was at the heart of preparation programs. There was also growing criticism of a field "that depended heavily upon individual perceptions and the vagaries of individual experience" (Goldhammer, 1983, p. 250) to form its knowledge base—a knowledge base that, as we have seen, was "little more than practitioners' prescriptive judgments on their experience" (T. Greenfield, 1988, p. 133). At the same time, the explicit values orientation of the human relations movement and the prescriptive framework of the entire first half century of preparation programs were coming under increasing scrutiny (Culbertson, 1964, 1965). Concurrent with the debate over the proper knowledge base and the role of values in preparation programs, criticisms were being leveled at practicing administrators, and preparation programs were being exhorted to develop stronger programs "to protect the public against ill-prepared or indifferent practitioners" (Goldhammer, 1983, p. 250).

A number of significant events that transpired during the early years of the behavioral science era were to have profound effects on preparation programs for school leaders; "taken together, they constitute the ingredients which have revolutionized a whole field of human endeavor" (Griffiths, 1959, p. 3). The first of these events was the formation of the National Conference of Professors of Educational Administration (NCPEA): "Born as an idea during the 1947 convention of AASA" (H. Moore, 1964, p. 17), it started when 72 men gathered in Endicott, New York, at the International Business Machines Homestead to consider the status of the profession of educational administration (Campbell et al., 1987; H. Moore, 1964). The NCPEA "represented an important first step in linking educational administration scholars from across North America" (Campbell et al., 1987, p. 181). Throughout the 1950s, it was a "continuing force for the improvement of professors of educational administration and of strengthening programs of preparation for school administrators" (Gregg, 1960, p. 22).[1] Perhaps the most important NCPEA meeting was the one held in Denver in August of 1954—a meeting labeled a "benchmark" in the professionalization of school administration by Getzels (1977, p. 8). At that meeting:

A number of scholars from the social science fields of psychology, sociology, political science, and social psychology, and others well versed in the theory of human behavior met with the professors of educational administration. These men did two things: first, they challenged the type of thinking which had been prevalent in educational administration, and second, they offered many suggestions for new approaches to thinking in the field. (Griffiths, 1959, p. 3)

The Denver meeting added considerable energy to the critical reviews of existing preparation programs and helped buttress the belief that a science of administration could provide an appropriate new direction for the profession.

The NCPEA was influential in spawning a second important event during the period of transition from the prescriptive to the behavioral science era—the creation of the Cooperative Project in Educational Administration, a consortium of eight universities[2] having "a regional or national leadership character" (H. Moore, 1964, p. 19) and funded by the Kellogg Foundation.[3] CPEA projects contributed to the improvement of a wide variety of the profession's components (see Campbell et al., 1987; Griffiths, 1959; and especially H. Moore, 1964), encouraged scholars from various disciplines to study school administration (Culbertson, 1965), and "profoundly influenced the professional climate surrounding the study and practice of educational administration" (Gregg, 1969, p. 994). For our purposes here, its most significant aspect is the fact that during the five-year life of the CPEA, its primary goal was to function as "a large-scale improvement program [that] would result not so much in discovery or pronouncement as in changes in the institutions which prepare school administrators" (H. Moore, 1964, p. 19):

Many aspects of the general problem of the preparation of administrative leaders [were] investigated and numerous experimental approaches [were] explored. Aspects which . . . received particular attention include[d] recruitment and selection of students, evaluation of existing programs, development of new curriculum patterns, establishment of cooperative relationships with school systems, provision of significant field experiences, and the strengthening of the organization and financial support of graduate institutions. (Gregg, 1960, p. 23)

In 1955, the Committee for the Advancement of School Administration (CASA) was established. Its membership of 18 included the
8 directors of the CPEA centers and was evenly divided between
practitioners and professors. In discussing the activity of CASA, H.
Moore (1964) concludes:

> Perhaps the most significant work of the Committee revolved
> around the establishment (through political/professional sanc-
> tions) of standards for the preparation of school administrators.
> Essentially, this took the Committee into areas of state certification
> regulations and professional accreditation. (p. 27)

The Committee, at the behest of the National Council for Accreditation of Teacher Education (NCATE), spent several years outlining
both "important features of preparation programs for administrators which should be considered in any accreditation visit" (H. Moore,
1964, p. 28) and specific standards for review.

The final "milestone" (Griffiths, 1959, p. 5) of this transition period occurred in 1956, when, growing out of the CPEA (Gregg, 1969),
34 programs in school administration at leading universities formed
the University Council for Educational Administration. The primary purpose of the association was:

> to improve graduate programs in educational administration
> through the stimulation and coordination of research, the publica-
> tion and distribution of literature growing out of research and
> training activities, and the exchange of ideas. (Campbell et al.,
> 1987, p. 182)

During its first quarter century, the "UCEA helped set directions
and had great influence on educational administration in the university world" (Willower, 1983, p. 181). Under the leadership of Jack
Culbertson it "became the dominant force in shaping the study
and teaching of educational administration in the 1960s and 1970s
[and] a major force in the advancement of preparation programs"
(Campbell et al., 1987, pp. 182-183).[4]

THE PREPARATION PROGRAM

Faculty

Throughout the life of the era of professionalization, a number of scholars studied the professoriate in school administration. One issue that they all address is departmental size. Farquhar (1977) reports that in 1954 the typical department had two full-time faculty members.[5] Because faculties were so small, "the internal organization of the staff of a department of educational administration [was] a relatively simple matter" (Wynn, 1957, p. 490). By 1957, Wynn reported that the modal number of faculty was four and that more than two thirds of all departments had five or fewer faculty members, while only 8% had more than eight professors. Lest we conclude that substantial growth was occurring in the mid-1950s, Wynn's caveat should be noted:

> Observation indicates that in many institutions professors of administration are part-time people, combining teaching in that field with teaching in other areas of specialization, or working at other tasks. It is not known how many of the persons above are part-time professors of administration. Several observers have estimated that if the numbers above were reduced by one half, a more accurate picture would result. (pp. 490-491)

There is some evidence that departments expanded during the golden era of the 1960s and early 1970s; according to Farquhar (1977), the typical department had nearly doubled in size from 1964 to 1974 and contained 10 full-time faculty members. However, by the mid-1970s things looked much as they had some 20 years earlier. In 1978, Davis concluded that the average department had only 6.5 full-time professors. And in their comprehensive 1988 study, McCarthy and her colleagues found the mean number of full-time faculty members to be 5 and the modal number to be 2.[6] Overall, it appears that despite "a downward shift in size of departments in recent years" (Miklos, in press), and despite the fact that departments are now very small, during the behavioral science era departments roughly doubled in size in terms of the number of full-time faculty members.

The profession was so overwhelmingly male and Caucasian during the 1950s that analysts of the era did not even address the issue of the gender and racial compositions of departments. In 1973, in the first of a series of three UCEA-sponsored studies of the professoriate in school administration, Campbell and Newell reported that 98% of professors were male and 97% were white. By 1978, Davis found that females occupied approximately 10% of faculty positions. Ten years later that number had increased to 12%, while the number of minority faculty had grown to 8% (McCarthy et al., 1988).

In the early 1950s, faculty members were still oriented primarily toward the practice dimensions of the profession. Indeed, as we have already seen, many departments were staffed with practicing administrators who taught on a part-time basis (Wynn, 1957). Although larger faculties were characterized by some specialization, most professors of school administration were still generalists. What differentiation existed involved the functional responsibilities of practitioners, "according to administrative levels or task areas" (Farquhar & Piele, 1972, p. 47). Over the next 30 years, this situation underwent fundamental alterations. Beginning in the late 1950s and continuing throughout the 1960s and 1970s, professors in educational administration programs became "qualitatively different in their roles" (Gregg, 1969, p. 1001). As specialization in the various disciplines increased, administrative experience became less important in the selection process[7] and professors became less interchangeable (Gregg, 1969) and less connected to the world of practice (Goldhammer, 1983):

> Beginning in the 1950s a different breed of individuals entered the professorship—specialists in particular technologies of behavioral science disciplines, people who may not have had extensive field experience but who could bring technical or conceptual expertise to the education of administrators. (Silver, 1982, p. 51)

By 1964, investigators "found an almost equal distribution of responses [from university preparation programs] favoring practice-related categories of specialization and those seeming to favor discipline-related specialization" (Farquhar & Piele, 1972, p. 46). By the mid-1970s, according to Farquhar (1977), the professoriate was even more fragmented:

> There was no longer any way to identify a single rubric by which their specializations could be categorized: a few retained the specializations oriented toward tasks and levels that predominated in the 1950s; many still espoused the subdiscipline- and

theory-oriented specializations that emerged during the 1960s; but several of the newly appointed professors were specialists in particular administrative problems, functions, settings, or other bases of expertise that [were] represented in the immense diversity of preparatory programs in the mid-1970s. (pp. 342-343)[8]

More recent reports (Boyan, 1981; Erickson, 1979; Immegart, 1977; McCarthy et al., 1988; Willower, 1987, 1988) confirm the specialization and fragmentation of the field of educational administration in general and of the professoriate in particular. Calls for methods and frameworks to bring coherence to this diversity abound (Boyan, 1981; McCarthy et al., 1988) and specific integrative mechanisms have been proposed (Boyd & Crowson, 1981; Erickson, 1977, 1979; J. Murphy, 1990h). We shall return to this issue in the concluding chapter.

To a lesser extent, from the mid-1950s to the mid-1980s there was some specialization by functional responsibilities of the professoriate, where roles

vary depending on whether their activities are focused primarily on research (the pursuit and discovery of new knowledge), synthesis (the collation and codification of existing knowledge), or development (the application of knowledge to the resolution of problems in the field). (Farquhar & Piele, 1972, p. 48)[9]

Both the shift in faculty orientation toward specialized disciplines and the specialization of functions of the professoriate itself helped to redirect the spotlight from "perspectives which have their roots in practice [to those] which have their roots in the structure of knowledge as found in university communities" (Culbertson, cited in Farquhar & Piele, 1972, p. 46). Overall, these changes resulted in professors entering the profession at a younger age and with more education than their peers of earlier generations. For example, in 1972 the average professor entered a faculty position at the age of 39; by the mid-1980s the average age had fallen to 37 (McCarthy et al., 1988). In the middle of the prescriptive era, fewer than 50% of the professors had a doctorate. By 1969, that number had risen to 90% (Gregg, 1969).

Throughout the behavioral science era, the time of professors of educational administration was consumed by teaching and advising, and, to a lesser extent, by service demands. High student-faculty ratios were, and continue to be, a defining characteristic of most educational administration preparation programs (Farquhar, 1977; Miklos, in press). Although the amount of time devoted to scholarly activities in general and to research in particular increased over the years (Campbell et al., 1987; McCarthy et al., 1988), the rise was not dramatic (Immegart, 1977) and the average still did "not compare favorably with the mean for faculty across disciplines" (McCarthy et al., 1988, p. 80; also Immegart, 1977). For example, in 1965, Griffiths (p. 42) used the term "dubious dribble" to characterize the quantity of research in educational administration. In the mid-1980s, at the close of the behavioral science era, McCarthy et al. reported that although educational administration professors spent 40% of their time on teaching and advising, they devoted only 12% of their work week to research-related activities (compared to 18% for other disciplines). Nearly 68% reported teaching as their primary area of strength, as opposed to only 14% who reported primary orientation toward research. The overall picture painted by reviewers in this era is one in which most of the professors were "occupied with a range of duties that preclude[d] serious and sustained scholarship" (Campbell et al., 1987, p. 184).

Students

Information on students in preparation programs during the era of professionalization is less extensive than reports on faculty. One very useful source of data is the set of portraits compiled by Farquhar (1977) of the typical student in 1954, 1964, and 1974:

> The typical educational administration student following a doctoral program at "University X" during 1954 was probably a white male in his mid- to late-thirties and was admitted on the basis of his previous academic record and his performance on normed tests of cognitive ability. He was an established educational administrator and continued as such throughout the program, because no study beyond the master's level was required for administrative certification in his state, graduate assistantships and fellowships were extremely rare, and full-time residency was unnecessary for doctoral study. He and most of his fellow students thus held administrative positions within school systems in and around the city where the university was located, and they took most of their

courses in the late afternoons and evenings, on weekends, and during the summer months. (p. 331)

The typical student enrolled at that time [1964] was, like his predecessor a decade earlier, a white male—but he was about five years younger. While he, too, was admitted on the basis of his academic record, his motivation for applying had not been strictly intrinsic: the state now required that he complete a doctorate or seventy hours of graduate study before he could become a superintendent. He had been a school principal, but he gave up this post to pursue graduate study because the university required that he spend at least two consecutive trimesters in full-time residence. (p. 334)

The "typical" student [in 1974], like his predecessor ten years earlier, was a male in his early thirties; but, unlike his predecessor, he was black. . . . He was also pleasantly surprised to note that fully a third of his fellow students were black and nearly a quarter of them were women. (p. 338)[10]

By the 1980s, the "trend toward increased heterogeneity of students in educational administration" (Silver, 1974, p. 22) was accelerating. The typical student was likely to be a female with a full-time job as a teacher[11] attending a doctoral program on a part-time basis in the evenings, on weekends, and/or during the summer (Campbell et al., 1987)—a pattern that has continued into the early 1990s (Shakeshaft, 1988).

Methods used by students to learn about and find their way into preparation programs did not vary much during this period. As we discuss more completely later in this chapter and in Chapter 4, the majority of the programs were "geographically parochial" (Nagle & Nagle, 1978, p. 119):

Self-initiated inquiry and recommendations of friends appear[ed] to be the most common sources of awareness of the programs, and convenience of location as well as faculty and program reputation provide[d] the major impetus for enrolling in the program. (Silver, 1978b, p. 206)

There were two important changes in entrance criteria during this decade: greater reliance on more advanced measures of intellectual prowess and more specification of standards. In the 1950s, the primary ingredients of admissions decisions were teaching experience and possession of a teaching certificate and a bachelor's degree (AASA, 1960). Other measures were used either infrequently or were so vague as to be meaningless. For example, in their 1960 report, AASA found that the Graduate Record Examination (GRE) was not stressed in making admissions decisions to training programs in school administration. On the issue of the GRE and related test scores, AASA discovered that "with most institutions which reported the use of tests for admission no cut-off points were given, nor was there any indication as to how the test results were used" (p. 57). On the subject of grade point average, they reported that although a "sizable number" of institutions claimed to require "acceptable grades," few specified what "acceptable" meant (p. 56). And, addressing the matter of academic record, they concluded that "while 'Academic Record' was mentioned most frequently, what would be looked for in the record was not clear" (p. 60).

Because of periodic efforts during the 1960s and 1970s "to apply more rigorous intellectual criteria in screening applicants" (Culbertson & Farquhar, 1970, p. 11), things had changed sufficiently by 1978 for Nagle and Nagle to conclude that a new set of criteria were firmly in place in preparation programs:[12]

> Three traditional criteria—a particular grade point average, a particular score on a standardized test (e.g., the Graduate Record Examination), and a set of acceptable recommendations—continue to be the critical criteria for admission as described by 85% or more of the respondents. In addition, 62% of the respondents indicated that students were required to pass a departmental interview prior to admission. (pp. 120-121)[13]

At the same time, there is some evidence that preestablished standards—at least in the areas of grade point average and standardized tests (e.g., a score of 1,000 on the GRE)—became institutionalized in some programs during the behavioral science era.

Although admission to graduate study in educational administration seems to have become more difficult over the scientific period, improvement in the quality of candidates admitted was marginal. Most departments continued to follow procedure approximating open admissions policies. In the 1978 UCEA-sponsored study of preparation programs in the United States, Silver (1978b) discovered that "only about 12% of doctoral program applicants [were] denied admission" (p. 206). Consequently, the quality of students in preparation programs from 1946 to 1985 was not especially high (Silver, 1982).

Little is known about students' roles in departments during this phase of administrator preparation. They appear to have been no more empowered than were the students in elementary and secondary schools, despite a somewhat enhanced role in the mid-1960s (Farquhar, 1977). According to Davis (1978):

> students [had] a relatively limited role in departmental decision-making and. . .this role [was] an informal one. In fact, less than one-quarter of all institutions report[ed] the existence of a formally constituted student organization in the department. (p. 42)

Program Structure

During the behavioral science era, programs in educational administration were, as they continue to be, designed to prepare both professors and practitioners, although for most departments the emphasis has been on the practitioner. Programs in this period were offered at the master's, intermediate, and doctoral levels of graduate study, although there was a good deal of overlap in the coursework at the three levels (Silver & Spuck, 1978).[14] There was a rather noticeable expansion in the number of programs over the 40-year period of the behavioral science era. While in 1946 there were about 125 institutions in the United States offering training programs, from 1940 to 1970:

> the two-year specialist program grew twenty-fold, the number of master's and doctor of education degree programs tripled, and the number of doctor of philosophy degree programs nearly doubled. (Miklos, 1983, p. 155)

Thus, by the late 1960s the number of programs had grown to 212 (Gregg, 1969). By the early 1970s, further expansion had pushed the number to 299 (Campbell & Newell, 1973); by the late 1970s to 375 (Culbertson & Silver, 1978); and by the mid-1980s to more than 500

(NCEEA, 1987). Not unexpectedly, this growth in the number of degree-granting institutions was matched by an increase in the number of degrees awarded. According to Farquhar (1977), for example, the number of doctoral degrees continued to mushroom throughout the era of professionalism, doubling each 10 years from 1955 to 1975—"increasing by over 70 percent between 1965 and 1970 alone" (p. 344). In 1954, approximately 250 dissertations were completed (Immegart, 1977). By 1957, that number had grown to 450, by 1964 to 490, and by 1971 to 1,030 (Immegart, 1977; Silver, 1982). All of these numbers represent substantial growth from the 13 doctorates conferred each year between 1911 and 1933 (Newlon, 1934). In addition, in the 1970-1971 academic year more than 8,500 master's degrees in educational administration and educational supervision were granted (Silver, 1982).

According to Culbertson and Silver (1978), preparation programs during this era were widely dispersed throughout the United States[15] —"in small institutions that cater[ed] to local interests and in huge multiversities that serve[d] a national population; . . . in urban metropolitan areas and in quiet rural towns" (p. 6). The programs had, and continue to have, "primarily a local or provincial character" (Miklos & Nixon, 1978, p. 110; also Clark, 1988; Davis, 1978; Silver, 1978a, 1978b). Nagle and Nagle (1978) paint the following portrait of educational administration training programs of this period:

> They draw most of their students from their surrounding geographic regions, they orient toward the dynamics and events of those regions and perhaps to the state in which they are located, and most of their graduates return to (or simply continue in) positions in those same regions. For example, faculty responding to this survey estimated that approximately 30% of their students received undergraduate training at the same institution in which they engage in doctoral work; that approximately 41% of their students lived or worked within a 25-mile radius of the institution at the time they are admitted to a doctoral program; and that upon completion of their doctoral work, at least 40% of their graduates assume positions within 100 miles of the institution. (pp. 119-120)

Like their peers from the preceding generation, most students during the early years of the era of professionalization were part-time

students, holding down full-time administrative positions while
completing coursework at night and during the summer (Farquhar,
1977).

In the 1960s, however, a "trend toward full-time residence study"
(Culbertson, 1966, p. iii) was evident across preparation programs.[16]
For example, in the 1962-1963 school year, "90 of the 103 institutions
offering doctoral programs reported that a year of residency for the
doctor's degree [although not for the master's degree] was required"
(Gregg, 1969, p. 998; also Farquhar & Piele, 1972). In 1959, AASA
implemented a standard requiring members entering the associa-
tion after 1964 to have completed two years of graduate study at a
NCATE-accredited institution (H. Moore, 1964)—a standard which
Culbertson (1963) predicted would soon rise to three years.[17]

The last 15 years of this era were characterized by a significant
rollback in full-time study in preparation programs. Succumbing to
"such external pressures as dwindling job markets, heightened competition for students, and legislation rather than to internal pleas for
rationality, relevance, or cohesiveness" (Silver, 1974, p. 24), by the
late 1970s the vast majority of the programs were again populated
by part-time commuting students who were completing their coursework at night, on weekends, and during the summer (Davis, 1978).[18]

Progress on the matter of certification was mixed. On the one
hand, the number of states requiring administrative coursework
continued to grow. In 1939, fewer than 20 states required graduate-
level study for administrators. By the mid 1950s, more than 40 states
mandated such coursework (Miklos, in press). By the mid 1960s, almost all states required "between 30 and 50 graduate credit hours
for the principalship" and a "doctorate or seventy semester hours
of graduate study to qualify for the superintendency" (Silver, 1982,
p. 51). On the other hand, the method of certification criticized by
Wynn in 1957—in which states specified "certification in terms of
accumulation of specific courses 'cafeteria style' " (p. 470)—was still
largely in place as the professional era drew to a close.

Deep evaluations of preparation programs were limited throughout this era, especially outside of UCEA programs and NCATE-
accredited institutions. The most common assessments were follow-
up studies of graduates that were of limited scientific validity (Silver,
1982). Evaluation based on examinations of outcome measures was
conspicuous by its absence (J. Murphy, 1987).

Program Content

The predominant trend during this era was the infusion of theoretical knowledge from the behavioral and social sciences—with related methodological perspectives—into programs of study for school administrators. The overarching framework of this activity was the expansion of the knowledge base of the profession through the development of a science of administration. This was a movement "to produce a foundation of scientifically supported (hypothetico-deductive) knowledge in educational administration in place of the hortatory, seat-of-the-pants literature already in place" (Crowson & McPherson, 1987, pp. 47-48) and a trend "away from technique-oriented substance based upon practical experience and toward theory-oriented substance based on disciplines 'external' to education" (Culbertson & Farquhar, 1971b, p. 9; Culbertson, 1988a). Accompanying these trends was "the emergence of logical positivism as a widely accepted mode of knowledge production" (Silver, 1982, p. 52; see Culbertson, 1981, 1988a, 1988b; Griffiths, 1988a, for reviews).

> The new science of administration was to make a sharp distinction between philosophy and science; prescribing to administrators the actions they should take was seen as something distinctly different from describing and explaining administration through scientific concepts and theories. Those who adhered strictly to the new school of thought focused upon the description and explanation of administrative phenomena and avoided prescriptive statements. Thus, the authors of a major textbook on public administration published in 1950 argued that "a science (of administration) in the sense of an objective understanding of the phenomena without confusion between facts and values" is possible. The authors, therefore, concentrated on the scientific aspects of administration and consciously avoided stating what government *should* do.
>
> The new movement also placed high value on theory. Contrary to the popular view that theory is for those in ivory towers, adherents of the new science maintained that theory was one of the most practical of human inventions. It was judged practical not only for those interested in studying administration but also for those interested in controlling human events . . . therefore, courses on the "theory of administration" found their way into catalogues of different universities.

Those responsible for preparing administrators recognized clearly the complexities inherent in administration and delved into the social sciences in a search for concepts and theories to illuminate these complexities. (Culbertson, 1964, pp. 307-308)

This movement produced: a view of school administration as "an applied science within which theory and research are directly and linearly linked to professional practice [and in which] the former always determine the latter, and thus knowledge is superordinate to the principal and designed to prescribe practice" (Sergiovanni, 1991b, p. 4); the acceptance of a heavy reliance on social science content "as an indicator of a high quality program" (Miklos, 1983, p. 160);[19] "the borrowing and adopting of research techniques and instruments from the behavioral sciences" (Culbertson, 1965, p. 7); and an interdisciplinary—or at least multidisciplinary—approach to training (Culbertson, 1963; Farquhar & Piele, 1972; C. Hodgkinson, 1975).[20]

For the first time, the field of educational administration reached beyond the business management literature as scholars delved into sociology, psychology, anthropology, political science, and economics (Culbertson et al., 1973) for conceptual frameworks and theory-based empirical evidence relevant to the study of educational administration. As the professors who had been trained at these institutions began to populate the faculties of major universities, subject matter and research methods from the allied disciplines gained ascendancy in administrator preparation programs throughout the country. (Silver, 1982, p. 52)

This interdisciplinary, social science approach to training focused upon the model of the administrator as decisionmaker (see especially Griffiths, 1959; also Culbertson, 1964).

The 1950s. There is some evidence that by the late 1950s, "the almost complete lack of theory oriented research in the field of administration" (Griffiths, 1959, p. 4) was being addressed and that the theory movement was holding center stage among leading scholars in universities (H. Moore, 1964). It is also true, to some extent, that the textbooks of the late 1950s were "characterized by a search for

the substance of administration and for the *theory* which binds substance together" (Griffiths, 1959, p. 2)—a substantial advance from
the "exhortations, how-to-do-it prescriptions, catalogues of opinion, or normative 'status' investigations" that filled the literature of
the prescriptive era (Halpin, cited in Griffiths, 1959, p. 4).

However, widespread incorporation of ideas from the theory movement into preparation programs was not a reality at this time—a fact
that should not be surprising considering, as we reported earlier,
that it generally takes a decade or more for new ideas in the field to
penetrate training programs. In their 1960 report, the AASA observed—in addition to an absence of attention to human relations
courses, a lack of interest in field experiences, and unintegrated core
experiences—"a complete lack of course titles referring to theory of
administration" (p. 64) in the preparation programs they reviewed.
In examining courses taken outside the field of education, they
found that "professors of educational administration, not knowing
what their students should study, [were] sending them to the social
scientists on a helter-skelter basis" (p. 67). The AASA, as well as
others, called for the development "of some sort of systematic process . . . for identifying [social science] concepts relevant to our purposes" (Cunningham, Downey, & Goldhammer, 1963, p. 101) and for
the establishment of programs containing those elements. As the
1950s came to an end, the AASA's assessment was that "the courses
currently offered [did] not reflect, in their titles or patterns of titles,
the groundswell of change which [was] evident in the field of administration" (p. 64).

Farquhar (1977) tells us that the typical student's program in 1954
looked as follows:

> About a third of the student's program consisted of courses in his
> major area of study—educational administration. These included
> a required core of four credit hours in "Current Practices in School
> Administration" (which emphasized school law, school system
> organization, the administration of personnel and the instructional
> program, school finance, pupil accounting, public relations, and
> building construction and maintenance) plus a variety of courses
> in which he could study more intensively the specialized task areas
> to which he was introduced in the core offerings. About a quarter
> of his program was devoted to courses in a minor field of study—
> normally either elementary or secondary education. He was also

required to take about one-sixth of his courses in the "foundations" field of educational history, philosophy, and psychology. The remaining quarter of his program was divided almost equally between courses in statistics and research methods and electives in areas outside of his minor field (including a couple of courses in disciplines other than education). In addition, he could gain limited credit for participation in a school survey, and he completed a dissertation on a problem concerning staff supervision, pupil accounting, educational finance, or school facilities. (p. 332)

Throughout this decade, the lack of good internship opportunities continued to plague preparation programs:

> The two most commonly mentioned weaknesses have to do with "in the schools" activities—the on-the-job experiences which the Commission encourages. In comparing the list of strengths with the list of weaknesses, it appears as though the colleges and universities agree to the value of the internship and field experiences yet have not been able to find ways of putting them into operation. (AASA, 1960, p. 74)

The 1960s. Throughout the 1960s, changes in the content of preparation programs became more noticeable. By 1964, Culbertson (1963) claimed that "the subject matter of school administration [had] undergone radical changes" (p. 35) and that training programs were employing "more encompassing and more rigorous types of content as bases for preparation" (Culbertson, 1964, p. 329). He listed these changes as follows: "shifts from a practical orientation to a more theoretical one, from the use of one discipline to the use of several disciplines, [and] from a technical orientation to a more general one" (Culbertson, 1963, p. 35). A study that contrasted courses offered in 1962-1963 with those offered in 1958-1959, although it uncovered a good deal of similarity, discerned two important changes that were consistent with the ideology of the behavioral science movement: "a completely new emphasis on instruction in administrative theory and additional stress on student competence in research" (Gregg, 1969, p. 997). A 1964 study by the AASA found that the integration of content from sociology, psychology, economics, political science, anthropology, and public administration represented a fundamental shift from the program content of the late 1950s (Farquhar &

Piele, 1972). A third study by the CASA reached the same conclusion: "the most frequently reported change for the period of 1958-1962 was the increased use of the social and behavioral sciences in preparatory programs for administrators" (Culbertson, 1965, p. 18).

The remainder of the 1960s saw both the continuation of these trends—especially the tendency for "discipline-based content . . . to displace practice-based content in preparation programs" (Farquhar & Piele, 1972, p. 7)—and the beginning of new ones as well. By the middle of the decade, Culbertson (1964) was reporting that:

> the administrator, as an efficient performer of a job (an image which characterized the earlier "scientific-management" movement), or the administrator as one skilled in interpersonal relations (an image which characterized the "human-relations" movement), no longer was the *central* target of training programs. Rather, the core facet of the administrator image in the new movement was that of a skillful decision-maker gifted in analysis and in the application of concepts and theories. (p. 308)

In turn, "many of the strictly technique courses in preparatory programs were replaced or supplemented by courses which utilized, to varying degrees, content and concepts from certain disciplines among the social sciences" (Farquhar, 1968, p. 100). An AASA study in 1962-1963 spelled out a variety of ways in which this shift was occurring:

> (a) courses in the disciplines are required; (b) professors of these disciplines teach certain courses designed especially for school administrators, often in the college of education; (c) professors of educational administration learn from their colleagues in these disciplines that content and those concepts that apply to school administration, and introduce them in their own courses; (d) professors of educational administration and professors of other disciplines teach courses jointly. (cited in Farquhar & Piele, 1972, p. 10)

Although option (c) would become the dominant pattern in the mid-to-late 1970s and continue throughout the-1980s, during the 1960s and early 1970s, "outside courses" (option [a]) were the preferred strategy. For example, during the mid-1960s, Goldhammer and his colleagues found that about two thirds of the preparation programs they surveyed were mandating cognate work in the social sciences, with a mode number of hours between 12 and 15 (Farquhar & Piele, 1972).[21]

A later study completed by Culbertson and Farquhar (1971b) discovered that 59% of all coursework external to education taken by school administration students was in the social sciences (as opposed, for example, to 20% in management science and 9% in the humanities). Sociology, political science, psychology, and economics were the most popular areas of study. By the close of the decade, Gregg (1969) was able to report that although specialized areas in students' programs were still often configured in terms of management functions or positions (see also Immegart, 1977), there was "an increasing emphasis on specialization with respect to disciplinary bases such as the sociology, politics, or economics of education" (p. 1001). Although the AASA's options (b)—behavioral science professors teaching special courses for school administration students— and (d)—joint teaching—do not appear to have been systematically employed during this decade, the seeds for cooperative instruction were planted when, "for the first time in history," interdisciplinary research teams of professors of school administration and the social sciences were formed (Culbertson, 1964, p. 308). It is also important to note that throughout this era scholars from varied disciplines "increasingly participated in the *study* of administration" (Culbertson, 1965, p. 9, emphasis added).

Before proceding to other content issues in the 1960s, several further points about the behavioral sciences are worth mentioning. First, in many respects, effects are in the eye of the beholder. As we discussed earlier (see Note 19), progress on infusing social science content into training programs has received mixed reviews. Second, as Gregg (1969) astutely discerned, two fundamental problems that prevented the successful marrying of educational administration and the behavioral sciences went largely unattended during this decade:

> No general effort [was] . . . made by education specialists and social scientists to identify cooperatively the knowledges and skills which the social sciences should contribute to the education of administrators, nor [was] any general pattern of relationships between departments of educational administration and other departments . . . established. (p. 1000)

Third, the first voices were heard suggesting that disproportionate attention to developing a science of administration could—either because of flaws endemic to the theory movement or through a diversion of energy—cause other important areas of study, as well as issues of ethics and purposes, to be devalued (Culbertson, 1964, 1965; Cunningham et al., 1963; Farquhar, 1968; Goldhammer, 1963; Halpin, 1960; Harlow, 1962).

Other issues of content also attracted attention during the 1960s. Continuing a trend that had begun in the 1950s (W. Anderson & Lonsdale, 1957), emphasis on field experiences became somewhat more pronounced. For example, Gregg (1969) reported that the number of field experiences quadrupled between 1958-1959 and 1962-1963, although only half of all training programs were offering internships, only a small percentage of students participated in them, and efforts to define the internship[22] continued to be largely unsuccessful (see also Farquhar & Piele, 1972). During the later half of the decade, nearly all institutions in a UCEA study reported that internship[23] opportunities had been increased in their programs (Culbertson & Farquhar, 1971c).

The 1960s were also characterized by "a definite trend toward a greater amount of common content in preparatory programs for principals, superintendents, supervisors, and assistant superintendents" (Culbertson, 1963, p. 34). Although some efforts at flexibility and specialization were made during this decade (Culbertson & Farquhar, 1971a; Farquhar, 1977), by and large there "was no agreement on differentiating the preparation of a principal from that of a superintendent" (Gregg, 1969, p. 1001) and most students experienced a large block of common learning.[24] The view that "administrative processes are similar even though they take place in diverse organizations" gained wide acceptance during the 1960s (Culbertson, 1965, p. 5). This, in the most general sense, led to a focus on administration qua administration in preparation programs:

> The rationale for the generic approach was grounded in the view that there were substantial similarities across the adjectival forms of administration, that administrator preparation should focus on conceptual rather than technical content, and that the interchange among administrators from different institutional settings could be a source of important learning. (Miklos, 1983, p. 163; see also Boyan, 1963)

In a practical sense, this meant the infusion into training programs of administrative concepts from other applied areas of study as well as an increase in the number of administration courses from outside the college of education completed by school administration students. More specifically, the effect was that students were "being exposed to a growing amount of content from business and public administration" (Farquhar & Piele, 1972, p. 10).[25]

A final content trend of the 1960s was the expansion in the amount of research and statistics material to which students were exposed (Gregg, 1969). Culbertson and Farquhar's (1971c) study reveals that throughout the decade, there was "increased sophistication of student research, as represented by more use of advanced statistics and computer technology in analysis" (p. 12).

The 1970s. In the 1970s, program content—as well as other elements of preparation programs—was shaped to a large extent by three major phenomena:

> One, a legacy from the 1960s, was the phenomenon of growth— both in the level of sophistication of preparatory programs and in the variety of content and activities comprising them. A second was the phenomenon of relevance—concern with the application and utilization, rather than merely the production and dissemination, of knowledge, concern with assessment and accountability, and concern with performance and competence. The third basic phenomenon was that of democratization, reflected in efforts to open up access to preparation programs, to involve students in departmental decision-making, and to increase flexibility and individualization in program determination. (Farquhar, 1977, p. 340)

The result of this momentum meant that the late 1960s and most of the 1970s were an era of change, high expectations, and expansion in departments of educational administration (Culbertson & Farquhar, 1971c): "Everywhere one looked, there seemed to be something promising that could be incorporated into our preparation programs" (Farquhar, 1977, p. 337). By the middle of the decade, when the first systemic attacks were being mounted on the scientific movement, "*most* universities were using some means to incorporate social science content into preparation programs" (Miklos, 1983, p. 160, emphasis added), although all the difficulties with developing theory-based content noted in the 1960s were still evident and some forces were working to shift emphasis "from discipline-oriented program design to career-oriented program design" (Farquhar, 1977, p. 341). Consistent with the maturation of the influence of the social and behavioral sciences, integration of educational administration with other departments continued (Silver, 1974).

The comprehensive study of doctoral programs in the United States conducted for the UCEA by Nagle and Nagle (1978) provides the most thorough description of training program content during the 1970s. The Nagles reported that, overall, professors believed there to be a fairly balanced treatment of conceptual, human relations, and technical skills in these programs. However:

> [in terms] of specific topics emphasized in coursework, the responses of both faculty and students reinforced [a] dominance of attention to developing conceptual skills. By far the most often-cited topic was administrative theory, for it was cited as a high priority topic by 81% of the respondents. The next most frequently cited topics included decision-making (47%), education law (47%), leadership (44%), and finance (42%). (p. 117)

The typical program required students to complete 82 hours beyond the baccalaureate degree, with a range from 60 to 105. Required course hours ranged from 33 to 50. The average student spent 57% of his or her time in formal instruction. Sixty percent of that time was spent in educational administration courses, 25% in courses in other departments

> in the college of education, and only 15% in courses outside the college.[26] To a great extent, despite the influence of the social sciences on the field of educational administration during the past decade and despite the presumed flexibility and breadth of doctoral programs in the 1970s, the actual coursework taken by students in the surveyed programs tends to be concentrated either in educational administration *per se* or in foundation courses that are taught in the college of education and are directly relevant to doctoral comprehensives. (p. 117)

Nagle and Nagle sum up the self-contained aspect of training programs as follows:

In sum, without question, the doctoral degrees offered by educational administration programs appear to be essentially professional school degrees. The typical student is required to complete 8 hours in research and statistics, 4.4 hours in a survey of educational administration, 3.3 hours in curriculum, 2.7 hours in history and philosophy of education, and 1.4 hours in educational sociology. (p. 125)

Sixty-five percent of the programs in the Nagle and Nagle study required some type of field experience (up from less than 50% in the 1960s)—a requirement that consumed 15% of the typical student's doctoral program. The average doctoral student spent 29% of his or her time in research activities (as compared to 20% for master's degree students [Miklos, in press]) consisting of field studies, research projects, and doctoral research. As noted above, the largest number of mandated coursework hours (8) were in the area of research and statistics. Nearly all doctoral students, whether Ed.D. or Ph.D. students, were required to do original research for the doctoral dissertation.[27]

Preparation program content in the 1970s was shaped by two additional developments. Although there was a great deal of overlap in program requirements for all students in training institutions (Nagle & Nagle, 1978), there is some evidence of an increase in specialization[28]—the opportunity for students to complete course-work that would prepare them for diverse positions in schools or to focus on a particular set of skills (Silver, 1974). Second, a number of analysts of the period confirm that programs were shifting "toward a competency-based format or increasing the amount of competency-related content" (Griffiths, et al., 1988b; Silver, 1978a, p. 190). By the early 1970s, "about one-third of programs in the United States were orienting some aspects of their preparation to the development of competencies" (Miklos, 1983, p. 168) and by the mid-1970s, competency-based education had become one of the most pronounced trends in school administration training programs (Silver, 1978a; 1982).[29]

The 1980s. By the end of the behavioral science era, what Cooper and Boyd (1987) labeled a "One Best Model" of training appeared to be deeply ensconced in university departments of educational leadership:

The content of these courses of study [was] basically the same. The programs typically focus[ed] on the study of administration, leadership, and supervision, and include[d] an introduction to school law, planning, politics and negotiation, finance and budgeting, and some gesture at research methods and evaluation. These courses generally rel[ied] on a small number of rather similar textbooks, cite[d] articles from the management and educational administration journals, and [were] taught by professors from this same tradition. . . . The programmatic content of the One Best Model [rested] on an intellectual paradigm borrowed from social psychology, management, and the behavioral sciences. The philosophical base of the One Best Model, one that evolved alongside the programmatic component, [was] an abiding belief in empiricism, predictability, and "scientific" certainty, taught by professors steeped in this approach. (p. 4)

Despite a rising crescendo of criticism of the influence of the theory movement in educational administration (J. Murphy & Hallinger, 1987), Silver (1982) reminds us that the social science intellectual paradigm was comfortably entrenched in training programs at the end of this era of professionalism:

Behavioral science content prevail[ed] in . . . programs in the form of courses devoted to administrative theory or organizational behavior as well as in the fairly widespread expectations that students complete cognate courses in behavioral science disciplines, conduct research in the hypothetico deductive mode, and include in their dissertation committees a member of one of the allied discipline departments. (p. 52)

Two investigations by M. Norton (M. Norton, 1991; M. Norton & Levan, 1987) shed some light on coursetaking patterns of educational administration students in the 1980s.[30] Norton found that about 33% of all their doctoral work was completed in educational administration, roughly 20% in foundations, 15% in research and statistics, 7% in cognates, 5% each in field experiences and workshops/seminars, and 3% in dissertation work. Within educational administration itself, 60% of the courses were taken in the areas of organization and administration, personnel, law, and finance. In the general area of research, students took 56% of their work in statistics and 44% in research methods. Other information on program content in the early-to-mid-1980s has been provided by Miklos (1983; in press), who reported that: (a) about one fourth of courses completed by doctoral students were external to educational administration; and (b) although roughly two thirds of all programs continued to require field experiences, less than 10% of student work time was spent in this area (down from 15% in the 1970s).

Instruction

Discussions of pedagogy in preparation programs were relatively infrequent before the behavioral science era (Wynn, 1972). What we do know is that as the ferment in this era began to be felt, "the learning of administration [was] still a bookish chore" (AASA, 1960, p. 67), that programs were "sterile, classroom bound, and unaffected by newer techniques such as simulation and field studies" (Gregg, 1969, p. 998), and that the textbook had become the primary tool in the preparation of educational administrators (Eaton, 1986).

We also know that, somewhat tentatively in the 1950s and with a quickening pace in the 1960s, programs began experimenting with a spate of activities designed to diversify instructional strategies, especially to move away from the traditional lecture-discussion format (W. Anderson & Lonsdale, 1957; Wynn, 1972). To a large extent, this expansion was made possible by instructional innovation in other areas, especially in business management, and by "the creation in 1955 of the University Council for Educational Administration, which accepted responsibility for the development of instructional materials and the enrichment of instructional method" (Wynn, 1972, pp. 12-13). Perhaps the most prevalent rationale for developing more varied approaches to instruction was the need to narrow the practice-theory gap that developed as efforts to create a science of administration moved preparation programs further and further away from the practice orientation of the prescriptive era (Miklos, 1983; J. Murphy & Hallinger, 1987). Culbertson (1964) captured this perspective at the zenith of the theory movement in preparation programs:

The discontinuity between the study of administration and its practice is widely recognized and, as knowledge about administration increases, this discontinuity may well become greater. One

way to avoid such a development is to use, in preparatory programs, those instructional methods which will effectively relate
emerging concepts to practice, thus helping to insure that the latter
is improved and the former is responsibly tested. It is in part to
achieve this purpose that cases, simulated situations, field study,
and the internship have been developed. Their use in preparatory
programs has been strongly influenced by emerging social science
concepts. (p. 329)

He argued that "simulated materials provide countless opportunities for relating social science concepts to administrative situations
and problems" (p. 327). Earlier, Griffiths (1959) suggested that case
materials could (and should) be employed "to try out theoretical
concepts" (p. 7) from the administrative science movement. Discussing the same strategy, Culbertson (1964) maintained that "cases
can encourage and help guide the organization of relevant content
about administration" (p. 325).[31] Gregg (1969) reached a similar
conclusion: "simulated situations give an opportunity to involve
the student emotionally as well as intellectually and also help bridge
the gap between theory and practice" (p. 988).

The desire to employ methods that would prepare "administrators to cope with purpose and policy" in an increasingly complex
world also provided impetus to the movement to diversify pedagogy in training programs (Culbertson, 1964, p. 329). A third purpose was simply to make learning more lively and interesting
(Miklos, 1983), in a response to what Wynn (1972) labels "the dis-
comfort of the profession with the sterility of 'classroom-bound'
instruction" (p. 10). A fourth rationale for pedagogical diversity—
one that emerged toward the end of the era of professionalism—was
the wish to bring instruction in line with the principles of adult
learning (Levine, Barth, & Haskins, 1987; J. Murphy & Hallinger,
1987; Pitner, 1987).

Institutions experimented with incorporating a variety of instructional approaches into their preparation programs during this period. Wynn (1972) informs us that "by the early 1960s a substantial
movement from 'sterile' to reality-centered methods of instruction
was clearly underway" (p. 9). A 1964 study by AASA discovered that

the use of simulated situations, game theory, cases, theory development and problem-oriented seminars, in addition to or without

the usual textbook-lecture-discussion technique, is mentioned in a majority of the questionnaires (from 212 of 289 institutions offering graduate work for superintendents of schools) even though no specific question was directed toward these approaches to learning. How prevalent they are is unknown, but they certainly form a part of the frontier in the teaching of school administration. (cited in Wynn, 1972, p. 2)

Also in 1964, Culbertson concluded that "with the emergence of pertinent content from the social sciences during the last few decades, cases have been used increasingly to relate concepts to 'facts of administrative life' " (p. 325). Wynn (1972) reported that "by 1964 at least sixty-five universities were using simulated materials in either preservice or inservice programs" (p. 9). In a review of instructional strategies toward the end of the 1960s, Gregg (1969) documented extensive application of the "in-basket" method of simulation,[32] revealing that the original UCEA "in-basket" materials had been used by 20,000 students in some 90 universities. However, his assessments in the areas of cases, gaming, and laboratory training were more guarded. Although he acknowledged that cases were indeed being employed in training programs, he saw little evidence of increase in this strategy during the early years of the professionalization era.[33] He claimed that use of gaming and laboratory training had not penetrated preparation programs deeply.

By the early 1970s, instructional innovation continued on the upswing. In their 1971 report, Culbertson and Farquhar (1971c) revealed:

The use of simulation has reportedly been introduced or expanded in almost 80 percent of the universities included in the survey. Increases in the use of cases and seminars were reported by about one-third of the respondents. In addition, experimentation with such less widespread methods as micro-training, computer-based simulation, gaming, and the use of tapes, films, and television were indicated to be underway in about one-tenth of the institutions. Less frequent employment of group dynamics techniques and laboratory training exercises was reported, although a growth in the popularity of these methods has been apparent since the UCEA study was completed.

It can be concluded, then, that there is a variety of instructional ap- proaches being introduced to increase student involvement in reality- oriented classroom experiences. (p. 2)

A year later Farquhar and Piele (1972) also argued that two "less traditional approaches to simulation" (p. 29)—gaming and computer-based simulation—were being increasingly employed in preparation programs. In his 1972 treatment of unconventional instructional methods, Wynn reached a similarly sanguine conclusion. He maintained that a "substantial amount of similarly persuasive evidence disclose[d] that remarkable progress [had] been made since 1960 in the development of instructional methods and materials for programs in educational administration" (p. 2). And finally, according to Farquhar (1977), in the typical school administration program in 1974:

"Lecture-and-textbook" courses began to be replaced by seminars and workshops relying heavily on the use of reality-oriented multimedia instructional materials and methods (including extensive work with cases, simulations, games, laboratory training exercises, computer-aided instruction, sensitivity training, tapes, films, etc.). (p. 337)

According to Miklos (1983), "the major characteristic of all these methods was an increased reality orientation" (p. 165).

Studies conducted closer to the end of the behavioral science era that reviewed the entire instructional program, rather than focusing on unconventional and alternative strategies, arrived at less euphoric positions (Alkire, 1978; Davis & Spuck, 1978; Erlandson & Witters-Churchill, 1988; Miklos & Nixon, 1978; Silver, 1978b). All of these authors found that "lecture and discussion in a classroom setting based on the use of the textbook remain[ed] the dominant mode of instruction" (Silver, 1982, p. 53). In addition, there was little evidence of the expanded diversification of instructional methods that occurred in the late 1960s and early 1970s. Nor was there much evidence that the earlier period of diversification had had a great impact. At the end of the 1970s, Nagle and Nagle (1978) summed up developments as follows:

In effect, then, despite the abundance of new instructional modes, techniques, and materials relevant to university classrooms, educational administration courses, at least in the 60 programs surveyed, continue[d] to be characterized by lectures and/or large group discussions in traditional classroom settings of between 10 and 30 students. Alternative approaches to instruction that employ one-to-one settings, programmed modules, and/or independent study [were] still very much the exception rather than the rule. (p. 126)

On the one hand, then, the assortment of instructional approaches visible in preparation programs did expand over the 40 years of the professionalization era. New methods were introduced and, although none were used extensively (Miklos, in press), collectively they offered a richer pedagogy to students than had been available in the prescriptive era. A few strategies, simulations and case studies in particular, penetrated fairly deeply into training programs. On the other hand, however, it is clear that as the behavioral science era drew to a close, the lecture method of instruction was still fairly well entrenched, despite the unfavorable light in which it was seen by students and in the literature (Miklos, 1983). Like their colleagues in public schools (see Cuban, 1984), professors in 1985 were teaching much as they had for the past half century.[34] We close with an excellent summary of progress in the area of instruction provided by Miklos (1983; see also Hoyle, 1987; J. Murphy & Hallinger, 1987):

The general outcome of attempts to improve the teaching of educational administration [during the theory era] seems to be that innovative instructional practices have been incorporated into preparation programs, but not to a revolutionary extent. These methods and materials have probably achieved the goal of more interesting and lively instruction; whether they have made a major contribution to bridging the gap between the study and practice of administration is doubtful. The challenge to develop additional reality-oriented materials and to use them more effectively appears to be as great now as it was some years ago. (p. 166)

Epistemology and Philosophy

Following the framework we outlined at the beginning of Chapter 2, we close our analysis of this section by highlighting two issues ingrained in much of the discussion to date—the epistemological and philosophical orientations of the era of professionalism. In moving from the prescriptive to the behavioral science phase of training:

> The essential shift was from conceiving of educational administration as a domain of action only to conceiving of it as a domain of study also. The shift moved the focus of effort from an orientation based on solutions, where experienced administrators gave answers to questions of "how to do it," to an orientation based on inquiry, where problems were posed and understanding was sought regarding the phenomena of administration in their own right. (Getzels, 1977, p. 9)

On the knowledge front, this meant a movement away from information drawn from practice to an understanding extracted from theoretical constructs within the disciplines. The epistemological foundations of this era were constructed with scientific knowledge, culled from the behavioral and social sciences, which provided an accepted "set of rules for what constituted truth" (T. Greenfield, 1988, p. 135). Despite well-articulated cautions (Culbertson, 1963, 1964, 1965; Halpin, 1960), theory and research became the only acceptable source of understanding (Sergiovanni, 1991b). Equally important, the methods of acquiring knowledge derived from the behavioral sciences also became firmly established (Culbertson, 1981, 1988a), particularly the tenets of logical positivism. As we discuss more fully below, these trends resulted in the entrenchment of a "philosophy of science" (Silver, 1982, p. 52) in preparation programs in educational administration. For those at the helm of training programs throughout this era, the humanities, philosophy, and values were all either consciously discarded or relegated to positions of minor importance.

The Dialectic Era

So the plan did not "come off." The profession has not emerged as it gave promise of doing thirty years ago. It has not become more solidly grounded in a knowledge base which provides standards and criteria for effective performance. It has not produced the type of symbiosis and adaptive relationship between the field and the preparatory and research programs that enables each to feed off the other in a combined effort to adapt, flourish, and build upon their commonality of interests. It has remained an adaptive profession, unable to determine its own destiny or to shape schools on the basis of its knowledge and experience. Its power remains fragmented, and the ability to control its own destiny is still underdeveloped. (Goldhammer, 1983, p. 269)

In Chapters 5 and 6 we look ahead to see what the future holds for preparation programs in educational administration. Here we are concerned with current events. Our focus is on the period of ferment that is accompanying the transition from one phase of training—the behavioral science era—to the next—what we refer to as the "dialectic era," what Kerchner (1988) labels the "period of choice," and what Sergiovanni and his colleagues (Sergiovanni, Burlingame, Coombs, & Thurston, 1987) call the "cultural era" (see Table 2.2).

SETTING THE STAGE

School administrators risk becoming an anachronism if their preparation programs in schools, colleges, and departments of education do not respond to calls for change in preparing them for professional leadership functions. (AACTE, 1988, p. 1)

The early phase of the dialectic era is experiencing the turbulence or "turmoil" (Griffiths, 1979) that is accompanying the movement of preparation programs in educational administration away from their young adulthood. As was true for earlier periods, the dialectic era also is being ushered in on the wings of widespread environmental pressure for the reform of American society, growing disillusionment with the guiding values and cognitive base undergirding existing preparation programs, a felt need to enhance the professional stature of school leaders,[35] and emerging views about a better future. As contrasted to earlier eras, however, a widely accepted perspective about an appropriate path to follow is slow in forming.[36]

To date, the transition from the behavioral science era has been a dark one for educational administration (Griffiths, 1988b; J. Murphy, 1990e). Although "the mood in educational administration in many universities continued to be upbeat in the 1970s" (Willower, 1983, p. 181), an underlying "sense of disillusionment" (Crowson & Mc-Pherson, 1987, p. 46) broke through the surface by the middle of that decade, when "the elements of optimism that [had] characterized ... the field for a good part of the last thirty years" were largely gone (p. 46). Although critiques of existing conditions are being promulgated with increasing frequency and alacrity by an ever-expanding number of professors and practitioners, clues required to address critical issues have been more difficult to find. In many places, the value and meaning of the available clues are being vigorously debated. In others, they are simply being ignored. And all the while, preparation programs go about their business poised on the brink of extinction (AACTE, 1988; Beare, 1989; Griffiths, 1988b).

Pressures for Change

Pressures feeding the current ferment in the field of administrator training can be sorted into two categories—those that emerge from analyses of existing preparation programs and those that arise from a desire to bring school leadership in line with a postindustrial view of education and schooling. We tackle the first group in Chapter 4 and the second in Chapter 5. Here we limit our discussion to the examination of an irreparable tear in the fabric of preparation programs that has acted as a catalyst for the current era of turmoil. We refer specifically to attacks from a variety of quarters on the administration-as-science perspective that dominated training programs for 40 years following World War II.

Although over the life of the theory movement "training programs increased in formality, structure, and complexity, much as did the school system: from amateur to professional, from simple to complicated, and from intuitive to 'scientific' " (Cooper & Boyd, 1987, p. 7), the outcomes of the quest for a science of administration were considerably less robust than had been anticipated. By the mid 1970s, this failure of the theory movement to deliver on its promises was brought to a head in a "well-documented bombshell" (Walker, 1984, p. 15) delivered by T. Greenfield (1975) at the Third International Intervisitation program in Bristol, England (Griffiths, 1988a). Although other scholars had been drawing attention to the limitations of a near-exclusive emphasis on a scientific approach to training for some time, T. Greenfield unleashed the first systemic broadside attack on the central tenets of the theory movement, especially of its epistemological roots and guiding values. In a word, he found the scientific era of educational administration to be impoverished. T. Greenfield's paper demarcates the beginning of the transition from the behavioral science period to the dialectic era in school administration.

Over the past 15 years, other thoughtful analysts have joined the debate about the appropriate value structure and cognitive base for educational administration in general and for preparation programs in particular. On the knowledge base issue, there has been increasing agreement—although with noticeable differences in explanations[37]—that "a body of dependable knowledge about educational administration" (Crowson & McPherson, 1987, p. 48) did not emerge during the behavioral science era. This condition, plus an expanding "variance in informed opinion about what educational administrators need to know" (Nunnery, 1982, p. 48) means that exiting the behavioral science era, there was not much "conceptual unity" to the field (Erickson, 1979, p. 9). In practical terms, Erickson (1979) concluded that "the field consist[ed] of whatever scholars associated with university programs in 'educational administration' consider[ed] relevant. It is, to say the least, amorphous" (p. 9). In his review, Boyan (1988a) concurred, arguing that "the explanatory aspect of the study of administrator behavior in education over 30 years appears to be an incomplete anthology of short stories connected by no particular story line or major themes" (p. 93). Given this absence of conceptual unity, there has not been much common agreement about the appropriate content for the next generation of preparation programs, either. Thus, as the behavioral science era drew to a close, Goldhammer (1983) reported that although there were "general areas of concern that might dictate to preparatory institutions the names of courses that should be taught, . . . there [was] less agreement on what the content of such courses should actually be" (p. 269).

At the same time, a pattern of criticism was forming about both the definition of legitimate knowledge and the accepted ways in which it could be generated. As Crowson and McPherson (1987) reported, during this transition phase critics "questioned with increasing vigor the appropriateness of traditional research methods and assumptions as a guide to an understanding of practice" (p. 48). Analysts called for both re-legitimization of practice-based knowledge:

Theory and research are only one source of knowledge, and this knowledge is always subordinate to the principal, teacher, or other professional, serving to inform but not to prescribe practice. Indeed, professional knowledge is created in use as principals and teachers think, reflect, decide, and do. . . .

Craft knowledge represents an anchor equal to and sometimes superior to theoretical knowledge in making up one's theories of prac- tice and informing one's professional practice. (Sergiovanni, 1991b, pp. 6, 8; see also Blumberg, 1984; C. Hodgkinson, 1975; Sergiovanni, 1984)

and the acceptance of:

an increasing diversity of research methods, including attempts at qualitative ethnographic, naturalistic, phenomenological, and critical studies. . . [and] an effort to generate "theories of practice" that incorporate both objective and subjective ways of knowing, both fact and value considerations, both "is" and "ought" dimensions of education within integrated frameworks for practice. (Silver, 1982, pp. 56, 53)

Finally, there was a deepening recognition that the knowledge base employed in preparation programs had not been especially useful in solving real problems in the field. Bridges (1982), Blumberg (1984), Carver (1988), Goldhammer (1983), and Immegart (1977) all concluded that the behavioral science knowledge base had little effect; the science "stipulated to solve administrative problems had notably failed to do so" (T. Greenfield, 1988, p. 137). This questioning of the relevance of theory to practice can be traced to a number of causes. Deeply ingrained methods of working that assumed that one could discover theory that would automatically apply itself to situations of practice was the first (Goldhammer, 1983). A second was the emergence of a "parochial view of science" (Halpin, 1960, p. 6)—one in which social scientists became "intent upon aping the more prestigious physical scientists in building highly abstract, theoretical models" (p. 6) at the expense of clinical science. A third was the proclivity of educational researchers employing social and behavioral sciences to contribute to the various disciplines rather than to administrative practice (Campbell, 1981)—administrative "structure and process were studied mostly as a way of adding to disciplinary domains" (Erickson, 1977, p. 136). Along these same lines, during this entire era there was a lack of effort on the part of professors to distinguish systematically those aspects of the social and behavioral sciences that were most appropriate for practitioners (Gregg, 1969). Largely because of the overwhelming nature of the task (Culbertson, 1965), the weakness of the theory movement noted by the AASA in 1960 (p. 57)—the failure "to work out the essentials in the social sciences for school administrators and to develop a program containing these essentials"—was still a problem as the sun set on the era of professionalism. There was throughout the era "a scarcity of consistent programs with well-developed rationales for the use of behavioral sciences in preparing administrators for the achievement of specified goals" (Goldhammer, cited in Farquhar & Piele, 1972, p. 9). Or, as Cooper and Boyd (1987) concluded, simply "placing educational administration in the mainstream of social science research did not seem to solve the dilemmas of what to teach practitioners" (p. 12). Finally, the relevance of theory was diminished by the failure to integrate the disciplines themselves in the service of practitioners. As Erickson (1977, 1979) and Miklos (1983) discerned, expanding the number of disciplines within preparation programs, or integrating by expanding boundaries, is not at all the same thing as integrating concepts from various disciplines around problems of practice (see Note 20).

A number of critics have also pointed out that regardless of its usefulness, the knowledge base constructed during the scientific era gave rise to a "narrowly defined concept of administration" (T. Greenfield, 1988, p. 147): "the educational administrator as the corporate chief executive" (Bryant, 1988, p. 7). This line of analysis (see also Chapter 4) has less to do with assessing the quality and usefulness of extant program content than it does with critiquing training programs for failing to include critical concepts, materials, and ideas. To begin with, by taking a "neutral posture on moral issues" (Culbertson, 1964, p. 311) the theory movement largely excluded value issues from preparation programs. When the term *value judgment* did surface, it was "frequently as an epithet indicating intellectual contempt" (Harlow, 1962, p. 66). Throughout the behavioral science era, there was "little serious, conscious effort to develop demonstrably in students the skills or behavioural propensities to act in ways that could be considered ethical" (Farquhar, 1981, p. 199). Attention to the "humanities as a body of 'aesthetic wisdom'

capable of contributing its own unique enrichment to the preparation of school administrators" (Popper, 1982, p. 12) was conspicuous
by its absence (see also Farquhar, 1968, 1981).

Also neglected during this period of administration qua administration[38] were educational issues—a phenomenon exacerbated by
efforts to professionalize administration and thereby distinguish it
from teaching (J. Murphy, 1990d; Sergiovanni et al., 1987). As we see
more fully in the next chapter, what W. Anderson and Lonsdale
reported in 1957—that "few items in the literature of educational
administration . . . say much about the psychology of learning"
(p. 429)—and what Boyan concluded in 1963—that "the content of
the advanced preparation tends to focus on the managerial and
institutional dimensions as compared to teaching, the technical base
of educational organizations" (pp. 3-4)—is still as true today.

Finally, because of the low status afforded practice-based knowledge, the world of educational practice was generally ignored
throughout the behavioral science era. Or, as Farquhar (1968)
concludes:

> Whatever success has been experienced in this "movement," how-
> ever, has been accompanied by some equally notable failures—
> probably reflected most clearly in the ample body of literature
> devoted to the so-called "theory-practice dichotomy." (pp. 111-112)

Early Activity

A variety of interrelated activities has helped fuel reform initiatives in educational administration training programs over the last
decade. A number of comprehensive educational reports and studies during the current era of more generalized educational reform
have addressed issues of administrator preparation (see J. Murphy,
1990a, 1990c, for reviews). Documents that specifically address educational leadership have also been released by various groups. The
1985 National Association of Secondary School Principals (NASSP)
study, *Performance-Based Preparation of Principals,* and the 1990 National Association of Elementary School Principals (NAESP) document, *Principals for the Twenty-First Century,* have both received a fair
amount of attention, as has the 1988 AACTE report, *School Leadership
Preparation: A Preface to Action.* The UCEA-sponsored investigation by
McCarthy and her colleagues (1988) on the professoriate in educa-

tional administration has also helped to shape thinking about training programs.

The event that really began to rivet attention on new approaches to preparing school leaders, however, was the formation of the National Commission on Excellence in Educational Administration (NCEEA) in 1985 under the leadership of Daniel E. Griffiths. Three documents growing out of the Commission's work —the 1987 report *Leaders for America's Schools*,[39] Griffiths's seminal address at the AERA (subsequently published as a UCEA paper—[Griffiths, 1988b]), and an edited volume containing most of the background papers commissioned by the NCEEA (Griffiths et al., 1988a)—were influential in generating discussion among and providing helpful guidance to those engaged in reforming preparation programs in the dialectic era.

During the 1988-1989 academic year, under the direction of David L. Clark at the University of Virginia,[40] and with financial support from the Danforth Foundation, the National Policy Board for Educational Administration (NPBEA), consisting of the heads of the 10[41] most influential groups with an interest in school leaders, was established. The NPBEA published its highly visible report, *Improving the Preparation of School Administrators: The Reform Agenda* (1989a), in May of that year (see J. Murphy, 1990b, 1990g). The document presented an extensive agenda for the post-behavioral science era of preparation. It recommended:

> that a common core of knowledge and skills in preservice programs be defined to include the following: societal and cultural influences on schooling, teaching and learning processes and school improvement, organization theory, methodologies of organizational studies and policy analysis, leadership and management processes and functions, policy studies and politics of education, and moral and ethical dimensions of schooling. The content of these areas is to be grounded in the "problems of practice" and supported by an increased emphasis on clinical experiences. (Miklos, in press)

Other major proposals included calls for national accreditation of training programs and national certification of graduating students. "Although some observers felt that the agenda was 'old wine in new bottles,' it became evident that national attention had been placed on the administrative and leadership functions of education" (Cunningham, 1990a, p. 3).[42]

As the debate about the next generation of preparation programs unfolded, a number of institutions throughout the nation—many with support from the Danforth Foundation—set about overhauling their departments and their training programs consistent with the spirit of the NCEEA and NPBEA reports. The NPBEA continued to release documents designed to spur further discussion and action. Additional institutions began to respond to the reform agenda, although somewhat cautiously and mostly on the margins (J. Murphy, 1991a). The extent to which the pressures for change and these early activities herald a new era of preparation for school administrators or are simply further indices of turmoil remains to be determined.

Part II

The Current Scene

Educational Administration as a field is at a delicately critical phase. In fact, there is a rumbling in the clouds above us—they are no longer merely on the horizon—which could in fact blow the whole field of Educational Administration apart, for both practitioners and the scholars in the field. (Beare, 1989, p. 3)

Four

The Current Scene: A Critical Analysis

> In comparison with political and organizational context and general social characteristics, formal training in educational administration has had marginal impact on the character of educational leadership. (Tyack & Cummings, 1977, p. 50)

> Administrator training appears to be an unusually "weak treatment" relative to professional preparation in other fields. (Sykes & Elmore, 1989, p. 80)

Criticism of the ways in which men and women are prepared for school leadership positions enjoys a long history. Perhaps the only thing more depressing than an honest appraisal of current educational administration programs is the knowledge that so little progress has been made in resolving the deeply ingrained weaknesses that have plagued training systems for so long. In 1960, the AASA, after a rather even-handed analysis, characterized the preparation of school superintendents as a "dismal montage" (p. 84). Twelve years later Farquhar and Piele (1972) coined the term *dysfunctional structural incrementalism* (p. 17) to describe university-based preparation programs. More recently, Pitner (1990) has portrayed the "zombie programs" (p. 131) in educational administration.[1]

These and other reviewers have chronicled a system of preparing school leaders that is seriously flawed and that has been found wanting in nearly every aspect. Specifically, critics have uncovered serious problems in: (a) the ways students are recruited and selected

into training programs; (b) the education they receive once there—
including the content emphasized and the pedagogical strategies
employed; (c) the methods used to assess academic fitness; and (d)
the procedures developed to certify and select principals and superintendents. In the remainder of this chapter,[2] we analyze the problems that currently confront preparation programs, reminding the
reader from time to time as we progress that these weaknesses have
deep roots. We revisit these issues again in Chapter 6 when we
address new perspectives on administrator preparation.

Recruitment and Selection

> Self-selection is still the only selection that is to be found in many
> of our institutions. Taking all of our programs over the nation as a
> whole, the main admission requirement is that the person be pres-
> ent. On second thought, he doesn't even have to be present—we'll
> take him sight unseen. (McIntyre, cited in Farquhar & Piele, 1972,
> p. 26)

> The lack of sound recruitment programs may be the most serious
> problem of all. (AACTE, 1988, p. 12)

Analysts of the recruitment and selection processes employed by
institutions in the administrator training business have consistently
found them lacking in rigor (Farquhar & Piele, 1972; Gerritz, Koppich,
& Guthrie, 1984; McIntyre, 1966). Procedures are often informal,
haphazard, and casual (AASA, 1960; Clark, 1988; Goodlad, 1984).
Prospective candidates are often self-selected, and there are few
leader recruitment programs (Achilles, 1984; AACTE, 1988; Miklos,
1988). Fewer than 10% of students report that they were influenced
by the recruitment activities of the training institutions. As has been
the case over the last 50 years, "the predominant [recruitment]
methodologies still consist of chance encounters with potential
candidates, randomly distributed bulk-mail brochures, and self-re-
cruitment by prospective students" (Culbertson & Farquhar, 1970,
p. 11). Despite well-documented, if commonsensical, reminders that
training outcomes depend on the mix of program experiences and
the quality of entering students, or, as Campbell and his colleagues
(Campbell, Charters, & Gragg, 1960) remind us, as "the training

charge is pursued it will be found that selection of candidates for administrative posts will be fully as critical as the training program itself" (p. 185), research on the recruitment of school administrators has been anemic. So impoverished is work in this area that McIntyre (1966) concludes "that seldom in the history of human endeavor have so many done so little about so important a problem" (p. 3).

Silver (1978a) lists "the general parochialism or provincialism of graduate programs in educational administration [as] another area of concern" (p. 204) in the recruitment and selection of students— what Cooper and Boyd (1987) refer to as built-in "inadequacies of candidates for training" (p. 13). They, along with other analysts (Clark, 1988; NPBEA, 1989a), see at least two problems with this parochialism. First, because the catchment area for most programs is quite local—within a 25- to 50-mile radius of the university—and because nearly all entering students are functioning as teachers or administrators, these reviewers question whether students will be exposed to new ideas and wonder about students' receptivity to alternative views that clash with accepted local norms (see also Cooper & Boyd, 1987; Silver, 1978a).[3] Mann (1975) speaks eloquently on this issue:

> Another characteristic applies only to part, although a large part, of the practitioner/student population. They are a group oriented to the status quo. Mustangs, who are tapped for advancement, are more often identified because they fit in than because they stand out. Many practitioner-students are already responsible for significant portions of the schooling operation and thus have a personal and professional identification with the very thing the university would have them learn to criticize. Moreover, they have acquired obligations to it for past successes, and expectations about their future role which depress anything but the tiniest bit of incremental proclivity to change. The real-world experience of the practitioner-student convinces him of the blunt and inadequate nature of academic tools. Since these tools aren't proof against an unyielding reality, why then not ride with the inevitable inertia of the existing system? All of this enhances a credentials-oriented conservatism and depresses the acquisition of any more substantive knowledge. (p. 144)

Silver (1978a) also views the fact that almost all candidates retain their full-time positions as contributing to this provincialism. The

AASA (1960) also notes the problems that accompany an emphasis on part-time study:

> If the colleges and universities continue to struggle along with few full-time students, they will never develop adequate internships and field experiences. The part-time student is much more of a weakness than the frequency of mention indicates, because many of the instructional program weaknesses are traceable to part-time students. (p. 76)

Standards for selecting students into preparation programs are often perfunctory: "It seems completely fair to say that the procedures generally employed by colleges and universities are *admission* rather than *selection* procedures" (AASA, 1960, p. 83); "in fact, most programs have 'open admissions,' with a baccalaureate degree the only prerequisite" (Griffiths et al., 1988b, p. 290); "For too many administrator preparation programs, *any body* is better than *no body*" (Jacobson, 1990, p. 35). The UCEA-sponsored study of the mid-1970s (Silver, 1978a) discovered that the rejection rates to preparation programs were quite low—about 12% for master's students, 14% for sixth-year students, and 25% for doctoral students. In 1984, Gerritz et al. found that only about 1 in 30 applicants was denied admission to certification programs in California. Part of the reason for this nonselectivity can be traced to the use of questionable methods and procedures and poorly articulated standards for entry. Miklos (in press) claims, for example, that "although various selection criteria are used, the dominant one is grade point average; only limited attention is given to factors associated directly with administrative potential. Scholastic aptitude tests may be required but do not appear to be weighted heavily in the selection of students" (p. 3). Gregg (1969) writes that "the usual procedures used in selecting and admitting students are the unproductive ones of interviews, letters of recommendation, rating scales, and transcripts of college credits" (p. 996), what McIntyre (1966) calls "a mish-mash of mysticism, myth, and automorphism" (p. 16). Miklos (1988) laments that "the relative weights assigned to various criteria are seldom made explicit" (p. 55). If, 50 years ago, all one needed to enter a training program in educational administration was a "B.A. and the cash to pay tuition" (Tyack & Cummings, 1977, p. 60), the situation does not seem to have improved much over the last half century.

Not surprisingly, the quality of applicants is, and has been for some time, rather low. In 1957, Hall and McIntyre reported:

> According to the nation-wide 1955 report, graduate students in education scored lower—almost one standard deviation lower— on verbal ability than graduate students in any other college. The comparison in quantitative ability portrayed education candidates equally uncomplimentarily. (p. 395)

In 1965, McIntyre (cited in Gregg, 1969) reported:

> Of 83 fields of study, including 18 in education, the field of educational administration and supervision ranked third from the bottom in the percentage of students with high academic competence. Only 2 percent of its students were in this superior group. (p. 995)

One year later, McIntyre (1966) concluded that "the average student of educational administration is so far below the average student in most other fields, in mental ability and general academic performance, that the situation is little short of being a national scandal" (p. 17). Nearly a quarter of a century later the situation was basically unchanged. In 1988, for instance, Griffiths (1988b) revealed that "of the 94 intended majors listed in [the] Guide to the Use of the Graduate Record Examination Program 1985-86 . . . educational administration is fourth from the bottom" (p. 12).

This lack of rigorous recruitment and selection procedures and criteria has several negative effects:

> First, it lowers the level of training and experience possible, since courses are often geared to the background and intelligence of the students. Second, "eased entry downgrades the status of the students in the eyes of the populace." Third, the candidates themselves realize that anyone can get in and that nearly everyone will get the license if he or she just keeps paying for credits. In part, this lack of rigor at entry reflects a lack of clear criteria for training or clear vision of what candidates and graduates will look like, and the realization that the graduate school experience itself is not very demanding. (Cooper & Boyd, 1987, p. 14)

This lack of rigor also contributes to the serious oversupply of credentialed administrators in the United States (Boyan, 1963; Culbertson & Farquhar, 1970; NPBEA, 1989a).

The scenario outlined so far reinforces political conservatism and adversity to risk taking in educational administration (Achilles, 1984) —one in which automorphism reigns and "good old boys" (McIntyre, 1966, p. 17) flourish, where "savvy, risk-taking, entrepreneurial educational leaders" are conspicuous by their absence (Conway & Jacobson, 1990, p. 191).[4] Or, as Stout (1973) captures it: "the typical potential recruit to administration is one who has stayed in teaching and, presumably, has come to accept the dominant mores of his occupation . . . [and] demonstrates greater compliance with implicit work rules" (p. 17; see also Miklos, 1988). As a group, the pool of prospective students does not reflect the diversity that characterizes American society (Griffiths, 1988b; McIntyre, 1966; Stout, 1973) and as such is unlikely to alleviate the problem of "gross underrepresentation of ethnic and racial minority persons in executive leadership positions in education" (Contreras, 1989, p. 8).[5] It should come as a surprise to no one, then, to discover that "selection practices yield minimally different administrators" (Pitner, 1990, p. 131).[6]

Program Content

Two major research studies, by Hemphill and others (1962) and by Gross and Herriott (1965), have revealed no significant positive relationships between amount of professional preparation and effectiveness of elementary-school principals. (Gregg, 1969, pp. 999-1000)

A more extensive knowledge base is needed in educational administration, yet no one is doing much about it. (Immegart, 1977, p. 320)

Much of the curriculum in preparation programs in educational administration is neither intellectually challenging nor useful to practitioners. At the most general level of analysis, there is a profound lack of agreement about the appropriate content for training programs and a seemingly endemic unwillingness on the part of the professoriate to address the issue (Goldhammer, 1983; Griffiths, 1988b; McCarthy et al., 1988; Nunnery, 1982). This fragmentation and complacency result from a variety of factors, two of which are noteworthy at this point—the absence of "over-arching gestalt conceptions shaping preparation programs" (Culbertson & Farquhar, 1971a, p. 11) and an impoverished knowledge base.

Although a good deal of consideration has been devoted to examining deficiencies in the cognitive base of training programs (see Chapters 2 and 3), a more serious issue—the absence of a collective vision about the purposes informing training experiences for school leaders—has been regularly overlooked. Thus most builders and critics of preparation programs have put the cart before the horse. Embedded in much of the literature in this field, especially in the critical analyses, is a belief that program vision will flow from the codification of an appropriate knowledge base.[7] The reality is the opposite. The knowledge base for training should be constructed from a blueprint that specifies what the role of the school administrator is and ought to be. We return to this issue later in this chapter and in the concluding part of the book.

WEAK KNOWLEDGE BASE

> Given the suspect quality of much research in . . . educational administration, the "hit and miss" nature of investigative efforts, and the effect of such research on the literature and practice, it seems that, while we know more, we still do not know very much. (Immegart, 1977, p. 319)

> The bloom is now well off the rose. A body of dependable knowledge about educational administration has not been forthcoming. (Crowson & McPherson, 1987, p. 48)

Turning directly to the knowledge base, we are confronted with the following tragedy: the indiscriminate adoption of practices untested (Culbertson, 1988a) and uninformed by educational values and purposes (Bates, 1984); serious fragmentation (Erickson, 1979; Willower, 1988); the separation of the practice and academic arms of the profession (Carver, 1988; Farquhar, 1968; Goldhammer, 1983); relatively nonrobust strategies for generating new knowledge (Achilles, 1990; Immegart, 1977), the neglect of ethics (Farquhar, 1968); an infatuation with the study of administration for its own sake (Evans, 1991), and the concomitant failure to address outcomes

(Boyd & Crowson, 1981; Erickson, 1977, 1979). The result has been the development of an impoverished—and often inappropriate— knowledge base and, as a consequence, an ersatz mission for training programs. In short, preparation programs as a group are not only failing to address the right things, they are also doing a fairly poor job of accomplishing the things on which they have chosen to work. It is almost as if the old saw "if it's not worth doing, it's not worth doing well" had guided our thinking.

The fact that the "knowledge base available to the profession that manages our schools is not well developed" (Crowson & McPherson, 1987, p. 45) was acknowledged quite widely at the tail end of both the prescriptive and behavioral science eras. For example, the anemic nature of our understanding of administration as we head into the dialectic era has been captured by Immegart, Bridges, Foster, Blumberg, and Carver:

> The relationship between research and practice was little improved from 1954 to 1974; some evidence indicates that the relationship may have deteriorated. Analysis yielded little evidence that research and inquiry have had any substantial impact on practice. (Immegart, 1977, p. 317)

> The research seemed to have little or no practical utility. In short, there is no compelling evidence to suggest that a major theoretical issue or practical problem relating to school administrators has been resolved by those toiling in the intellectual vineyards since 1967. (Bridges, 1982, p. 25)

> The practical wisdom of the social sciences seem[s] ephemeral at best. (Foster, 1989, p. 7)

> My bets are that one cannot point to a single administrative practice that has been influenced in any significant degree by research on the behavior of administrators. (Blumberg, 1984, p. 27)

> Some might say it [the behavioral science theory engine] was yanked off front and center stage because it did not yield descriptions, explanations, and predictions that were judged sufficiently useful to warrant its continuance as the driving force in the study of educational administration. (Carver, 1988, p. 1)[8]

The reasons for the "shaky" (Immegart, 1990, p. 8) cognitive foundations in school administration have been well-documented. They include: our ardor to borrow ideas before they are tested (Culbertson, 1988b); the lack of theory upon which to ground resarch efforts (Griffiths, 1965); a failure to focus on educational administration as an area worthy of study in and of itself (Miklos, 1990); poor scholarship habits within the field (Griffiths, 1965; Immegart, 1990); and an absence of a sense of vision about the profession.

FRAGMENTED PROGRAMS

Preparation programs are essentially diverse collections of formal courses that, taken together, do not reveal consistent purposes or a systematic design. (NASSP, 1985, p. 2)

Given the above-noted description of the knowledge base, it should surprise no one to discover that "course content is frequently banal" (Clark, 1988, p. 5): "Where the student should be fattened by a rich diet of multidisciplinary fare, he is starved by the lean offerings of provincial chow" (AASA, 1960, pp. 83-84). Nor do training programs exhibit much internal consistency. Students "often confront a confusing melange of courses, without clear meaning, focus, or purpose" (Cooper & Boyd, 1987, p. 14). They end up taking "a succession of three-semester-hour courses . . . thrown together in a tasteless potpourri" (AASA, 1960, p. 178). There is an absence of a "continuum of knowledge and skills that become more sophisticated as one progresses" (Peterson & Finn, 1985, pp. 51-52). What all this means is "that most administrators receive fragmented, overlapping, and often useless courses that add up to very little" (Cooper & Boyd, 1987, p. 13; see also Hoyle, 1987).

The inability or unwillingness of educational administration program faculty to engage in serious curriculum development work over the past quarter century has not gone unnoticed. For example, in the late 1960s, "Goldhammer concluded that few institutions are actively engaged in curriculum development or in planning major revisions in their programs" (Farquhar & Piele, 1972, p. 42). Boyan in turn argued:

Curriculum development in educational administration today looks very much like the conventional local school system approach. It is disparate, fragmented, uneven, scattered, and mainly noncumulative. (cited in Culbertson & Farquhar, 1971a, p. 11)

Twenty years later, McCarthy et al. (1988) arrived at a similar position (see also Miklos, 1987):

Critics have charged that the educational administration curriculum has remained essentially unchanged for decades. This is not surprising since educational administration programs are bastions of conservatism in tolerant but risk-aversive universities. . . . Nothing less than a fundamental reordering of what is covered in graduate programs can respond to the current crisis in educational leadership. . . . [However,] systemic curriculum revision demands a level of commitment and effort from faculty members that they do not presently seem prepared to give. (p. 172)

LACK OF CONNECTION TO PRACTICE

School administration as practiced by superintendents and principals bears little resemblance to school administration as taught in graduate schools of education. (Pepper, 1988, p. 360)

Moreover, the knowledge and skills needed to become an effective educational leader and school manager are generally not those provided by current Administrative Service Credential Programs. (Gerritz et al., 1984, p. 1)

One of the most serious problems with the current cognitive base in school administration training programs is the fact that it does not reflect the realities of the workplace, "does not provide the kind of experiences or knowledge that practitioners feel they need" (Muth, 1989, p. 5), and is therefore, at best, "irrelevant to the jobs trainees assume" (Mulkeen & Cooper, 1989, p. 1) and, at worst, "dysfunctional in the actual world of practice" (Sergiovanni, 1989a, p. 18). As we saw in Chapter 3, as an antidote to the "naked empiricism" and "recipes" (J. Murphy & Hallinger, 1987, p. 260) of the prescriptive era, scholars of the behavioral science era attempted to develop a science of administration. One of the effects was an exacerbation of the natural tension between the practice and academic arms of the profession (Carver, 1988; Culbertson & Farquhar, 1971b). The nurturance and development of the social sciences became ends in themselves. Professors, never very gifted at converting scientific knowledge to guide practice (Immegart, 1990), had little motivation to improve (Miklos, 1987). As a result, "scholarly study of human behavior and the administration of human affairs [have not been] intimately connected" (Wengert, 1962, p. 36)—the theory and research borrowed from the behavioral sciences "never evolved into a unique knowledge base informing the practice of school administration" (Griffiths, 1988b, p. 19).

Processes and Procedures

Mann (1975), Bridges (1977), Muth (1989), Sergiovanni (1989a, 1991b), and others have all written influential essays in which they describe how the processes and procedures stressed in university programs are often diametrically opposed to conditions that characterize the workplace milieu of schools.[9] In one of the earliest and most important works on this topic, Mann reveals how the "academic requirements [of preparation programs] are very likely to violate the 'reality' of the protean cauldron in which the administrator knows himself to be" (p. 141). Bridges observes that although within the school context a premium is placed on verbal skills, the ability to make quick judgments, and activeness, we train our administration students to be passive, to use rational decision making models, and to develop their written skills to the near exclusion of their oral ones.

Muth in turn discusses how the research training offered to practitioners—the traditional Ph.D. research courses that emphasize methods and techniques only distally connected to the problems confronting managers—"may be not only inappropriate but also intellectually disabling" (p. 9). Writing in a similar vein, others have questioned the appropriateness of the traditional research dissertation for those oriented toward practice (J. Murphy, 1989c, 1990e); the dissertation is an activity that is, according to Muth, "often removed from field-related problems by several levels of abstraction" (p. 11) and "viewed as worthless" (p. 7) by administrators.

Finally, Sergiovanni (1991b), in extensions of his influential 1988 UCEA address, argues that a basic assumption of administration as science—the view "that a one-to-one correspondence exists between knowledge and practice" (p. 5)—runs counter to the reality of the messy world of school leadership. He points out that Schon's conception of administration as a process of managing messes more closely fits the reality of managerial work than does the view of the "principalship as a logical process of problem solving with the application of standard techniques to predictable problems" (p. 5) that is embedded in the perspective of administration as an applied science that dominates training programs.

Substance

Other thoughtful reviewers concerned with connections between training institutions and the field have addressed the substance of preparatory programs. They have found that programs are often developed with a "jaunty disregard for the demands of educational leaders" (AASA, 1960, p. 178): "Administrators-in-training are given a potpourri of theory, concepts, and ideas—unrelated to one another and rarely useful in either understanding schools or managing them" (Mulkeen & Cooper, 1989, p. 12). In their review of training programs at the outset of the dialectic era, Crowson and McPherson (1987) argue that institutions "that had emphasized a solid grounding in theory, the social sciences, [and] rational decision making . . . were discovered to be well off the mark as effective preparation for the chaotic life of a principal or superintendent" (p. 49). Jean Hills (1975), a professor who spent a sabbatical as a principal, offers equally unfavorable judgments about the usefulness of the content emphasized in educational administration preparation programs:

> Occasions on which I was able to catch myself drawing upon anything like organization theory or social-behavioral science materials were extremely rare. Try as I might, I could seldom catch myself thinking about problems or questions in these terms, and when I did, I seldom found it useful in deciding upon a course of action. (p. 2)

In terms of program substance, three somewhat distinct problems merit attention: lack of attention to "field-related substance dealing with current problems, needed skills, and administrative tasks" (Culbertson & Farquhar, 1971b, p. 9); the absence of robust clinical experiences; and marked deficiencies with regard to issues of diversity.

Lack of Attention to Skills. Evidence from nearly all fronts leads to the conclusion that the focus on the behavioral sciences during the scientific era of training resulted in a glaring absence of consideration of the problems faced by practicing school administrators (Farquhar & Piele, 1972; Griffiths, 1988b). The pervasive antirecipe, antiskill philosophy that currently characterizes many programs of educational administration has resulted in significant gaps in the prevailing knowledge base (J. Murphy & Hallinger, 1987): an almost complete absence of performance-based program components (NASSP, 1985); a lack of attention to practical problem-solving skills (Mulkeen & Cooper, 1989); "a neglect of practical intelligence" (Sergiovanni, 1989a, p. 17); and a truncated conception of expertise (see Kennedy, 1987). Administrators consistently report that the best way to improve training in preparation programs is to improve instruction of job-related skills (Erlandson & Witters-Churchill, 1988; Notar, 1988-1989; Weindling & Earley, 1987). Griffiths (1988b; see also Erlandson, 1979) has chronicled the costs of this knowledge gap in our training programs and of our consistent unwillingness to address the problem:

> Probably more school administrators fail because of poor skills than any other single reason, yet program and faculty in educational administration fail to do anything about it. It's as though a baseball team in spring training gave the player books to read and lectures on the theory of baseball and did not have the player practice hitting and fielding. Administrators have to perform, and in order to perform well they must have the basic skills of administration. (p. 17)

Weak Clinical Programs. Because "the state of the art of field training in educational administration remains rather primitive" (Cronin & Horoschak, 1973, p. 39), it is not surprising that the clinical aspects of most preparation programs in educational administration are notoriously weak (Milstein, Bobrofe, & Restine, 1991). Despite an entrenched belief that supervised practice "could be the most critical phase of the administrator's preparation" (Griffiths, 1988b, p. 17) and a long history of efforts to make field-based learning an integral part of preparation programs (see Daresh, 1987, for a review), little progress has been made in this area. And despite concern over the impoverished nature of clinical experience for nearly 30 years, Pepper was still able to report as late as 1988 that "few, if any, university programs in school administration offer a thorough clinical experience for future school administrators" (p. 361). The field-based component continues to be infected with weaknesses that have been revisted on a regular basis since the first decade of the behavioral science revolution in administrative preparation: (a) "unclear or even conflicting objectives" (Cronin & Horoschak, 1973, p. 16); (b) inadequate number of clinical experiences; (c) activities arranged on the basis of convenience; (d) overemphasis on role-centered as opposed to problem-centered experiences; (e) "lack of individualization in 'molding' field experiences to students' individual needs and goals" (Culbertson & Farquhar, 1971c, p. 12); (f) poor planning, supervision, and follow-up; (g) absence of "connecting linkages between on-campus experiences and field-based experiences" (Milstein, 1990, p. 121); and (h) overemphasis on low-level (orientation and passive observation type) activities (Clark, 1988; Daresh, 1987; Milstein, 1990).

Inadequate Attention to Diversity. Woven deeply into the fabric of "administration as an applied science" is the belief that there is a single best approach to educating prospective school leaders (Cooper & Boyd, 1987), including a dominant worldview of administration as an area of study (content) and method of acting (procedure). A number of thoughtful analysts, especially critical theorists and feminist scholars, have shown that this perspective has resulted in significant gaps in the knowledge base employed in current training programs (Foster, 1989). Missing is consideration of the diversity of perspectives[10] that inform scholarship and practice.[11] For example, in her review of the literature on women administrators, Shakeshaft (1988) discovered "differences between the ways men and women approach the tasks of administration" (p. 403). She concludes that although "these differences have implications for administrative training programs . . . the female world of administrators has not been incorporated into the body of work in the field . . . [n]or are women's experiences carried into the literature on practice" (pp. 403-406). Turning to the issue of racial minorities, Jackson

(1988) and Valverde and Brown (1988) also argue for diversification of training programs in order to capture worldviews of minority educators.[12] According to Valverde and Brown:

> Renovation of preparation is crucial also because the theoretical constructs that dominate preparation programs figure into the difference between the recruitment, selection, advancement, and socialization of minority and white administrators. (p. 153)

LACK OF ATTENTION TO EDUCATION AND ETHICS

> And when all of the strands of the story are woven together, it is clear that the essence of the tragedy was in adopting values and practices indiscriminately and applying them with little or no consideration of educational values or purposes. (Callahan, 1962, p. 244)

In many ways, educational administration preparation programs are empty bodies devoid of a heart and a soul. Undirected by a central mission and untethered to a unifying conception of the field, the profession has, over the last 90 years, drifted a long way from its roots—educational concerns and the ethical and moral dimensions of schooling.

Educational Concerns

> There is . . . a deafening silence concerning the fundamental message systems of schools: curriculum, pedagogy, and evaluation. (Bates, 1984, p. 261)

One of the most troubling aspects of preparation programs for educational leaders is that they have very little to do with education. On the most basic level, programs do not routinely provide the students themselves with a well-rounded education. Many programs are actively characterized by a nonintellectual (Foster, 1989), if not an anti-intellectual, climate (Callahan, 1962). Most programs show "little interest in exploring the historical roots and social context of schooling" (G. Anderson, 1990, p. 53), ignore the "critical examination of educational and social implications of the structures and procedures discussed" (Newlon, 1934, p. 93), and do "a very bad job of teaching . . . a wider vision of schools in society" (Mulkeen & Cooper, 1989, p. 12).

Furthermore, there is ample evidence that the content in training programs focuses on managerial issues and largely ignores matters of teaching and learning, of pedagogy and curriculum.[13] This focus, as we have seen in Chapters 2 and 3, can be traced to external pressures shaping the evolution of preparation programs during the prescriptive era and internal forces influencing the development of training during the behavioral science era.[14] According to Callahan (1962), educational administration, under considerable pressure and perceiving itself to be in a relatively weak position vis-à-vis the larger society, adopted wholesale "the basic values and techniques of the business-industrial world" (p. 244). This "American tragedy," as Callahan has labeled it, was (and is) fourfold:

> that educational questions were subordinated to business considerations; that administrators were produced who were not, in any true sense, educators; that a scientific label was put on some very unscientific and dubious methods and practices; and that an anti-intellectual climate, already prevalent, was strengthened. As the business-industrial values and procedures spread into the thinking and acting of educators, countless educational decisions were made on economic or on non-educational grounds. (pp. 246-247)

The result of all this activity continues to influence the training of administrators. Preparation for *educational* leadership is as problematic today as it was in the time about which Callahan wrote. Today's programs still tend to produce "bookkeepers and public relations men" (p. 259) who are not equipped "to ask or answer the really basic questions in education" (p. 247), and who have very little understanding of the "educational aspects" (p. 255) of their jobs (Bates, 1984; Evans, 1991; Foster, 1984, 1988; J. Murphy, 1990d, 1990e).

Most of the interest and scholarly activity of the succeeding behavioral science era heavily reinforced the "separation of problems in administration from problems in education" (T. Greenfield, 1988, p. 144) and the emphasis on noneducational issues in training programs. Driven by the intellect and will of a handful of scholars who were struggling to professionalize school leadership, considerable energy was invested in developing a science of school admin-

istration. Unfortunately, as Evans (1991) astutely chronicles, the era
sponsored discourse and training primarily on "the administration
of education" (p. 3), or administration qua administration—a major
shift from its formative years when the emphasis "was upon the
adjective 'educational' rather than upon the noun 'administration' "
(Guba, 1960, p. 115). Bates (1984), Evans (1991), T. Greenfield (1988),
and others reveal how during this era school management came to
be viewed as "two activities rather than *educational administration* as
a singular and unitary activity" (Evans, p. 3). Evans concludes that
the legacy of the scientific era is the fact that preparation programs
today are more concerned with the hole than with the doughnut.[15]
The separation of educational administration "from the phenomenon known as instruction" (Erickson, 1979, p. 10) means that the
typical graduate of a school administration training program can
act only as "a mere spectator in relation to the instructional program" (Hills, 1975, p. 4).[16]

Ethical and Moral Dimensions

For more than a quarter of a century, a fact-driven model of
decision-making and rationality has dominated training programs
for educational administrators. To the extent that these programs
embrace technically oriented notions of administration, they offer
less than they espouse. They miss the meaning of human action.
(T. Greenfield, 1988, p. 154)

Throughout its formative years, spiritual and ethical matters were
at the very center of school administration (Callahan & Button, 1964;
Tyack & Hansot, 1982). For example, Beck and Murphy (in press-a)
in their study of the metaphorical language of the principalship,
document that in the 1920s, "the work of principals [was] linked
with absolute, spiritual truth and values" (p. 22). They show how,
in making "ample use of religious imagery in their discussions of
education and of the people charged with administering education
in local schools . . . educational writers of the 1920s [were] continuing a trend established by the earliest chroniclers of school management" (p. 23; see also Johnson, 1925; Johnston, Newlon, & Pickell,
1922, and, for a review of earlier decades, Mason, 1986; and Tyack
& Hansot, 1982).

Ethics. By the early 1960s, the second major root of the field (values and ethics), like education before it, had atrophied. The result was reduced consideration of two issues: organizational values, purpose, and ethics; and organizational outcomes. According to T. Greenfield (1988), "the empirical study of administrators has eluded their *moral* dimensions and virtually all that lends significance to what they do" (p. 138). Despite some early notices that "educational administration requires a distinctive value framework" (Graff & Street, 1957, p. 120), pleas to reorient administration toward purposing (Harlow, 1962), and clear reminders that education is fundamentally a moral activity (Culbertson, 1963; Halpin, 1960) or "values in action" (W. Greenfield, 1988, p. 215; Foster, 1984, 1988, 1989), the problem of meaning in school administration as a profession and in its training programs has taken a back seat "to focus upon the personality traits of administrators—upon the mere characteristics of administrators rather than upon their character" (T. Greenfield, 1988, pp. 137-138).

The unfortunate outcome of this development "is that such conceptions of administrative training block the development of programs that might deal more openly and helpfully with the value problems that confront all those who manage organizations" (T. Greenfield, 1988, p. 149). In his study, Farquhar (1981) finds that "almost three-quarters of the universities contacted pay no conscious attention to the subject of ethics in their administrative preparation programs" (p. 195). In concrete terms, "very little in their preparation programs equips [prospective administrators] to deal with school organizations as a cultural or value system" (Popper, 1982, p. 15) and "available literature provides almost no guidance on how to prepare educational administrators for ethical practice" (Farquhar, 1981, p. 192). Thus administrators exit training programs unprepared to grapple with ethical issues and to address openly the values deeply embedded in schools that often hide behind "a mask of objectivity and impartiality" (T. Greenfield, 1988, p. 150).

Outcomes. As early as 1960, Chase was pointing out what was to become an increasingly problematic situation in educational administration in general and in training programs in particular—a lack of concern for outcomes. Seventeen years later, Erickson (1977) reports that studies in the field "between 1954 and 1974 provided no adequate basis for outcome-oriented organizational strategy in education" (p. 128) Two years later Erickson (1979) expands on the ideas of his earlier essay. He again documents "the tendency to neglect the careful tracing of connections between organizational variables and student outcomes" (p. 12). Like T. Greenfield (1988), he decries the focus on the characteristics of administrators at the expense of more useful work. He lays out his now famous line of attack on the problem: "the current major *emphasis*, in studies of organizational consequences, should be on postulated causal networks in which student outcomes are the bottom line" (p. 12). Preparation programs have yet to resonate to this idea.

Delivery System

Full-time graduate study in school administration is relatively rare. When it does exist the numbers of students are so small as to cast doubt upon the validity of the idea that *bona fide programs* actually exist. (AASA, 1960, p. 84)

STRUCTURAL ISSUES

There appear to be far too many institutions with small enrollments in the business of preparing school administrators (AASA, 1960, p. 68).

The presence of such unneeded institutions in the preparation field is a depressive factor on the profession as a whole. (McIntyre, 1966, p. 17)

The delivery system that shapes preparation programs is marked by a number of serious problems, most of which have a long history. Taking the profession as a whole, it is clear that there are too many institutions involved in the training business: "Many institutions lack sufficient facilities and adequate resources for the task" (Wynn, 1957, p. 472). The result has been "the dissipation of [scarce] resources on the extravagant luxury of maintaining hundreds of impoverished institutions competing with each other for the privilege of exposing a little circle of graduate students to a mediocre program" (AASA, 1960, p. 191). According to the NCEEA (1987), although "there are 505 institutions offering courses in school administration in the United States, . . . less than 200 have the resources and commitment to provide the excellence called for by the Commission" (p. 20)—an even smaller percentage (40%) than Campbell and Newell (1973) reported could do an effective job some 15 years earlier (50%). Despite both direct (Campbell & Newell, 1973) and indirect (AASA, 1960; NCEEA, 1987) calls for the discontinuation of weak programs, as we saw in Chapter 3, the number of training institutions has grown dramatically over the last half century. Many of these programs are cash cows for their sponsoring universities,[17] kept open more for political and economic than for educational reasons (Campbell & Newell, 1973). According to Willower (1983), many "offer graduate study in . . . name only. They seriously stint inquiry and survive by offering easy credentials and by working hard at legislative politics. Their faculties neither contribute to the ideas of the field nor are they actively engaged with them" (p. 194).[18] These institutions tend to be characterized by high student-faculty ratios and limited specialization among faculty (Miklos, in press).

A related problem is the framework in which students' educational experiences unfold: "Administrator training . . . is most often a dilatory option, pursued on a convenience basis, part-time, on the margins of a workday" (Sykes & Elmore, 1989, p. 80). Current programs have indeed drifted far from the traditional residency model: "The ideal of one or two years of full-time student life at the graduate level seems to be disappearing from our preparatory programs, and with it the notions of time for scholarly objectivity, student life, and colleague-like interaction between professors and students" (Silver, 1978a, pp. 207-208). As many as 95% of all students are now part-timers (Griffiths, 1988b), and "many students complete their training . . . without forming a professional relationship with a professor or student colleague" (Clark, 1988, p. 5). Conditions that Goldhammer observed in 1963 are as discernible today as they were then:

> There is currently a dangerous trend to offer a menu of courses in late afternoon and evening hours, on Saturdays, and through summer sessions. Advanced degrees are offered in many places which require no consecutive quarters of residence. Colleges and universities are reducing their requirements in order to attract a mass audience. Such programs are inevitably substandard. They make it

impossible to employ research and knowledge . . . effectively . . .;
they reduce the essential content to the least common (and least
significant) denominator; they prostitute the professional responsibility for the protection of the public against malpractice; and
they are an unwarranted appeal to the "glitter" of an advanced degree for status purposes, but without substance or quality. (pp. 32-33)

ARTS AND SCIENCE MODEL

Perhaps the single most destructive trend affecting professional
preparation during the last thirty years has been domination by an
arts and science model rather than a professional school model of
education. (Griffiths et al., 1988b, p. 299)

The attempt by professional educators to develop a pseudo arts
and science degree has been met with scorn in most universities.
(Griffiths, 1988b, p. 18)

The arts and science model that currently forms the core of preparation programs emerged more to help professors develop "greater
academic sophistication through their professional roles in order to
gain acceptance by their peers in other departments" (Goldhammer,
1983, p. 256) than in response to the needs of prospective administrators. Unfortunately, the arts and science model—"one grounded
on the study of the disciplines" (Miklos, in press)—has neither furn-
ished professors the status for which they had hoped (Clifford &
Guthrie, 1988; Griffiths, 1988b) nor provided graduates with the
tools they need in order to be successful practitioners (Peterson &
Finn, 1985). In addition, it has driven a wedge between professors
and practitioners, creating what Goldhammer (1983) has labeled the
"university-field gap" (p. 265). For these reasons, it has become clear
to many professors and administrators that a fundamental change
is required in the basic delivery system employed in preparation
programs. As we note more fully in Chapter 6, many analysts are
recommending that a new delivery system "should be conceived in
the framework of the professional school model, not the arts and
science model, meaning that the program should prepare students
to act, not merely think about administration" (Griffiths, 1988b,
p. 14; also Clifford & Guthrie, 1988; NPBEA, 1989a).

DEGREE STRUCTURE

> The apparent lack of distinction between Ph.D. and Ed.D. programs, particularly in research course requirements and culminating research products, might be another area of some concern. (Silver, 1978a, p. 210)

The emulation of the arts and science model has spawned a number of subproblems in preparation programs. One of the most serious is that education designed for practitioners (Ed.D. programs) has been molded to parallel the training provided to researchers (Ph.D. programs), in terms of both research requirements (Silver, 1978a) and general coursework (M. Norton & Levan, 1987). This blurring of requirements and experiences for students pursuing quite distinct careers has resulted in the development of ersatz research programs for prospective practitioners. Students, burdened with a variety of inappropriate activities (e.g., the dissertation, see J. Murphy, 1989c, 1990h), are prepared to be neither first-rate researchers nor successful practitioners. Not surprisingly, recent acknowledgment of the problem has produced calls for a more professionally oriented model of preparation—a program that is clearly distinguishable from the Ph.D. training sequence and that focuses on the problems of practice and on the clinical aspects of the administrator's role (AACTE, 1988; NCEEA, 1987).

FACULTY

> Most faculty are only marginally more knowledgeable than their students. (Hawley, 1988, p. 85)

No analysis of the delivery system employed in programs to prepare school leaders would be complete without a discussion of faculty. Two problems in this area are paramount. To begin with, because of the large number of colleges operating programs and because many of these programs are money "makers used to support the work that universities consider more important" (Hawley, 1988, p. 85), there is a good deal of understaffing of faculty in these programs: "Some institutions are obviously engaging in administrative preparatory programs without the number or quality of professors essential to provide the range of skill and knowledge needed" by practicing and prospective administrators (Goldhammer, cited in Farquhar & Piele,

1972, p. 47). Although analysts have argued that "a quality program requires a *minimum* of five full-time faculty members" (NCEEA, 1987, p. 20, emphasis added), the median number today is four and the modal number is two (McCarthy et al., 1988). Moreover, although faculty size increased during the behavioral science era (see Chapter 3), recently there appears to be a slight downturn in the number of faculty per department (Miklos, in press). It is also important to note that many faculty members in educational administration occupy administrative positions in addition to their regular professional roles (McCarthy et al., 1988; Wynn, 1957). Farquhar and Piele (1972) remind us that the problem of faculty understaffing in school administration is exacerbated by "the need to secure staff expertise in the skills of the profession for which students are being prepared and in the disciplines from which content is drawn for the preparatory program" (p. 44).

In attempting to address the need to develop intradepartmental balance between professor-scholars attuned to the disciplines and professor-practitioners oriented to the field, departments have generally produced the worst of both. Unclear about the proper mission of preparation programs (J. Murphy, 1990e), seeking to enhance the relatively low status afforded professors of school administration, and overburdened with multitudes of students, faculties in educational leadership are characterized by weak scholarship (Achilles, 1990; Campbell & Newell, 1973; Griffiths, 1965; Immegart, 1977, 1990; McCarthy et al., 1988) and problematic connections to the field (Griffiths et al., 1988b; J. Murphy & Hallinger, 1987; Willower, 1988). A number of reviewers have concluded "that only a relatively small number of those in the field of educational administration actively engage in scholarly activities" (Immegart, 1990, p. 11). Most "have little time for, or inclination toward research" (Campbell & Newell, 1973, p. 139). Even more disheartening are the assessments of the quality of the scholarship that does occur. In general, it is neither "very significant . . . nor regarded very highly by practitioners" (Griffiths, 1965, p. 28). Because of serious limitations in their own training, many professors "are not qualified to supervise research" (Hawley, 1988, p. 85). Coupling this deficiency in ability with the previously noted lack of effort results in a situation in which "very little good research is being conducted by [educational administration] faculty and students" (Hawley, 1988, p. 85) and in which students develop a truncated, academic view of scholarly inquiry (Immegart, 1990).

It would be nice to be able to report that the professoriate in educational administration was channeling energy uninvested in scholarship into efforts to forge better connections with the field and to attack the problems that infest training programs. Unfortunately, this is not the case. Faculty linkages to schools have actually atrophied over the last two generations. And, as Griffiths and his colleagues (1988b) have noted, professors are not seriously engaged in the work of strengthening preparation programs:

> In 1973 the authors of a major study of professors of educational administration were perplexed by the complacence of professors in the face of recognized problems with administrator preparation.... Today these professors continue to be complacent.... Fewer and older, these professors are faced with insufficient resources and small enrollments; they are less able and probably less disposed to improve administrator preparation now than they were in 1973. (p. 298)

Thus we find that most professors are adrift in roles that are esteemed neither by their peers in the university (the second-class citizenship syndrome) nor by their colleagues in the schools (the ivory tower syndrome).

INSTRUCTIONAL APPROACHES

> The predominance of traditional instructional modes might be some concern to those who seek improvement of preparation programs.... This traditionalism in instruction ... is particularly problematic in a field that purports to emphasize educational leadership. (Silver, 1978a, p. 205)

It is probably not surprising, although it is distressing, that inappropriate content ineffectively packaged should also be so poorly delivered in many training institutions. It is also disheartening that so little progress has been made in an area that has been so thoroughly critiqued (AASA, 1960; Culbertson & Farquhar, 1971c; Erlandson & Witters-Churchill, 1988; Farquhar & Piele, 1972; Hall & McIntyre, 1957; J. Murphy & Hallinger, 1987; Silver, 1978a) and about which we have learned so much over the last quarter century. In 1960, the AASA reported:

> The mediocrity of programs of preparation comes from the sterility of methods reported. Instruction is classroom bound; administration is talked about rather than observed, felt, and in these and other ways actually experienced. (p. 83)

> Teaching methods in general provided excellent demonstrations of what the students had been advised *not* to do in their previous education courses. (p. 178)

Thirty years later, "the dominant mode of instruction continues to be lecture and discussion in a classroom setting based on the use of a textbook" (Mulkeen & Tetenbaum, 1990, p. 20), even though such a method is "regarded unfavorably in the literature and by the students" (Miklos, 1983, p. 165). As we saw in Chapter 3, although some progress was made during the behavioral science era to infuse reality-oriented instructional strategies into preparation programs, the change has hardly been revolutionary and the use of innovative pedagogical methods is not prevalent. For example, in the Texas NASSP study (Erlandson & Witters-Churchill, 1988), principals report "lecture and discussion" to be the primary instructional mode used for eight of nine skill areas examined—and the ninth skill, written communication, is a close second! Mulkeen and Tetenbaum (1990) remind us that this approach not only is often sterile, but also assumes a fixed knowledge base—an assumption that is inconsistent with the realities of knowledge production in a postindustrial world (J. Murphy, 1991b).

Standards of Performance

> Most schools of education are embarrassed by the academic performance of the doctoral students in educational administration. The model grade given to students is an "A"; not because we have criterion referenced performance standards that all could ultimately meet but because we have given up on holding tired, end-of-the-day students to graduate level performance. (Clark, 1988, p. 4)

The lack of rigorous standards is a serious problem that touches almost every aspect of educational administration. Previously, we noted the general absence of standards at the point of entry into preparation programs: "If entrance requirements exist at all, they are not very competitive and most applicants are accepted" (Peterson & Finn, 1985, p. 51). Once students enter preparation programs, the situation does not improve: "The quality of [their] experiences is often abysmally low" (Mulkeen & Cooper, 1989, p. 1). They are not exposed to rigorous coursework: "Students move through the program without ever seeing a current research study (other than a local dissertation), without ever having read an article in ASQ or EAQ or AJS [*Administrative Science Quarterly, Educational Administration Quarterly*, and *American Journal of Sociology*, respectively]. They are functionally illiterate in the basic knowledge of our field" (Clark, 1988, pp. 4-5; see also AACTE, 1988). Because performance criteria are ill-defined and "vary considerably in how rigorously they are applied" (Nagle & Nagle, 1978, p. 123), there is also very little monitoring of student progress (Hawley, 1988). Not surprisingly, very few entrants to certification programs fail to complete their programs for academic reasons (Gerritz et al., 1984). Most former students indicate that their graduate training was not very rigorous (Jacobson, 1990; Muth, 1989). The delivery system most commonly employed —part-time study in the evening or on weekends—results in students who come to their "studies worn-out, distracted, and harried" (Mann, 1975, p. 143) and contributes to the evolution and acceptance of low standards (Goldhammer, 1963; Hawley, 1988; Mann, 1975). McIntyre (1966) has pointed out that:

> the organization, content, and methods characteristic of our preparation programs are not conducive to performance assessment— except for the performance of the professor. The typical three-semester-hour course, especially one meeting two or three times weekly, hardly provides a setting for the study of student behavior that might be relevant to effectiveness in school administration. (p. 12)

Exit requirements in turn are often "slack and unrelated to the work of the profession" (Peterson & Finn, 1985, p. 54). Compounding the lack of standards at almost every phase of preparation programs are university faculty who are unable or unwilling to improve the situation (Hawley, 1988; McCarthy et al., 1988). An even greater obstacle to improving standards are the bargains, compromises, and treaties that operate in preparation programs—the lowering of standards in exchange for high enrollments and compliant student behavior:

> The solution is often to conclude a treaty of mutual non-aggression with one's students. The terms of the treaty are usually that the professor won't plague the students with "irrelevant" ideas if the students will keep quiet about that professorial non-performance. The glue on the agreement is high grades based on low or no performance, which is traded for silence. (Mann, 1975, p. 144)[19]

The NCEEA (1987) and the NPBEA (1989a) have concluded that the time has come to elevate markedly standards in school administration.

Certification and Employment

CERTIFICATION

> Whether few or many, these requirements are nearly always stated in terms of paper credentials supplied by colleges of education—transcripts and credit hours that must parallel those on a list maintained by the certification bureau or the state education department. License-seekers rarely have to pass any sort of test or examination analogous to a bar exam or to medicine's "national boards," nor does the education profession enforce any substantial standards for those seeking administrative certification. (Peterson & Finn, 1985, p. 44)

Suggestions for the reform of educational administration extend beyond preparation programs to address problems with the certification and employment of principals and superintendents. The major criticisms of certification and accreditation processes are: they are unduly costly and cumbersome (Goodlad, 1984); they focus on requirements and skills different than those that administrators need to be successful on the job (National Commission for the Principalship, 1990); they reduce the pool of potential leaders to only those applicants who have worked in public schools (Bennett, 1986);

they operate at only one period of time, for example, at the completion of preparation programs (NCEEA, 1987); and, in total, they do not promote excellence in the profession (NCEEA, 1987).[20]

Advocates for reform have proposed a number of solutions for these problems. Perhaps the most controversial are those that establish alternative routes to certification, thus allowing prospective administrators to maneuver around educational administration programs altogether. Such proposals are designed "to encourage service in the public schools by qualified persons from business, industry, the scientific and technical communities and institutions of higher learning" (Education Commission of the States, 1983, p. 39; see also Bennett, 1986; Clinton, 1987). Other proposals call for bringing greater coherence to the licensing process by eliminating the piecemeal methods by which certification can be gained (Peterson & Finn, 1985) and by establishing a tighter coupling between certification requirements and the skills prospective administrators need in order to be effective (National Commission for the Principalship, 1990; NGA, 1986). A few influential reports have suggested the use of multiple levels of licensure. For example, the National Governors' Association (Clinton, 1987) and the NCEEA (1987) have both called for provisional or entry-level certification of new administrators to be followed by full certification after the documentation of successful performance. Coupled with these suggestions are proposals for recertification every few years "on the basis of successful performance and continuing professional development" (NCEEA, 1987, p. 27). Harking back to an early proposal by Grace (1946), some recent reports have called for a connection to be drawn between licensure and successful performance on a post-training examination (Gerritz et al., 1984; NPBEA, 1989a).

EMPLOYMENT

> Localism, limited esteem, and a baronial system of career management are not conducive to the innovative leadership that we are regularly advised is required in education. Quite the contrary. They seem likely to encourage the recruitment of individuals who are relatively uncreative and to extinguish administrative creativity if it should arise. (March, 1974, p. 22)

Observation leads me to conclude that the two most prevalent factors in selection of superintendents are seniority and political patronage. I am not sure which ranks first, but I regret that at the present time I must put both ahead of competency based on formal professional preparation. Other unsubstantiated observations convince me that a man has a better chance for promotion than a woman; a handsome man wins over a homely one; and an extrovert outclasses an introvert. It is common knowledge that racial, religious, fraternal, and political ties are fundamental in ruling on candidates for administrative posts. (Campbell et al., 1960, p. 186)

The first major problem in the area of employment deals with the processes used to select new administrators. Although "remarkably little is known about just how these critical educational leaders are chosen" (Baltzell & Dentler, 1983, p. 1), tentative evidence suggests that selection procedures are cloudy and quixotic (Boyer, 1983), random (Achilles, 1984), byzantine (Barth, 1988), chance-ridden (Baltzell & Dentler, 1983; Hall & McIntyre, 1957), and only distally connected to the ability to perform (Campbell et al., 1960, p. 178): "Access to the chance to perform still depend[s] on personality, presentability, 'street sense,' carefully cultivated connections, power and blind, dumb luck" (Mann, 1975, pp. 141-142); "The process [of principal selection] itself *cannot* be characterized as merit-based or equity-centered" (Baltzell & Dentler, 1983, p. 19). There is little evidence that educational leadership is either demanded of or sought in candidates. In general, the lack of criterial specificity—"relatively few school districts have written policies for recruiting and selecting administrators" (Miklos, in press)—

opens the way for widespread reliance on localistic notions of "fit" or "image" which emerged as centrally important. . . . However, time and time again, this "fit" seemed to rest on interpersonal perceptions of a candidate's physical presence, projection of a certain self-confidence and assertiveness, and embodiment of community values and methods of operation. (Baltzell & Dentler, 1983, p. 7)

The entire process is characterized by "limited resources" and "inadequate preparation" (Miklos, in press) and a bias toward local candidates (Miklos, 1988).

The most clearly developed proposal for reform in this area has been articulated by Baltzell and Dentler (1983, pp. 42-44). They suggest, among other things, the use of more highly focused selection criteria with better linkage to merit standards, a layered screening process, greater reliance on data and less on interpersonal judgments, and more direct attention to equity issues. On the matter of equity, Clark (1988) has examined the role that departments of educational administration have played in the selection process and found that they "are part of the problem, not the solution, in increasing the placement of women and minority groups in positions of educational leadership" (p. 8). He suggests renewed attention to equity issues in colleges of education. Finally, relevant reform reports consistently recommend that selection criteria be more heavily weighted in favor of educational leadership skills (Clinton, 1987; see J. Murphy, 1990c, for a review).

A second employment problem noted in recent reform reports is the lack of quality postemployment training opportunities for principals and superintendents. Three facets of the problem have been identified. To begin with, there is a virtual absence of induction programs for newly appointed administrators (Peterson & Finn, 1985). Nor are experiences in the assistant principalship being deliberately structured to nurture administrators for the principalship (Weindling & Earley, 1987); if anything, the assistant principal experience may be providing dysfunctional training (W. Greenfield, Marshall, & Reed, 1986). In addition, continued professional growth opportunities for administrators are limited, and these experiences often accumulate in an unsystematic manner (Daresh & LaPlant, 1984; Hallinger & Murphy, 1991; NCEEA, 1987). As difficult as it may be to believe after reading the rest of this chapter, continuing education programs in educational administration seem to be in even worse shape than preparation programs (Hallinger & Murphy, 1991). Reform proposals call for increased attention to ongoing professional development for administrators. Mentorships[21] and enhanced peer interactions are often emphasized in these proposals (U.S. Department of Education, 1987). The content foci are both educational and managerial skills, and, contrary to the thrust of a quarter century ago (Farquhar & Piele, 1972), the preferred delivery structures are networks and centers outside the control of colleges of education and educational administration faculty (Boyer, 1983; Education Commission of the States, 1983; J. Murphy & Hallinger, 1987).

Part III

The Future

One can never know certainly where one stands in history or society. Estimates of historical position and social situation are imprecise at best, and often contested. But we make estimates, thoughtful or not, and often act accordingly. Different estimates of where one stands in history—even among those who agree on where it is headed—can yield very different conceptions of what is possible, and what is to be done. (D. Cohen, 1988, p. 21)

Unfortunately, there are no research findings to describe the future. Lacking a crystal ball, the best one can do is to discern in current developments some portents of tomorrow. It may not even be possible to document with much finality the existence of the trends from which one extrapolates. One must use whatever evidence is available, whether or not it is conclusive. Further, when one has conjured up a number of these forces for change, several organizational responses to these forces are always possible, and a choice from among them necessarily reflects one's own values. (Erickson, 1964, p. 57)

We construct our own system of thought and value, and then live "as if" reality conformed to it. (Shattuck, 1960)

We must somehow get hold of some kind of eye-bath—something to cleanse our eyes of an accumulated grit of cliches, slogans, and meaningless words. (Halpin, 1960, p. 17)

Five

A New Vision of Education and Leadership

> Around the middle of the twentieth century, we entered the post-industrial information age, a new stage in the human evolution. This new age requires new thinking, new perspectives, and a new vision of education. Improving our educational system, which is still grounded in the industrial revolution of the late nineteenth century, will not do in this postindustrial information society. What we need is a new image of education attained by a broad sweep of a comprehensive transformation—a metamorphosis. (Banathy, 1988, p. 51)

Our conception of administrative preparation needs to be forged not only on the anvil of history, but also upon our best understanding of the future—for society, for education, and for school leadership. This chapter provides a picture of the future in these areas, which in turn informs our discussion in Chapter 6 of training programs for tomorrow's school leaders.

The first half of the chapter is devoted to schooling. It examines what movement from an industrial to an information society implies for the way schools relate to their environment, the methods used in managing school operations, and the structure of the core technology. The second half of the chapter addresses the topic of school leadership. It provides a metaphorical analysis of tomorrow's school administrators. Within that framework, it examines the major challenges confronting administrators and discusses qualities of leadership for tomorrow's schools. This composite portrait, juxtaposed with our understanding of the evolution of administrator preparation over the past 100 years, provides a springboard for the concluding chapter's discussion of new preparation programs for school leaders.

Documentation and analysis of the movement from an industrial to a postindustrial society—a phenomenon that undergirds the changes outlined in this chapter—have been provided by a number of scholars both within and outside of education (Banathy, 1988; Beare, 1989). All of these authors see widespread, fundamental, and systemic changes on the horizon as we continue our transition to the information age.[1] For the purposes of discussing the redesign of schooling and school leadership, two of their themes and four of their foci are most important. The themes are the development of a new "social physics" (Bell, cited in Campbell et al., 1987, p. 26) and a new "ecological ethics" (Banathy, 1988, p. 65), both of which promise to transform the basic fabric of society, to bring the human dimension in line with the extraordinary technological advances of the past 100 years. That transformation encompasses four interrelated elements: increased emphasis on human capital; democracy; social justice; and community.

Our efforts to extract knowledge about schooling for the twenty-first century from evolutionary trends in society are also grounded on the following six premises:

1. "For those who seek fundamental, second order changes [in schools] that will sweep away current structures and start anew . . . *basic social and political changes would need to occur outside of schools.*" (Cuban, 1988, p. 344)

2. "Organizations are a significant part of society and being more or less open, over time they become quite similar to the societies in which they exist. When societal changes occur, corporate organizations, institutions of higher education, and public schools undergo change in response." (Griffiths, 1988b, p. 33)

3. "Systems of learning and human development are evolutionary and should coevolve with the larger society as well as spearhead societal evolution." (Banathy, 1988, p. 68)

4. There exists "a dangerous evolutionary gap—a discrepancy between the recently emerged new societal image and the still-prevailing outdated image of education" (Banathy, 1988, p. 53), educational organizations, and educational leadership.

5. The purposes of schooling and the nature of the educational process itself are largely determined by the form of organizational structures, policies, and practices (Bates, 1984; McCartney & Schrag, 1990; Sizer, 1984) and by methods of organizing, governing, and managing (Clark & Meloy, 1989; J. Murphy, 1991b). The evolutionary gap noted above is most evident here: teaching and learning are being inappropriately defined by industrial management designs.

6. New perspectives on education and the redesign of schooling should backward map from rich conceptions of learning and teaching (Elmore, 1991; Evertson & Murphy, in press; J. Murphy, 1991b) and from analysis of the fundamental purposes of schooling (Foster, 1984, 1988).

Schooling for the Twenty-First Century

Today's schools aren't designed for an information-technological society. (Hutchins, 1988b, p. 75)

We are leaving behind the industrial age which gave birth to schools as we now know them and are moving into a knowledge/information age whose needs are not yet fully revealed. What is readily apparent even now, however, is that schools will need to undergo massive reconceptualisation if they are to keep pace with the ever-increasing and rapid changes of this new age. (Mulkeen & Tetenbaum, 1990, p. 14)

Recently, a number of thoughtful analysts have begun addressing what Banathy (1988) labeled our "crisis of perception" in education—our "lack of perception and vision of what could be and should be the function, the substance, and the form of education in the postindustrial information society"[2] (p. 53; see J. Murphy, 1991b, for a review). Some reviewers have traced the evolution of schooling from the agrarian era to the information age, using powerful metaphors to convey the needed redesign of educational organizations (Beck & Murphy, in press-b; Petrie, 1990; Schlechty, 1990). Other scholars in the area of organizational theory, especially critical theory, employ developmental lenses to discern the changing purposes of education in a transformed society (Bates, 1984; Foster, 1988; Giroux, 1988; Purpel, 1989). A third group focuses more directly on developing a portrait of tomorrow's schools based on new conceptions of student learning (Evertson & Murphy, in press; Marshall, in press-a). Still others have used critiques of current reform efforts, especially so-called Wave 1 reforms, as a springboard to develop "a new image of education that is compatible with the societal image of the current [postindustrial] age" (Banathy, 1988, p. 66; Carnegie Forum, 1986; Chubb, 1988; Sedlak, Wheeler, Pullin, & Cusick, 1986).

Although there are differences among these various groups of reformers, they share much in common. From their collective efforts emerges a vision of education quite unlike the "center of production" (Barth, 1986, p. 295) image that has shaped schooling throughout the industrial age. In its stead stand metaphors of "education as human development" (Clark, 1990, p. 27), school as a "community of learners" (Barth, 1986, p. 295), and administrators as "transformative intellectuals" (Foster, 1989, p. 1). Embedded in this emerging postindustrial conception of education and schooling are changes in three areas: the relationship between the school and its larger environment, the management and organization of schooling, and the nature of teaching and learning.[3]

RELATIONSHIP BETWEEN THE SCHOOL AND ITS ENVIRONMENT

The needs of children and youth are no longer satisfied by schools and schooling alone. (Cunningham, 1990a, p. 15)

The new vision encompasses a basic change in our view of the relationship between the school and its environment. The new design is "based on wide-scale participation of the stakeholders in American education" (Hutchins, 1988a, p. 49). Historically ingrained notions of schools as sheltered monopolies, or delivery systems, appear to be breaking down under the incursion of a market philosophy into education (Boyd, 1990; Boyd & Hartman, 1988). In schools of the information age, the traditional dominant-subordinate relationship between schools (and professional educators) and the public will be reworked in favor of more equal arrangements, that is, partnerships (Seeley, 1980, 1988). As the business of schooling becomes redefined in relation to the customer, there will be unprecedented inroads of market forces into the governance and organization of schools.

In the schools of tomorrow, these changes are likely to be expressed in a variety of ways. Governance will likely be opened up "to the full community of stakeholders in education" (Hutchins, 1988b, p. 77). Thus schools will empower parents and other community members, allowing them more control over school decisions than is currently the case. It also appears that in postindustrial schools parents will have expanded options about which facilities their children attend. The choice[4] movement that is currently receiving a good deal of attention may become part of the fabric of schooling. Finally, efforts to expand and integrate the services of an assortment of institutions in the larger school community are likely to occur.[5] In discussions of schools of the future, there is growing agreement on the desirability of: (a) uniting schools, businesses, universities, foundations, and so forth around the needs of children and their families; (b) meshing the efforts of the disparate variety of service agencies—including education—within the structure of schooling; (c) developing schools as educational service centers for all members of the community; and, to make all these changes more feasible, (d) "simplifying the authorizing environment of schools" (Sykes & Elmore, 1989, p. 89) or freeing individual schools from outside interference from district offices, unions, and regulatory agencies, especially state departments of education.[6]

SCHOOL ORGANIZATION AND MANAGEMENT

Too many schools are not manageable if judged against our deepest educational ideals. (Sykes & Elmore, 1989, p. 77)

The focus needs to shift to new designs, ones that are as different from the current notion of "keeping school" as a nuclear engine is from the internal combustion engine. (Hutchins, 1988b, p. 77)

The emerging vision of tomorrow's schools includes methods of organizing and managing schools (Beare, 1989; Clark & Meloy, 1989; Sykes & Elmore, 1989; Weick & McDaniel, 1989) that are generally consistent with the "quiet revolution [in] organizational and administrative theory in Western societies" (Foster, 1988, p. 71). In the still-forming image of schools for the twenty-first century, the hierarchical bureaucratic organizational structures that have defined schooling since the onslaught of scientific management give way to systems that are more organic (Griffiths, 1988b; Weick & McDaniel, 1989), more decentralized (Guthrie, 1986; Harvey & Crandall, 1988; Watkins & Lusi, 1989), and more professionally controlled (J. David, 1989; Houston, 1989; Weick & McDaniel, 1989), systems that "suggest a new paradigm for school organization and management" (Mulkeen, 1990, p. 105; Wise, 1989). The basic shift is from a "*power over* approach . . . to a *power to* approach" (Sergiovanni, 1991b, p. 57). This model of change spotlights "four interrelated values—participation, communication/community, reflection and experimentation" (Rogers & Polkinghorn, in press), an analysis consistent with the general themes and foci noted earlier.

In these redesigned, postindustrial school organizations, to which Louis and Miles (1990) have given the label "adaptive model" (p. 26),[7] there will be "very basic changes in roles, relationships, and responsibilities" (Seeley, 1988, p. 35): traditional patterns of relationships will be altered (Conley, 1989; Rallis, 1990); authority flows will be less hierarchical (Clark & Meloy, 1989), for example, traditional distinctions between administrators and teachers will begin to blur (Giroux, 1988; Petrie, 1990); role definitions will be both more general and more flexible (Corcoran, 1989)—specialization will no longer be viewed as a strength (Beare, 1989; Houston, 1989); because "organizational structures [will] promote authority based on ability" (Sergiovanni, 1991b, p. 62), leadership will be dispersed and will be connected to competence for needed tasks rather than to formal position (AACTE, 1988; Sykes & Elmore, 1989); and independence and isolation will be replaced by cooperative work (Beare, 1989; Maccoby, 1989). Furthermore, the traditional structural orientation discussed in our historical analysis of preparation programs will be overshadowed by a focus on the human element (Louis & Miles, 1990; Sergiovanni, 1991b). The operant goal will no longer be maintenance of the organizational infrastructure but rather the development of human resources (Clark & Meloy, 1989; Mojkowski & Fleming, 1988; Schlechty, 1990). Developing learning climates and organizational adaptivity will replace the more traditional emphasis on uncovering and applying the one best model of performance (Clark & Meloy, 1989; McCarthey & Peterson, 1989) and a premium will be placed on organizational flexibility (Banathy, 1988). The metaphors being developed for this new design for schools—for example, from principal as manager to principal as facilitator, from teacher as worker to teacher as leader—nicely portray these fundamental revisions in our understanding of social relationships and in our views of organizations and conceptions of management. They reveal a reorientation in transformed schools from bureaucratic to moral authority and from bureaucratic control to professional empowerment, or control through "professional socialization, purposing and shared values, and collegiality and natural interdependence" (Sergiovanni, 1991b, p. 60). They also reveal an orientation toward accountability through professionalization "rather than through micro*managing* what the professional does" (Petrie, 1990, p. 24).

THE NATURE OF TEACHING AND LEARNING

The advocates of adventurous instruction may be working near the beginning of a great, slow change in conceptions of knowledge, learning and teaching. (Cohen, 1988, p. 22)

Student learning will "look" different in redesigned schools than it does in non-redesigned schools. (Evertson & Murphy, in press)

When the curriculum is geared toward the goal of authentic achievement, new forms of teaching will be necessary. (Newmann, 1991, p. 461)

Preliminary sketches of redesigned schools suggest that we may be on the threshold of significant changes in the core technology of schooling (Marshall, in press-a; J. Murphy, 1991b). A more robust understanding of the educational production function is beginning to be translated into "dramatically different way[s] of thinking about the design, delivery, and documentation of instructional programs" (Spady, 1988, p. 8). The strongest theoretical and disciplinary influence on education—behavioral psychology—is being pushed off center stage by "cognitive or constructivist psychology" (D. Cohen, 1988, p. 18) and newer sociological perspectives on learning, especially "social cognitive theories of motivation and achievement" (Maehr & Midgley, in press). This shift away from a "science of teaching" (Rogers & Polkinghorn, in press) and toward "research on cognition as a basis for understanding how people learn casts an entirely different perspective on how the schooling process should be redesigned" (Hutchins, 1988a, p. 47).[8] Underlying this change are radically different ways of thinking about the "educability of humanity" (Purpel, 1989, p. 10). Those who are at the forefront of transforming schools that were historically organized to produce results consistent with the normal curve, to sort youth into the various strata needed to fuel the economy, see education being transformed to ensure equal opportunity for all learners (A. Collins, Hawkins, & Carver, 1991; Means & Knapp, 1991; J. Murphy, 1991c). This, as Barth (1988) reminds us, has "profound implications for instruction and students" (p. 130). Seeley (1988) concurs, arguing that this is indeed "a fundamental component of a new vision [for schools], since all other components gain motive force from this shift in goals" (p. 34). As we discuss more fully below, all of these changes lead to new conceptions of curriculum and instruction.

At the center of this newly forming vision about schooling for tomorrow are fairly radical changes in assumptions about intelligence and knowledge (Bransford, 1991; D. Cohen, 1988; Means & Knapp, 1991). The alpha paradigm of knowledge—the view that "knowledge can be assumed to be an external entity existing independently of human thought and action, and hence, something about which one can be objective" (Fisher, 1990, p. 82)—"dominant for so long in classroom practice, has begun to be critically examined in a new way" (p. 84). A new view, one that holds that knowledge is internal and subjective, that it "depends on the values of the persons working with it and the context within which that work is conducted" (p. 82), is receiving serious consideration (Lotto & Murphy, 1990). Thus, the new educational design considers "knowledge not as somehow in the possession of the teacher, waiting to be transmitted to the student or to be used to treat the students' problems, but as mutually constructed by teacher and student in order to make sense of human experience" (Petrie, 1990, pp. 17-18). "Knowledge is a human creation rather than a human reception" (D. Cohen, 1988, p. 12). Knowledge is personal and the learning of skills is embedded in a "social and functional context" (A. Collins et al., 1991, p. 173; Brown, Collins, & Duguid, 1989). Learning is seen as a social phenomenon and considerable attention is devoted to the social origins of cognition and "the social and cultural context in which learning takes place" (Prestine & LeGrand, 1990, p. 8).

Consistent with Banathy's (1988) assertion "that societal evolution and characteristics of its current stage are primary sources in determining the content of learning" (p. 68), new views about what is worth learning characterize emerging perspectives on schooling for the twenty-first century. The traditional emphasis on acquiring information is being replaced by a focus on learning to learn and on the ability to use knowledge (Bransford, Franks, Vye, & Sherwood, 1989; Newmann, 1991). Maintenance learning that "involves acquiring fixed outlooks, methods, and rules for dealing with known events and recurring situations" (Banathy, 1988, p. 58) takes a back seat to evolutionary learning that empowers students "to anticipate and face unexpected situations" (p. 59). New perspectives on the context of learning are also being developed, directing attention to active learning. A century-old concern for independent work and competition—a focus on the individual dimension of human existence, especially on individual ability—is slowly receding in favor of more cooperative learning relationships—a focus on the social dimensions of human existence (J. David, 1989; Maehr & Midgley, in press).

A "whole new orientation in providing experiences for learning intellectual skills and pursuing methods of inquiry" (Banathy, 1988, p. 64) is being foreshadowed in early reports about schooling for the information age. Vigorous attacks on the practice of tracking (Oakes, 1985; Page, 1984) are accompanied by calls for a core curriculum for all students (Boyer, 1983; Goodlad, 1984). Reformers involved in the redesign of education are also tackling the traditional emphasis in schools on a "splintered view of knowledge" (Sizer, 1984, p. 133), content coverage, rote learning of basic skills, and reliance on textbooks as the primary source of knowledge. They promulgate an alternative image of a core technology that: (a) reflects "a new interdisciplinary vision" (Boyer, 1983, p. 115; O'Neil, 1989); (b) features a curriculum that is more vertical and less horizontal—that covers fewer topics in more depth (Corcoran, 1989; Newmann, 1988; Sizer, 1984); (c) highlights higher-order thinking skills for all students (A. Collins et al., 1991; Means & Knapp, 1991); (d) "de-emphasize[s] the use of predigested information found in textbooks and put[s] emphasis on helping students learn to search for and organize material from a variety of resources" (Hutchins, 1988a, p. 48), especially original source documents (Bradley Commission, 1988; National Commission on Social Studies, 1989); and (e) underscores the use of a broadened evaluation system that highlights authentic measures of assessment (Newmann, 1991; Wiggins, 1989; Wolf, Bixby, Glenn, & Gardner, 1991).

"An elevated conceptualization of teaching" (Rallis, 1990, p. 193) consistent with the changes noted above is an integral part of almost all visions of schooling for the twenty-first century. The view of the teacher as a professional rather than as a technician is finding more and more acceptance (Holmes Group, 1986; Petrie, 1990), as the humanistic focus of redesigned schools provides an "alternative to the culture of schooling dominated by a technocratic mindset" (Rogers & Polkinghorn, in press). The conception of the teacher as reflective practitioner is becoming increasingly embedded in discussions of schooling for the twenty-first century (Zeichner & Tabachnich, 1991), as are the metaphors of teacher as leader, decision maker, learner, and colleague (McCarthey & Peterson, 1989). Knowledge from the science of teaching is no longer "epistemologically privileged" (Sergiovanni, 1991b, p. 327). Thus, craft knowledge, or the "epistemology of practice" (Zeichner & Tabachnich, 1991, p. 2), receives new-found respect in emerging images of tomorrow's schools (Bransford, 1991). Rather than seeking ways to simplify instruction, to uncover a scientifically correct method, the complexity of teaching is acknowledged and nurtured (Petrie, 1990).

Analysts of tomorrow's schools envision teachers, freed from their role as technicians, being much more concerned with the purposes of education than with implementing predetermined goals (Conway & Jacobson, 1990). They argue that teachers will have "a good deal of freedom and flexibility in setting appropriate goals for the kinds of students they have" (Petrie, 1990, p. 23). They also see teachers exercising considerable discretion over pedagogy (Bolin, 1989; Carnegie Forum, 1986), curricular materials (Boyer, 1983), and the "way in which the school's resources [money and people] are employed to support teaching and learning" (Mojkowski & Fleming, 1988, p. 4).

In schools of the postindustrial era, a learner-centered pedagogy replaces the more traditional model of teacher-centered instruction. The model of the teacher as "a pipeline for Truth" (D. Cohen, 1988, p. 12) or a "sage on a stage" (Fisher, 1990, p. 83), in which instructors are viewed as content specialists who possess relevant knowledge that they transmit to students through telling, is replaced by an approach in which "teaching is more like coaching, where the student (as opposed to the teacher) is the primary performer" (p. 83). Substantive conversation replaces conventional classroom talk (Newmann, 1991) and didactic instruction (Bransford, 1991). Dialogue becomes "the central medium for teaching and learning" (Means & Knapp, 1991, p. 12). Analysts believe that in the twenty-first century, schools will be conceived of as "knowledge work" organizations (Schlechty, 1990, p. 42), learning will be seen as "meaning making" (Petrie, 1990, p. 19), and teaching will be viewed "as facilitating the construction of meaning" (p. 18). Thus, in tomorrow's schools, teachers will act as facilitators (McCarthey & Peterson, 1989), modelers (Spady, 1989), guides (D. Cohen, 1988), scaffold builders (A. Collins et al., 1991), and coaches (Sizer, 1984) who invest "students with increased power and responsibility for their own learning" (Elmore, 1988, p. 3). Students are seen as "producers of knowledge" and teachers "as managers of learning experiences" (W. Hawley, 1989, p. 23). The focus is on learning, not on the delivery system (Seeley, 1980). Teaching methods are "designed to give students the opportunity to observe, engage in, and invent or discover expert strategies in context" (A. Collins et al., 1991, p. 178). "Teaching for meaningful understanding" is the concept most generally employed by reformers to capture this emerging vision of instruction for tomorrow's schools (Marshall, in press-b; J. Murphy, 1991b).

Leaders for Tomorrow's Schools

The most critical challenge ultimately facing school administrators is that of being prepared to deal with tomorrow's problems in tomorrow's schools. (Watson, 1977, p. 92)

The over-riding challenge before tomorrow's school leaders, then, is . . . to help articulate and implement an educational vision for a new society. (Culbertson, 1988a, p. 9)

There is widespread belief among scholars of educational administration that "school leadership in the future will be more challenging, more difficult than ever before" (Cunningham, 1990b, p. 42). At the most fundamental level, the challenge is to keep alive the vision of public education for all students, to prevent the "development of a system of elitism and a trend toward the public school serving a welfare role" (Rogers & Polkinghorn, in press). This is not a new challenge (Culbertson, 1988a): as McPherson (1990) notes, one task of tomorrow's school leadership is to continue to address the very issues we have handled with insufficient success for the past half century:

> The same might be said for the challenges to school leadership in the 1990s. . . . The ones that will bedevil us are the ones we either have ignored or only partially addressed in the past—racial and social inequities; failures in productivity and accountability; professional insularity; isolating, bureaucratic (rather than collegial) organizations; inadequate funding; little attention to human resource development of education professionals and non-professionals; misplaced authority and responsibility; and ignorance regarding the special needs of children emerging from generations of poverty. In my judgment, the failed agenda of the last fifty years is still our appropriate agenda. (pp. 94-95)

At the same time, immense new social and economic challenges have been added to the leadership agenda. The fabric of American society is being rewoven in some places and unraveling in others, resulting in changes that promise to have a significant impact on schooling. At the core of these revisions are demographic shifts that threaten "our national standard of living and democratic foundations" (Carnegie Council on Adolescent Development, 1989, p. 27) and promise to overwhelm schools as they are now constituted. Minority enrollment in America's schools is rising as is the proportion of less advantaged youths. There is a rapid increase in the number of students whose primary language is other than English. The traditional two-parent family, with one parent employed and the other at home to care for the children, has become an anomaly. At the same time that these new threads are being woven into the fabric of American society, a serious unraveling of other parts of that fabric is occurring. The number of youngsters affected by the ills of the world in which they live—for example, poverty, unemployment, crime, drug addiction, malnutrition—is increasing, as is the need for a variety of more intensive and extended services from societal organizations, especially schools (M. Hodgkinson, 1991; Kirst et al., 1989; Natriello, McDill, & Pallas, 1990; Quality Education for Minorities Project, 1990; Wagstaff & Gallagher, 1990).

To restore America to its preeminent position in business, science, and technology, tomorrow's leaders will also face the challenge of helping to jump start a failing economy by improving educational productivity.[9] At no time in our nation's history have schools been under such sustained and comprehensive scrutiny and widespread condemnation (J. Murphy, 1990a). Although part of this increasingly critical scrutiny can be traced to the turmoil accompanying the evolution from the industrial to the information age, a good deal of the critique is grounded on fairly persuasive evidence that American public schools are failing to educate the bulk of our students well. As I have reported elsewhere (J. Murphy, 1990a):

> indices of less-than-satisfactory student performance have been documented in seven areas: (1) academic achievement in basic subject areas—compared to historical data about the United States and to student performance in other countries; (2) functional literacy; (3) preparation for employment; (4) the holding power of schools (dropout rates); (5) knowledge of specific subject areas such as geography and economics; (6) mastery of higher-order skills; and (7) initiative, responsibility, and citizenship. (p. 10)

The task confronting tomorrow's leaders is both direct and exceedingly complex: to reform schooling to improve performance on the above-noted measures.

In addition to addressing the unfinished agendas of the past and tackling current crises, administrators of tomorrow's schools will face the challenge of leading schooling into the information age, of shaping the metamorphosis of educational purpose and organizational structures. The task is even more arduous than it appears at first sight. Not only are school administrators being challenged to help transform schooling consistent with the evolution of values and organizational structures in the larger environment, they are also being asked to take a leading role in forging the vision of the postindustrial world to which they must direct the educational enterprise. Thus they are being asked both to help discern the larger forces that will influence education in the twenty-first century and to shape and define those forces.

What emerges from these challenges of the past, of today, and of tomorrow is a belief that society needs better schools. The first corollary in the area of administration is that if "we want better schools, we are going to have to manage and lead differently" (Sergiovanni, 1991b, p. x). The second corollary is that different leadership will require a transformation of our conception of administration, that leaders and leadership in the postindustrial age must look radically different from what they have looked like in the past.[10] The remainder of this chapter sketches a picture of leadership for tomorrow's schools. Because "changing our metaphors is an important prerequisite for developing a new theory of management and a new leadership practice" (Sergiovanni, 1991b, p. 68), it employs a metaphorical approach.[11] It attempts to describe school leadership for the twenty-first century by using metaphors that portray fundamental shifts in our conception of school administration, metaphors that convey changes from what leadership is today to what leadership needs to be in tomorrow's schools.

ADMINISTRATOR AS SERVANT LEADER

> Long considered a school manager, the principal might more adequately be considered a school leader. (Foster, 1988, p. 79)

> One cannot become a leader without first becoming a follower. (Sergiovanni, 1991b, p. 327)

If there is an all-encompassing challenge for administrators of tomorrow's schools it is to lead the transition from the bureaucratic model of schooling, with its emphasis on minimal levels of education for many, to a postindustrial adaptive model, with the goal of educating all youngsters well. At the same time, "school leaders will have to adjust their own definition of what it means to be a school leader" (Hallinger, 1990, p. 76). The first challenge, then, is to reorient the principalship from management to leadership, and to do so in ways consistent with the principles of postindustrial organizations (Beare, 1989; Sergiovanni, 1991b). Given the penchant noted in Chapter 1 for society in general, and for members of organizations in particular, to look to leadership in periods of crisis, it should come as little surprise that during this era of unrest in education, reform reports call for administrators to don the mantle of leadership (J. Murphy, 1990c). Discounting the rhetoric and the calls for saviors, these reports confirm a rather deep leadership void in America's schools (J. Murphy, 1990f). Administration has evolved to meet the clerical needs of schools, and nearly all of the forces exerted on the administrative role over the past 150 years—including, as we have documented, administrative training—have reinforced the administrative nature of the position (March, 1978; J. Murphy, 1990d). Bureaucratic schools require managers and shape the activities of the men and (to a lesser extent) women who occupy their administrative roles accordingly (Foster, 1989). Competent management, however, is likely to prove insufficient to meet the challenges of leading schools into a new age. Schools need leadership—the combining of "management know-how with values and ethics" (Sergiovanni, 1989b, p. 39)—and the administration of tomorrow's schools must change to meet that need (Culbertson, 1965).

The leadership challenge for administrators is quite complex. Not only must they accept the mantle of leadership—changing from implementors to initiators, from a focus on process to a concern for outcomes, from risk avoiders and conflict managers to risk takers—but they must also adopt leadership strategies and styles that are in harmony with the central tenets of the heterarchical school organizations they seek to create (Clark & Meloy, 1989; Louis & Miles, 1990). They must learn to lead not from the apex of the organizational pyramid but from the nexus of a web of interpersonal relationships (Chapman & Boyd, 1986)—with people rather than through them (Clinton, 1987). Their base of influence must be professional expertise and moral imperative rather than line authority. They must learn to lead by empowering rather than by controlling others, or as Barth (1988) puts it, "perhaps the most important item in the list of effective principals is the power to relinquish [decision-making authority] so that the latent, creative powers of teachers may be released" (p. 138). Leadership in tomorrow's schools becomes "a support function for teaching rather than a mechanism for the control of teaching" (Bolin, 1989, p. 88). Servant leaders will understand that the "world can and will go on without them. Leaders don't create . . . transformations, but rather they know how to place the props carefully and wisely on the educational stage so as to be so inviting that individuals are enticed to transform themselves" (J. Collins, 1990, p. 34).

Servant leadership will differ from more traditional views of management in a number of other ways as well. "Such concepts as purposing, working to build a shared covenant" (Sergiovanni, 1989b, p. 33), and establishing meaning—rather than directing, controlling, and supervising—are at the core of this type of leadership: "Empowering leadership is based on dialogue and cooperative, democratic leadership principles" (Bolin, 1989, p. 86). Enabling leadership also has a softer, less heroic hue (J. T. Murphy, 1989, 1991; Tonnsen, 1990). It is more ethereal and less direct: "Symbolic and cultural leadership are key leadership forces" (Sergiovanni, 1989b, p. 33). There is as much heart as head in this style of leading (Moorman, 1990; Roberts, 1990). It is grounded more upon teaching than upon informing (Lam, 1990), more upon learning than upon knowing (Barth, 1988; Deck, 1990), and more upon modeling and clarifying values and beliefs than upon telling people what to do (Bredeson, 1989; NAESP, 1990; Petrie, 1990). Its goals include "ministering" (Sergiovanni, 1991b, p. 335) to the needs of organizational members rather than gaining authority over them and creating "new structures that enable the emergence of leadership on a broad basis" (Sykes & Elmore, 1989, p. 79). It is more reflective and self-critical than bureaucratic management (Bates, 1984; Foster, 1984).

ADMINISTRATOR AS ORGANIZATIONAL ARCHITECT

> The task of fundamentally reforming the structures of schooling is perhaps the most challenging opportunity that faces school leaders in the 1990s. (Roberts, 1990, p. 133)

> What we have learned and are learning about children, their families, their teachers, their schools, their communities, and about how children learn and how they are taught is important for how we plan to organize and administer tomorrow's schools. (Cunningham, 1990a, p. 2)

There is a fair amount of agreement that existing organizational structures and arrangements contribute to the problems that currently confront schools, that these conditions either support or cause the educational negligence that often characterizes the schooling enterprise (Clark & Meloy, 1989; Cuban, 1989). The attack on the existing bureaucratic infrastructure of schooling follows two separate but parallel courses, both of which are based on the belief that "the institution itself impedes the performance of all those working within it—students, teachers, and administrators" (Sykes & Elmore, 1989, p. 83). In the first camp are those who see the current hierarchical system as counterproductive to the development of the professional workplace that, it is being argued with increasing vigor, is essential for the transformation of schooling. In this group are those who claim that the "bureaucratic structure inhibits the motivation and creativity of teachers and administrators" (Hutchins, 1988b, p. 76; Frymier, 1987; Sizer, 1984). Others maintain that the current structure "is impractical, and it does not fit psychological and personal needs of the workforce" (Clark & Meloy, 1989, p. 293). Some reviewers argue that bureaucratic structures are inconsistent with professional work (Weick & McDaniel, 1989). Still others maintain that bureaucratic management is incompatible with the sacred values and purposes of education. They question "fundamental ideological issues pertaining to bureaucracy's meaning in a democratic society" (Campbell et al., 1987, p. 73; Foster, 1989) and in schools that serve the modeling and promulgation of democratic ideals (Beck & Murphy, in press-b; Bolin, 1989; McDonald, 1988).

In a second camp are analysts who maintain that "bureaucratic controls . . . undermine educational goals" (McNeil, 1988, p. 344) and that "bureaucratic management practices cause unacceptable distortions in [the] educational process" (Wise, 1989, p. 301), that they are "paralyzing American education . . . [and] getting in the way of children's learning" (Sizer, 1984, p. 209; Goodlad, 1984; Sedlack et al., 1986). Some devote special attention to the harmful effects of bureaucratic management practices on at-risk students (Cuban, 1989). Also included here are those reviewers who claim that the existing organizational structure of schools is neither sufficiently flexible nor sufficiently robust to meet the needs of pupils in a postindustrial society (Banathy, 1988; Harvey & Crandall, 1988).

What is clear from this analysis, and from our earlier discussion of organization and management for tomorrow's schools, is that if schooling is to be reformed, restructured, or reborn—in short, if all youngsters are truly to be well-educated—then the organizational and governance structures of the current system will need to be systemically reconfigured. Leaders for tomorrow's schools will face the great challenge of helping define and breathe life into these new forms of governance, organization, and leadership. The task will be akin to redesigning a 747 in flight (Maccoby, 1989). The work will be neither easy nor comfortable. Furthermore, because "the prospect is for a continuous prospect of reconstruction" (Sirotnik, 1989, p. 104), we will need to "build with canvas" (Sergiovanni, 1989b, p. 34).

In becoming organizational architects, tomorrow's leaders must replace a traditional focus on stability with a focus on change (Louis & Miles, 1990; NAESP, 1990). They will need to function less as classical managers and more as change agents (Kanter, 1983):

> The new manager . . . will not be a classical, hierarchically oriented bureaucrat but a customized version of Indiana Jones: Proactive, entrepreneurial, communicating in various languages, able to inspire, motivate and persuade subordinates, superiors, colleagues and outside constituents. (Gerding & Serenhuijseur, cited in Beare, 1989, p. 19)

Tomorrow's leaders will need to disavow tenets of organizing consistent with bureaucracies (controlling, directing, supervising, evaluating, and so forth) and embrace those principles associated with heterarchies (cooperation, empowerment, community, participation, and so forth) (Beare, 1989; Clark & Meloy, 1989; Sergiovanni, 1991b; Sykes & Elmore, 1989).

The specific challenge, then, is to use these new principles of organization in service of the creation of adaptive and organic forms for schooling. These new structures need to promote the development of a professional workplace (AACTE, 1988; Boyer, 1983):

> Our analysis suggests that people who create organizational designs for schools should construct forms that aid the articulation and development of professional values, since these values are sources of guidance when people process nonroutine information. Our review also suggests that organic organizational forms are better designs both for developing values and for clarifying vague causal structures than are mechanistic forms. Since organic forms also encourage the development of substitutes for leadership, they encourage professional development as well as utilize current skills and attitudes. (Weick & McDaniel, 1989, p. 350)

Even more important, construction of new forms must advance from blueprints based on our best knowledge of student learning (Sykes & Elmore, 1989). We now know that "the organization of schooling appears to proceed as if we had no relevant knowledge regarding the development of children and youth" (Goodlad, 1984, p. 323). Thus the "main challenge facing educational leaders is . . . to reconstruct conceptions of authority, status, and school structure to make them instrumental to our most powerful conceptions of teaching and learning" (Elmore, 1990, p. 63).

ADMINISTRATOR AS SOCIAL ARCHITECT

It is the changing demographics that may be the biggest challenge our school leaders face. (Thompson, 1990, p. 163)

Now they [school leaders] face a situation in which the efficacy of their organizations, and the well being of our society, will be tested by their ability to be effective leaders in schools that must become centers of learning and development for children who have not previously prospered in these environs. Our least well served student populations are rapidly becoming the majority population in schools. (Clark, 1990, p. 25)

At a recent conference on Reinventing School Leadership sponsored by the National Center for Educational Leadership, educational scholars from across the nation underscored the need for leaders of tomorrow's schools to address the rapidly changing complexion of society. Some analysts approach these changes in terms of the family (Pitner, 1990; Shakeshaft, 1990; Spaedy, 1990), others in terms of demographics (Ortiz, 1990; Wright, 1990), and still others under the larger rubric of diversity (W. Greenfield, 1990; Tonnsen, 1990). All of them reinforce the message developed earlier in this study: the social fabric is changing. Society is becoming increasingly populated by persons of color and people from linguistically different groups. The citizenry is aging and becoming more mobile. Income is being distributed less equitably. The "condition of the family" (Pitner, 1990, p. 129) is changing so that an increasing "number of children come from homes without strong support systems" (Shakeshaft, 1990, p. 147) and from "economically-stressed families" (p. 147):

What this means for schools is that the body of students is increasingly made up of many minority groups and language groups, poorer, unprepared for schools' conventional kinds of social interaction and intellectual engagement, disengaged from much of life and society, lacking sound parental or adult support, in poor health, victims of unemployment, crime, teen pregnancy, and racism, and so on. (Moorman, 1990, p. 99)

The task, then, is to restructure schooling completely in order to address these needs and problems (Astuto, 1990; Spaedy, 1990). Especially prominent is the need "to respond effectively to the children of poverty" (Clark, 1990, p. 28)—to increase the well-being and the "achievement of the socially and economically disadvantaged" (Hutchins, 1988b, p. 77). Exacerbating the situation is the fact that up to this point, we have largely failed the challenge. Schools, as Tyack (1974) reminds us, "have rarely taught the children of the poor effectively—and this failure has been systemic, not idiosyncratic" (p. 11). If our response in the future is no more successful,[12] the result is likely to be the emergence of a dual-class society not unlike that found in many third-world countries (Natriello et al., 1990; Scribner, 1991). As with many other social issues, schools will have a good deal to say about the adequacy of the nation's response. Administrators, in turn, will play a significant role in determining whether the efforts of our schools are successful or not.

In his 1990 UCEA Presidential address, Scribner (1991) raises the key question: "Do these trends have implications for the kind of values, content, and skills needed by those who will manage our schools in the years ahead?" (p. 5). The answer is yes. The metaphor of administrator as social architect has clear implications for the role of leaders in the twenty-first century: "Because schools as they are organized and operated are not able to be responsive to this increasingly diverse student body" (W. Greenfield, 1990, p. 73), the "leadership challenge in this instance is to develop more responsive schools" (p. 73). Because it appears that "these children require different approaches to instruction/schooling" (Thompson, 1990, p. 163), and because the exact nature of "the type of educational services to be delivered to these groups has [yet] to be determined" (Ortiz, 1990, p. 115), "the first challenge for school leaders will be to be active in the search for the solution to this dilemma" (Thompson, 1990, p. 163). Although the specifics are not yet clearly discernable, the overall solution strategy for tomorrow's leaders is clear: "They must invent and implement ways to make schools into living places that fit children rather than continuing to operate schools for 'good kids' who adapt to the existing structure" (Clark, 1990, p. 26; Astuto,

1990). A second challenge to administrators is to exercise leverage over institutional structures and arrangements, such as ability grouping and tracking, that disproportionately disadvantage students in slower groups and nonacademic tracks—tracks overrepresented by low-income pupils, students of color, and other at-risk youth (see Good & Marshall, 1984, and J. Murphy & Hallinger, 1989, for reviews). At the same time, "the school leader . . . must have a general appreciation for cultural diversity and understand how to make it work in the educational setting" (Thompson, 1990, p. 164).

Finally, because "schools must provide much more of the basic human support students need in their lives than they did when parents and grandparents, neighbors, churches, merchants and other figures at home and in the community provided such support" (Moorman, 1990, p. 99), school leaders, in their role as social architects in the postindustrial age, must see schooling as one element of a larger attack on the problems facing youth: "School leaders need to have an expansive view of the charge to and possibilities of schooling. Instead of trying to artificially limit the roles of schools, they need to expand the influence of schools to each child, each family, the community, the political infrastructure" (Astuto, 1990, p. 3). To accomplish this, they will need more effectively to "bring together the home/family and school in a concerted effort to enhance the quality of education" (Hinojosa, 1990, p. 81). They will also need to be at the forefront of efforts to design and construct an integrated social agency network to address the conditions confronting many of their pupils and their families. The school may well find itself at the hub of this network. Thus school administrators in a postindustrial society will be busy not only redesigning the purposes and structures of their own institutions to better service our changing student population, but also developing integrated networks of services with other groups.

ADMINISTRATOR AS MORAL EDUCATOR

Tomorrow's school administrators, residing in between the industrial and the telematic cultures, will face, as already noted, the highest of all leadership demands: namely, that of helping redefine the ends of schooling and of meshing these ends with the needs of an altered society. (Culbertson, 1988a, p. 14)

At the time when change is a constant, the school leader must be a visionary rooted in educational morality against which every goal, program, activity, and service must be measured. (Frank, 1990, p. 70)

We reported in Chapters 3 and 4 that both the educational and value dimensions of leadership have atrophied since the formative era of school administration when superintendents were thought of as philosopher-educators. Throughout most of this century, the field has gravitated toward conceptions of leadership based on scientific images of business management and social science research. There is an expanding acknowledgment of "the pathology of such an approach to educational administration" (Bates, 1984, p. 26) and a growing belief that to prepare leaders for the twenty-first century, the pendulum must swing back.

The metaphor of the administrator as moral educator takes on many forms. At its root are two fundamental beliefs: that "the deep significance of the task of the school administrator is to be found in the pedagogic ground of its vocation" (Evans, 1991, p. 17); and that "the new science of administration will be a science with values and of values" (T. Greenfield, 1988, p. 155). Moral leadership acknowledges that "values and value judgments are the central elements in the selection, extension, and day-to-day realization of educational purpose" (Harlow, 1962, p. 67) and that "deeply educative and pedagogic interest in the lives of children and young people" is critical to administering schools (Evans, 1991, p. 17). Thus at the most basic level, there is an emerging consensus that "educational administration must find its mission and purpose in the purpose of schooling generally" (Foster, 1988, p. 69) and that with a postindustrial "reformation of the purpose of education a reconceptualization of school administration [is] in order" (Parker, 1986, p. 59).

As moral educators, administrators of tomorrow's schools will be much more heavily invested in "purpose-defining" (Harlow, 1962, p. 61) activities and in "reflective analysis and . . . active intervention" (Bates, 1984, p. 268) than simply in managing existing arrangements. This means that "persons wishing to impact society as school leaders must be motivated by a set of deep personal values and beliefs" (Spaedy, 1990, p. 157), by "a guiding set of academic and social values that can provide a rudder" (Wimpelberg, 1990, p. 177); "they must also have a view of the future that is significantly different from how schools have been" (Spaedy, 1990, p. 157). In short, they must have a "critical spirit" (Foster, 1989, p. 17) and "visionary capacities" (Culbertson, 1988a, p. 28) and "bring to their enterprise a certain passion that affects others deeply" (Sergiovanni, 1991b, p. 334). They must view their task more as a mission than a job (J. T. Murphy, 1991), "as a meaningful calling of the highest order" (Roberts, 1990, p. 134); "they must develop strong commitments to important things and model them persuasively" (Moorman, 1990, p. 101); "the task of the leader is to create a moral order that bonds both leader and followers to a set of shared values and beliefs" (Sergiovanni, 1989b, p. 34). Therefore, moral leadership means that tomorrow's school administrators must use their personal platform to "engage participants in the organization and the community in reinterpreting and placing new priorities on guiding values for education" (Moorman, 1990, p. 98) and in reconstructing "structures so that they celebrate the intended educational purposes of the school community" (Bates, 1984, p. 268).

The pedagogic dimensions of moral leadership are also becoming more clearly defined. Tomorrow's leaders must provide "students with a more complex and demanding educational experience than ever before" (Shakeshaft, 1990, p. 148). At the same time, they must reach a large portion of the students who have not experienced success even under less demanding standards and expectations (J. Murphy, 1990a, 1991b): "The school that formerly graduated 60%, one third of whom were able workers and citizens, now has to pull them all through" (Moorman, 1990, p. 99). To accomplish this, leaders in a postindustrial society will need to be much more committed to education and "invested in children" (J. Murphy, 1990f, p. 110) than they have been previously. Because the challenge for tomorrow's leaders will be "to refocus the structure [of schooling] on some new conception of teaching and learning" (Elmore, 1990, p. 63), they will need to be more broadly educated in general (Culbertson, 1988a) and much more knowledgeable about the core technology of education in particular (J. Murphy, 1990d; NAESP, 1990). "Instructional and curricular leadership must be at the forefront of leadership skills" (Hallinger, 1990, p. 77) and administrators must "maintain a focus on teaching and learning in the school" (p. 76). In a rather dramatic shift from earlier times, school and district administrators of tomorrow's schools will be asked to exercise intellectual leadership not as head teachers, but as head learners (Barth, 1986, 1988).

The belief that the activities of administrators are deeply inter-twined with critical and ethical issues is central to the metaphor of administration as moral educational leadership. As we have seen, this belief means sensitivity "to racial issues and to the goal of equal educational opportunity" (Culbertson, 1988a, p. 28). In tangible terms, it suggests changing schooling to be responsive to the needs of his-torically disenfranchised and undereducated pupils rather than attempting to mold children to fit currently dysfunctional organiza-tional forms (Astuto, 1990; Clark, 1990; W. Greenfield, 1990); it calls for us to examine current arrangements from a critical viewpoint, to educate the whole child, and to ensure success for all students.

The centrality of values for administrators for the twenty-first century is clearly evident in the call for leadership of the school community. In their role as transformative leaders, school heads are being asked to nurture the development of learning, professional, and caring communities based on the values of "reflective inquiry and democratic participation" (Foster, 1988, p. 71; Bolin, 1989). In developing "communities of learning" (Zeichner & Tabachnich, 1991, p. 9), tomorrow's leaders must promote an atmosphere of inquiry. They "must be curious and inquiring about schooling prac-tices and effective learning conditions, and they must instigate curiosity and inquiry among others" (Roberts, 1990, p. 135). These "leaders will need to know how to find, interpret and use important information to weave plausible scenarios of future conditions that will challenge educators" (Achilles et al., 1990, p. 16). They "must develop the capacity to reflect on their practice" (Deck, 1990, p. 50) and promote self-inquiry among other members of the school com-munity. Particular attention must be given to examining organiza-tional values that provide meaning to community activity (Driscoll, 1990; Sergiovanni, 1991b). Our earlier comments about the admin-istrator as head learner are relevant here as well.

In developing democratic, professional communities, tomorrow's leaders must operate from moral authority based on ability (Angus, 1988), commitment to the values of the school (Sergiovanni, 1991b) and "to serving the best interests of the children in their schools" (W. Greenfield, 1990, p. 74), and "courageous tenacity" (Sanford, 1990, p. 145), or "the courage to persist in what is right" (Moorman, 1990, p. 101). In working with others, they must widen the circle of participation in schools (Blackman, 1990; J. Collins, 1990), "focus on collaboration and shared decision making" (Hinojosa, 1990, p. 83), enhance "the feelings of self-efficacy among . . . organizational members so that they can work to develop new organizational forms and functions based on the emerging needs of our culture and society" (Deck, 1990, p. 49), and encourage "others to be leaders in their own right" (Sergiovanni, 1991b, p. 335); "this expanded vision of leadership [for tomorrow's schools is both more] accessible and cooperative" (Lam, 1990, p. 86).

Finally, in facilitating the development of a caring community, "school leaders need to demonstrate the ethic of care to all members of the school community" (Astuto, 1990, p. 4).[13] They can bring this about by: (a) attending to the "human factor" (Frank, 1990, p. 69) or "human infrastructure" (Cunningham, 1990a, p. 13) directly—by "concentrat[ing] on people first" (Sergiovanni, 1991b, p. 52); (b) "valuing each of them as ends [and by being] alert to their unique qualities and needs" (Moorman, 1990, p. 101); (c) "ministering" to their needs "by furnishing help and being of service" (Sergiovanni, 1991b, p. 335); and (d) "developing people as human resources" (Vazquez, 1990, p. 174)—"by building capabilities of people . . . and by encouraging them to develop the ways and means for using their capabilities" (Sergiovanni, 1989b, p. 39).

We have now come full circle. We have seen how preparation for school administration has developed over the past century. We have examined in some detail problems with current training programs. And we have provided a portrait of schooling and leadership for the twenty-first century. One task remains: to use this knowledge of the past, present, and future to craft a new model of preparation for school leaders. We turn to that task in Chapter 6.

Six

Preparing Leaders for Tomorrow's Schools

> Undergirding these continuing reports, conversations and critical exchanges is the inescapable conclusion that substantive changes are needed in educational administration programs. (Prestine & LeGrand, 1990, p. 1)

> To cultivate and develop school leaders who can meet the challenges of creating new structures and reforming schooling practices will require a dismantling and restructuring of the ways in which such leaders are prepared and trained. (Roberts, 1990, p. 135)

> We cannot advocate practices for . . . schools that we are not willing to advocate and practise ourselves. (Fullan, 1991, p. 3)

This final chapter sketches a design for transforming preparation programs to meet the challenges of educating leaders for tomorrow's schools. Because, as Cuban (1988) says, "defining problems carefully at the outset is far more important than generating clever solutions to ill-defined problems" (p. 343), and as Reyes and Capper (1991) report, "how a problem is defined can determine if and how the problem is addressed" (p. 551), considerable effort has been devoted in earlier chapters to framing the nature of the problem. Building on that work, the guidelines presented here are grounded upon three propositions: (a) that the "proper means for reconstructuring our social institutions are best suggested by a careful accumulation and analysis of our institutional experience and [that a] wider accumulation and saner interpretation of the facts of our educational history" (Cubberly, cited in Culbertson, 1988a, p. 9) can help establish a framework for the transformation of leadership preparation programs; (b) that new training models must unequivocally address the weaknesses that plague current programs; and (c) that the transformation must fit our vision of society, schooling, learning, and leadership for the twenty-first century. The guidelines themselves are presented in two sections. The first section examines the objectives of proposed reconstructed preparation programs. We discuss values, education, inquiry, and knowledge of the human condition. The second half of the chapter develops a set of principles to shape the knowledge base, delivery systems, and support structures that would comprise these alternative educational programs for school administrators.

It is difficult to analyze the state of affairs in administration programs without becoming despondent. Indeed, the fundamental tenet of this volume is that we must be about the business of improving things dramatically. At the same time, however, we must avoid the sins of past reforms, especially that of zealotry. We need to examine alternative perspectives critically. The history of shifts from the ideological to the prescriptive era and from the prescriptive to the social science era reveals three types of overzealousness: *excessive criticism*—the demand "that almost everything that had been done in the past . . . be changed" (Callahan, 1962, p. 191); a belief that *one* true path had been discovered (e.g., scientific management, behavioral science research); and a virtual absence, especially in the yeasty time of ferment, of close scrutiny of the "new" model.

Caveats introduced in Chapter 1 are also worth revisiting, especially a warning against March's (1974, 1978) ideology of administration—the rational,[1] linear "conceit" (1974, p. 21) that training will noticeably enhance leadership, which in turn will significantly improve education and schools, resulting in solutions for the complex problems confronting society. As previously documented, all the links in this chain have been subject to fairly persuasive criticism. Particularly troublesome in this discussion is the first coupling—improved training to better leadership.[2] Because "graduate training [is] a low-gain enterprise" (Tyack & Cummings, 1977, p. 59), "it is important to have a realistic understanding of possible reform of educational leadership through improved training" (p. 63).

It is also useful to remind ourselves that nearly every dimension of preparation programs treated below (e.g., emphasis on training the person versus training for organizational roles, generic versus specialized training content) has been debated throughout our field's short history (Campbell et al., 1987). Different answers have found acceptance in various eras.[3] Therefore, it may be naive to assume that the resolutions proposed here for recurring issues will hold over time. It is perhaps unrealistic even to believe that they will take root.[4] As D. Cohen (1988), Cuban (1984, 1988), Elmore (1987), and other scholars have shown, fundamental change in educational institutions is rare indeed. Changes in programs of educational administration may be even more problematic (J. Murphy, 1989b, 1991a). Although Milstein (1990) argues persuasively that "it is clearly to our advantage to take the leadership" (p. 130) in the effort to improve preparation, we have been reluctant to do so (Griffiths et al., 1988b; McCarthy et al., 1988). Furthermore, because institutions of higher education are characterized by a good deal of "organizational sediment" and inherited "instructional guidance" (D. Cohen, 1989, pp. 6, 8) most changes in preparation programs have been "superficial, reactive, and cosmetic" (Griffiths et al., 1988b, p. 299) or at best evolutionary in nature (Miklos, 1983).

Campbell and Miklos also add some cautionary comments to our discussion. Campbell and his colleagues (1960) reinforce a point made in Chapter 4—that a clear path of what needs to be done is far from obvious:

> I see us in a forest replete with trees, vines, and brambles, with a number of open spaces generally scattered. There are few clearly marked trails or signposts—worst of all, we administrators are not quite sure from which side of the woods we hope to emerge. (pp. 188-189)

Miklos (in press) in turn maintains that the knowledge base necessary to inform change efforts is far from robust:

> Not only is there an uncertain knowledge base for administrator preparation, there is also an inadequate research base for efforts to improve programs. Most of the current proposals for reform—even though they may be persuasive—are not grounded in an extensive body of research. If there is to be a sound base for future reforms, various aspects of administrator preparation must be subjected to more intensive research than has occurred in the past.

Program Purpose and Goals

> Shaping the character and the scope of every preparatory program
> is a set of educational goals. Sometimes relatively implicit and some-
> times more explicit, these goals reflect the image of the adminis-
> trator which a given program would produce. Defining the desired
> facets of the image is the most fundamental of all acts in program
> development; the definition attained will and should affect every
> major aspect of preparation. (Culbertson, 1962, pp. 151-152)

Material for the design of preparation programs presented herein
is drawn from the three areas described in Chapters 2 through 5: a
deep understanding of our history; analysis of current conditions in
training programs; and a vision of the future of society, education,
and leadership. Given our understanding of that material, the following purpose of training programs for school leaders emerges: to
provide leadership to communities so that children and young adults
are well educated, in the deepest sense of the term. The key words
here are *leadership* and *education*. Yet the sad fact is, as we have discovered repeatedly throughout this volume, that current preparation programs have little to do with either of these core dimensions
of school administration: "Much . . . training is at best tangential
and often merely conjectural with respect to the goals our institutions strive to achieve" (Erickson, 1977, p. 125). Taking this purpose
seriously, then, will require a quite different set of goals for training
programs than those currently driving the education of prospective
administrators.

PROGRAM GOALS

> [A] critical challenge facing those involved in preparation and
> training programs for school leaders is to help these potential leaders
> purposefully shape their own leadership paradigms in ways that
> enable them to take on the role of school leadership with vision-
> driven, action-oriented, and reflective confidence in their ability to
> instigate reform and stimulate success. (Roberts, 1990, p. 136)

As we have seen throughout earlier chapters, the implicit—if not explicit—goal of most preparation programs has been to help students of administration master a body of knowledge, often for a specific role (Campbell et al., 1987). For approximately the first 50 years of this century, that content consisted of rough-hewn principles of practice couched in terms of prescriptions. Since the end of World War II, the focus has been on knowledge from the social science disciplines. In both eras, administrators were to apply the knowledge acquired at the university to the problems they confronted at the school or district site. Thus, throughout its brief history, the field of school administration in general, and preparation programs in particular, have been defined primarily by reference to a body of knowledge. This is not a particularly surprising finding given the drive to professionalize administration and anoint it as an area of study (applied or otherwise). Although it is perhaps inappropriate to argue that this was the wrong way to define the field and to establish goals for school administration training programs, it is fair to suggest that it was not the most appropriate method of proceeding (Sergiovanni, 1991b). Indeed, as Evans (1991) correctly concludes, the attempt in educational administration "to *construct* a field of study on a 'body of knowledge' or a set of propositional findings . . . diverts our thinking onto the wrong path" (p. 19). It seems more useful to suggest that the content in training programs should backward map from the goals of preparation, rather than vice versa,[5] or, as Culbertson and Farquhar (1971a) captured it nearly a quarter of a century ago, "the search for more effective structure must be based upon the search for more clearly defined program goals" (p. 12).[6] Four such goals for preparation programs for practitioners[7] are discussed below: helping prospective leaders to become moral agents, educators, inquirers, and students of the human condition. The discussion is based on the belief that tomorrow's preparation programs should highlight "the centrality of ethical and intellectual qualities" as opposed to administrative roles, and that their goal is to "prepare the person" rather than to prepare the person for the role (Campbell et al., 1987, p. 192).

Values

It therefore follows necessarily that one of the principal emphases in the training of educational administrators—possibly the critical emphasis—must be placed on training in educational purpose and in the processes through which such purposes are defined. No amount of empirical description of schools or management, regardless of frame of reference, can supply the insights necessary for this task. (Harlow, 1962, p. 63)

If preparation programmes for school administrators are to acknowledge the surfing characteristics of administrative life they will need to give far more emphasis to a concern for values. (Sergiovanni, 1989a, p. 11)

The first goal of preparation programs should be to help students articulate an explicit set of values and beliefs to guide their actions—to become moral agents (Beck & Murphy, in press-b), or what C. Hodgkinson (1975) calls "valuationists" (p. 16). This goal is based on the belief that "the specific things (answers) that can be taught to prospective administrators may be less useful in many ways than a set of values behind the answers" (Crowson & McPherson, 1987, pp. 50-51). This is a radically different starting point for program development than the one that has been used for the past 90 years (Evans, 1991; Sergiovanni, 1989a). Because "acts of leadership at critical junctures in human events seldom involve choices in which the implications are clearly evident" (Popper, 1982, p. 16), and therefore "one cannot act on the basis of knowledge alone" (Hills, 1975, p. 17), values may well be the appropriate starting point. Behavior in the absence of these values is little more than "artificial posturing" (Hills, 1975, p. 16).

Because administrators are "representatives of values" (T. Greenfield, 1988, p. 152)—that is, "since administrators occupy and operate within a value-saturated universe" (C. Hodgkinson, 1975, p. 17; Starratt, 1991)—and "because administrators perform acts which flow from value judgments" (Carlson, 1963, p. 25), the focus on "deliberate moral choice" (Willower, 1988, p. 737), the "ethics of administration" (Watson, 1977, p. 91; Farquhar, 1981), "ethical inquiry" (Starratt, 1991, p. 186), and purposing (Carlson, 1963; Culbertson, 1963, 1964; Harlow, 1962) must be conscious goals of preparation programs (Carlson, 1963; Culbertson, 1962; Farquhar, 1968; Harlow, 1962; Wengert, 1962). Adherence to this goal shifts the focus in training programs from characteristics of administration to the character of administrators and from "administration as a science" to administration as a "moral act" (T. Greenfield, 1988, p. 137):

> [T]he determination of educational purposes is not a matter simply for an exercise in group dynamics. Neither is it a platform for the exhibition of a persuasive and charismatic personality. It is a matter for the most carefully reasoned, most carefully disciplined intellectual effort. It is in this fact that there is to be found an opportunity for the improvement of training programs for prospective educational administrators. (Harlow, 1962, p. 68)

Education

> [I]t must be asserted with some force that educational administration must derive its position and principles from more general assumptions about the nature of education in our society. (Foster, 1988, p. 69)

> The changing context in which we'll operate during the twenty-first century will place an even greater obligation on the principal to possess broader knowledge about teaching, learning, and curriculum. . . . What is involved here is more than the acquisition of recent research. It is an attitude of not only becoming expertly informed but of remaining informed and of preserving a habit of inquiry and reflection about the teaching and learning processes. (NAESP, 1990, pp. 13, 26)

Helping students become educators should be the second goal of restructured preparation programs. Earlier we cited the work of Bates (1984), Callahan (1962), Evans (1991), Foster (1988, 1989), and J. Murphy (1990d, 1990e, 1990f) and his colleagues (J. Murphy et al., 1983; J. Murphy, Hallinger, Lotto, & Miller, 1987) which reveals that school administration became "conceived as a special field within a larger field of Administration" rather than as "a special field within the larger field of Education" (Boyan, 1963, p. 12). We saw how the focus in preparation programs—first on scientific management and then on the social sciences—and the desire to create a profession separate from teaching (Goldhammer, 1983) contributed to: (a) the institutionalization of administration qua administration (Boyan, 1963); (b) the "separation of problems in administration from problems in education" (T. Greenfield, 1988, p. 144) in general; and (c) a heavy "accent on administrative and maintenance functions" (Watson, 1977, p. 89) in preparation programs in particular.

Because this approach to the field produces men and women who, in Hills's (1975) eyes, are little more than spectators in their own schools, we now know that "there is room for, and need for, dramatic changes in how principals understand their vocation" (Miklos, 1990, p. 339). The organizing framework for school administration as a field of activity is student learning, the effects of schooling on children and young adults (Erickson, 1977, 1979). Or, as Evans (1991) puts it, "the deep significance of the task of school administration is to be found in the pedagogical ground of its vocation"; it is, in fact, "the notion of *education* that gives the idea of leadership its whole purpose" (pp. 17, 3). Therefore, "the first quality . . . educational leaders of the future should have is a deep, empirically grounded, and unsentimental understanding of some aspect of teaching and learning" (Elmore, 1990, p. 64). The school administrator of the future "needs to be reasonably well grounded in developmental psychology, learning situations, socialization, cultural variation, instructional methods and materials, and curricular development" (Hills, 1975, p. 13). Programs for tomorrow's leaders need to restore "to educational administration what belongs to it, namely a deeply educative and pedagogic interest in the lives of children and young people" (Evans, 1991, p. 17). This shift in goals leads to a redirection in training programs from management to education by reconnecting administration with its original roots in teaching (Goldhammer, 1983).

Inquiry

[W]e need to reconceptualize our research training [for professional educators] so that the process of inquiry becomes central. (Muth, 1989, p. 5)

Facilitating the development of inquiry skills, or enhancing the thinking abilities of students, should be the third goal of reconstructured preparation programs. Consistent with the tenets of the behavioral psychology approach to learning that undergirds existing preparation programs (see Chapter 5), the operant goal in training programs is the transfer of knowledge from faculty to students. Furthermore, "most programs have emphasized the solutions to algorithmic tasks as opposed to heuristic ones" (Bryant, 1988, p. 10). In addition to the weaknesses of the transmission model of learning discussed in Chapter 5, knowledge *transfer* is an inappropriate primary goal for a variety of reasons. To begin with, as we have noted repeatedly, the process of defining educational administration by establishing a knowledge base and then backward mapping preparation from this content leads to distortions and dysfunctions in training programs. Furthermore, since it is becoming more obvious that there is not a codifiable knowledge base in educational administration and that efforts to develop one are not likely to be especially fruitful, making the transfer of predefined chunks of information the center of preparation seems counterproductive.[8] Such a process is also inconsistent with the dynamics of the administrative environment, a "scruffy" world (Sergiovanni, 1991b, p. 4) "full of unknowns where creative problem solving is likely to pay more dividends over the long run than superficial answers in the short run" (Bryant, 1988, pp. 13-14). Finally, as Culbertson (1964) reminds us, inquiry is central to the moral and educational goals discussed earlier, especially "in updating the meaning of educational purposes" (p. 321).

In programs to prepare tomorrow's leaders, it is important that inquiry occupy the high ground—that our students "acquire, above all else, the attitudes and skills of inquiry" (Erickson, 1964, p. 60). The focus should be less on acquiring information and discrete technical skills than on "cognitive and metacognitive processes" (Prestine & LeGrand, 1990, p. 13) and on learning the skills and habits of "conceptual literacy" (Giroux, 1988, p. 8) and "clinical reasoning" (Copeland, 1989, p. 10). Within the context of values, and based upon firm pedagogical foundations, process issues should displace content coverage at center stage (Hills, 1975). Procedural knowledge —"knowledge about how to perform various cognitive activities" (J. Anderson, 1990, p. 219)—rather than declarative knowledge— knowledge about facts, things, and associations—becomes the primary focus (Ohde & Murphy, in press). Construction of knowledge should move to the foreground, the dissemination of information to the background (Bransford, 1991; Fisher, 1990; Stigler & Stevenson, 1991); "Course content becomes a part of the process rather than an end in itself" (Prestine & LeGrand, 1990, p. 15). The spotlight should be on "those thought processes that precede purposeful . . . action" (Copeland, 1989, p. 10), on the construction of knowledge, and on

understanding: "A preparation program with an inquiry orientation . . . would have the virtue of producing seekers of knowledge
rather than the providers of answers" (Bryant, 1988, pp. 14-15).
Specific inquiry foci that would shape educational experiences—
within the framework of practice-driven, problem-based activities
—include ways of perceiving and knowing[9] (e.g., seeing issues from
multiple perspectives, reading situations), interpreting (e.g., critical
analysis and reflection, including unpacking the concepts, language, and values of daily life[10]), and shaping activity (e.g., problem
framing). "The common language and skills developed in such programs would be those [of] inquiry, problem finding, problem defining, and problem solving" (Muth, 1989, p. 12). The paradigmatic
shift here is from behavioral psychology to cognitive constructivist
approaches to learning.

The Human Condition

> The significant influence of study comes . . . through altering the
> conceptions . . . of the human being and of human behavior which
> serve as the context for administrative practice. (Hills, 1975, p. 3)

The final major goal of preparation programs for the future is to
help our students learn to work productively with people, to lead
in the broadest sense of the term. Although we have known for some
time now "that the crucial task of the school administrator is that of
helping people make good decisions" (AASA, 1960, p. 176), we have
not approached this goal with much reflection or imagination in our
training programs. As we saw in Chapter 5, the bureaucratic conception of management has focused on people as means rather than
as ends. If Hills (1975) is right, and I think he is, that "the heart of
the matter [educational leadership] seems to be how one behaves toward people," and that it is "far more important . . . that [the leader]
have a reasonably adequate conception of the human condition than
he have at his fingertips the most recent work in 'the politics of
education,' 'the economics of education,' or 'organizational change' "
(p. 12), then we need to rethink strategies to ensure that our preparation programs more effectively promote understanding of the
human condition and more systematically provide a context for
bringing that knowledge to bear on problems of education. Changes
required in preparation programs in order to highlight this goal

include: the creation of learning communities that incorporate understandings of the human condition; the infusion of content from a greater variety of areas, especially the humanities; and the use of instructional approaches that promote cooperative effort, dialogue, and reflection.

Principles for Developing New Programs

> The paradigm shift and the presence of alternative perspectives in administrative theory suggest that the time is right for allowing administrator preparation programs to reconsider their standard coursework and to try out different training models. (Foster, 1988, p. 78)

> Perhaps the day may come when entire preparation programs in educational administration are focused on the development of ethical competence, with the selection of social science and humanistic content and of instructional materials and field experiences being determined by the nature of a few crucial ethical problems around which the programs are built. (Farquhar, 1968, p. 203)

As with the issue of goals, the essential problem in defining principles consists of clearly identifyinig a few broad areas. In educational administration, we have invested considerable energy in trying to develop analogs to the periodic table—especially lists of functions, competencies, skills, courses, and so forth. Similar efforts at this juncture in our history may not present us with an especially clear path. What the field lacks is not lists but "over-arching gestalt conceptions shaping preparation programs" (Culbertson & Farquhar, 1971a, p. 11). Perhaps it makes most sense at this transition period to develop a relatively short but robust set of principles that comprise a gestalt of preparation and then to orient the education of school administrators toward these ideas. This strategy is both different from the catalog development procedures currently employed and consistent with the emerging views of knowledge construction presented in Chapters 5 and 6. For organizational purposes only,[11] essential principles for the development of preparation programs for leaders of tomorrow's schools are divided into two sections—curricular and instructional revisions.

CURRICULAR REVISIONS

> More of the same—more courses, more requirements, more pro-
> grams—may not be the best way to improve training and prepare
> administrators for the 1990s and beyond. (Mulkeen & Cooper,
> 1989, p. 10)

The curriculum in reconstructed preparation programs should be
characterized by authenticity, complexity, and interrelatedness. The
following principles appear particularly appropriate for the redesign work:

1. The program should be designed to help students develop the
   capacity to learn (as opposed to accumulating information).
2. The program should feature multisource, interrelated content (as
   opposed to a single-source, multidisciplinary approach).
3. The curriculum should be constructed "out of *generative topics*"
   (Perkins, 1991, p. 6), "essential questions" (Wasley, 1991, p. 42), or
   around authentic problems of practice (as opposed to being based
   on roles or academic disciplines).
4. The emphasis should be on depth of experiences (as opposed to
   content coverage).
5. The program should use original source documents (as opposed
   to textbooks).
6. The program should feature a single core curriculum (as opposed
   to specialized programs).
7. Professor choice is a key to developing good curricular experiences (as opposed to prescribed learning sequences).

Implicit in these principles is a rejection of the following norms that
characterize current preparation programs: (a) the belief the administrators can be prepared to deal with the specific content of their
jobs, and that we can do this better by preparing people for ever
more discrete roles; (b) equating preparation with the transmission
of a "systematized body of knowledge" (Gregg, 1969, p. 997)—
either discrete technical skills[12] or discipline-based content; (c) the
separation of administration from education and values; and (d)
distinctions between theory and practice.

In the stead of the above norms stand a variety of new conceptions about preparation content. At the most fundamental level, the principles listed above portray a dramatic shift in our understanding of knowledge. Knowledge is a tool, not a product. Starting from this viewpoint,

> whether or not one finds specific applications for specific learnings, is less important than the general orientation, world view, or whatever, that one constructs out of the variety of things experienced and learned. (Hills, 1975, p. 15)

At the same time, we are experiencing a shift in the nature of knowledge—to "a kind of knowledge that is rooted in action rather than cognition" (Petrie, 1990, p. 20; see also Perkins, 1991). The principles that should guide the restructuring of program content are grounded in the belief that the type of "knowledge needed to act competently as a principal relies more on the capacity to grasp meaning (a hermeneutic activity) than it relies on the possession of an abstract body of empirically derived skills and knowledge" (Evans, 1991, p. 7). Because administrative behavior in reality is "governed to a considerable degree by a rather generalized, closely interrelated mixture of empirical beliefs and values" (Hills, 1975, p. 2), they also acknowledge the fact that meaning is best nurtured in a context that underscores the development and use of three types of knowledge —craft, scientific, and moral. The design principles also reveal that educational administration needs to be studied as "a field of practice on its own turf and in terms of its own dynamics" (Immegart, 1990, p. 6; see also Cunningham, 1990a; Miklos, 1990). Finally, founded on the belief that the theory-practice dichotomy is largely an artifact of perspective and that efforts to bridge this perceived gap will fail as long as we continue attempting to map one domain onto the other, the view of knowledge contained in the seven principles outlined above is based on a model of integrated spirals of ways of knowing and acting. This mindscape both rejects out of hand the separation of theory from practice (and practice from theory) and, within the context of preparation, links these two formerly discrete concepts in such a way as to render meaningless a discussion of one without the other (Prestine & LeGrand, 1990).

These principles differentiate content in the new preparation programs from more traditional ones in other ways as well. To begin with, they require a multisource approach to providing students with educational experiences. Such an approach stands in stark contrast to earlier attempts to identify the one most appropriate content base for preparation programs. Equally important, the "multisource approach suggests abandoning the practice of simplification by isolation and adopting the strategy of simplification by integration" (Iran-Nejad, McKeachie, & Berliner, 1990, p. 513). The multisource strategy, developed "out of the vastness of organized knowledge . . . that appears most relevant to the practitioner's tasks" (Walton, 1962, p. 93), focuses attention on three broad areas or ways of knowing: philosophy (Culbertson, 1962; C. Hodgkinson, 1975) and the humanities (Culbertson, 1964; Farquhar, 1968; Halpin, 1960; Harlow, 1962; Popper, 1982, 1987); the social and behavioral sciences (see Chapters 3 and 4); and other professions (Soder, 1988), especially the helping professions (Cunningham, 1990a; Harbaugh, Casto, & Burgess-Ellison, 1987). It is humanities-oriented, scientifically grounded, and interprofessional in conception. It focuses on values, on education broadly defined, and on "the uniqueness of administrative functions in education" (Miklos, 1983, p. 164). In terms of integration, the new design encompasses two changes. The construction principles facilitate the fusing of knowledge from the three sources noted above by situating learning in context. Establishing interconnectedness through simplification also means a shift from macro-level integration strategies that focus on developing multidisciplinary expertise, often at high levels of abstraction, to micro-level strategies that highlight an "ongoing process that brings together diverse influences of many sources bearing on the solution to a complex problem" (Iran-Nejad et al., 1990, p. 511) of practice. Separate disciplines are accepted for what they are: "artificial partitions with historical roots of limited contemporary significance" (Perkins, 1991, p. 7).

These principles signal a fairly substantial shift in the way we think about the content that shapes learning experiences. At the structural level, the design acknowledges "the inadequacies of the usual course-added-to-course approach to the preparation of school administrators" (McIntyre, 1957, p. 4). It also makes clear that "departments which undertake to nurture educational vision will

also have to eliminate content from established programs" (Culbertson, 1988b, p. 30) and that developers will need to value the depth
of learning experiences more highly than the number of courses completed. At the heart of the new structure is a substantive change in
the conception of program content, a shift from the nearly exclusive
focus on the liberal arts/philosophy of the ideological era, from the
folklore base of the prescriptive era, and from the behavioral science
methods of the scientific era. The change is to a " 'learning-in-action'
context for graduate education" (Silver, 1978a, p. 205), or what are
becoming known as "real people, real life" (Willower, 1988, p. 731),
clinically based (Griffiths, 1977), and problem-based strategies
(Bridges & Hallinger, 1991).[13] The "alternative model . . . recognizes
the legitimacy of, and addresses, the practitioner orientation" (Muth,
1989, p. 9). It locates the development of needed knowledge and
"research skills in the problems and contexts with which practitioners must contend" (p. 9). The seven design principles address the
calls of both humanities-oriented and social science-oriented professors for a more inductive approach to preparation—one that "starts
with a primary focus on real, contemporary ethical problems confronting educational administrators and then delves selectively into
humanistic content from time to time as circumstances dictate"
(Farquhar, 1981, p. 200), and one that begins "with a specification of
the substance of administration and attempt[s] to identify the areas
in which this overlaps with the substance of the various social
sciences" (Cunningham et al., 1963, p. 97).[14]

The problem-based framework draws upon a variety of forces. To
begin with, this approach recognizes "that attention to administrative functions such as budgeting, finance, school law, organizational
theory, curriculum development, and supervision lacks transformative power" (Cunningham, 1990a, p. 5) and is consistent with a
growing recognition of the need for the development of a "knowledge base organized around problems of practice" (Griffiths et al.,
1988b, p. 301; see also J. Murphy, 1990h; Silver, 1986, 1987). It re-
orients preparation in such a way that the "distinctive quality" of
the knowledge base becomes its *relevance* to the problems faced by
practitioners" (Lortie, 1962, p. 78). At the same time, there is a developing belief in the field that this approach is particularly useful
in meeting the four program goals discussed earlier (J. Murphy,
1990h). For example, because many "of the past findings have
simply shown that our approaches to direct teaching of values or

teaching by example have been dysfunctional" (C. Hodgkinson, 1975, p. 13), Farquhar (1981) suggests that "ethical competence . . . should be approached inductively in an educational administration problem solving way" (p. 203). Evans (1991) makes a similar claim when he argues that "questions of meaning cannot be addressed in the abstract but must be referred to the practical world of the here and now, the experienced and experienceable world of concrete acts and real events" (p. 5). Similar arguments for mastery of the other preparation goals—education, inquiry, and knowledge of the human condition—have been drawn by J. Murphy and Hallinger (1987), Muth (1989), and Hills (1975), respectively.

Considerable support is also being generated for the propositions that: (a) anchoring learning in "macrocontexts" or "complex problem spaces" (Cognition and Technology Group, 1990, p. 3) for extended periods facilitates learning to learn or the construction of meaning (Bransford, 1991; Brown et al, 1989; A. Collins et al., 1991); (b) "the most important goal of education is to prepare students for action . . . and that the best way to do this is, presumably, to provide students with problem-solving experiences that are similar to situations that they will encounter later on" (Bransford et al., 1989, p. 493); and (c) "problem-oriented learning environments" (p. 470) that focus on "complex, meaningful task[s]" (Means & Knapp, 1991, p. 9) and "situated cognition" (Brown et al., 1989, p. 32) promote clinical reasoning and the use and transfer of knowledge more effectively than do more traditional learning formats (Cognition and Technology Group, 1990; Copeland, 1989; Stigler & Stevenson, 1991).

Finally, the practice-oriented, problem-based approach is drawing momentum from the fact that it provides a learning context more consistent with the context that students face on the job (Bridges & Hallinger, 1991). In an influential 1974 essay, March reminded us that one

of the persistent difficulties with programs for reform in the training of administrators is the tendency to try to improve managerial behaviour in ways that are far removed from the ordinary organization of managerial life. Unless we start from an awareness of what administrators do and some idea of why they organize their lives in the way that they do, we are likely to generate recommendations that are naive. (p. 25)

The real-life, real-people model proposed to prepare leaders for tomorrow's schools confronts this issue directly. Its framework reflects the beliefs: "that the most obvious characteristic of school
administration is the job's uncompromising insistence that a host of
things *get done*" (AASA, 1960, p. 175); that "understanding practice
is the single most important precondition for improving practice"
(Levine et al., 1987, p. 160); and that this understanding is best forged
in an environment—one more disorderly than orderly (Erickson,
1977; Sergiovanni, 1991b)—that matches the one confronting administrators. Underlying these beliefs is the tenet that "clinical reasoning . . . appears to develop as a consequence of experiences with
clinical environments" (Copeland, 1989, p. 12). Implicit in the design is recognition of T. Greenfield's (1988) admonition that "administrators know administration, scientists don't" (p. 155). The
focus of attention is thus on real issues in the field (Crowson &
McPherson, 1987; Muth, 1989).

How would a curricular program based on the ideas and principles noted above differ from current practice?[15] To begin with, most
discrete courses in preparation programs would disappear. There
would be no courses in school law, politics of education, administrative theory, statistics, or any of the other titles that combine to create
the curriculum in most preparation programs. Specialized courses
designed to prepare learners for roles such as the principalship, the
superintendency, the department chair, and so forth, would be elimi-
nated as well. The somewhat confusing segregation of inquiry skills
into separate research methods courses would cease (Muth, 1989).
The function of preparation programs—having students cover 8, 10,
or 12 essential blocks of knowledge (i.e., separate courses) that they
need to be certified and/or to graduate—would change. The goal
would be to help students develop the capacity to learn, a foundation from which they can acquire information and develop understanding.

What, then, would a restructured curriculum in these preparation
programs look like? Something like this makes sense: During the
course of their tenure at the university, students would grapple with
a select number of authentic and significant *educational* problems.
Because this plan acknowledges that no particular discipline is
essential, the particular nature of the problem is less critical than the
extent to which it promotes the development of the four program
objectives discussed earlier. In addition, the issue selected should

be an authentic aspect of practice rather than discipline-focused concern. That is, the design is both practice-driven and problem-based. Discipline-based knowledge can then be brought to bear on the problem as appropriate and needed. Knowledge would be linked to problems and the disciplines would be employed in the service of the profession, which, as we have seen, is a reverse of the current order. The opportunity is also created for the humanities to become an integral and integrated aspect of preparation programs. What students learn about the particular problem under study would be much less important than their ability to employ the solution strategies in dealing with future problems (Hills, 1975). The goal is to allow students "to construct their own cognitive understandings which could then be used for future clinical reasoning" (Copeland, 1989, p. 14).

How might this type of curriculum unfold in the real world? A cohort of students would matriculate in the fall. During their first year in the program they would tackle a real problem, similar to the following, for which they would receive 12, 15, or 18 hours of traditional course credit:

> The Cleveland City Schools are seriously considering "restructuring" their schools. We have been asked by the superintendent to work with her and her staff to study the issue and develop a plan of operation. Your responsibility is to conduct the study and develop the plan.

The learning activity would be shaped, facilitated, and evaluated by a core team of instructors working cooperatively. It is critical that the team be interdisciplinary in nature and include instructors from both the university and the field. The interdisciplinary (and/or interprofessional) team might include university faculty with interests in organizational theory, educational ethics, finance, qualitative research methods, and the principalship, as well as full-time adjunct professors from the field who have additional expertise (especially craft knowledge) to offer on this particular topic. If thoughtfully planned and guided by the faculty team, the learning activity would form a tapestry in which practice and theory could be inexorably linked, and in which the individual disciplinary threads and understandings from philosophy and the humanities would be tightly interwoven. Comprehensive contact with a small number of issues (depth) would be the focus, rather than maximum exposure to a variety of knowledge domains (breadth). Original sources—such as reports of original studies, analyses of major theoretical constructs as first developed by their authors, and studies conducted (by students and others) in service of the problem under investigation— would be used. The hodgepodge of textbooks common to most preparation programs would be conspicuous by its absence. Much of what would be needed to solve this problem could be anticipated and structured for students (for example, readings about attempts to implement school-based management in other localities, site visits to districts/schools that are pioneering restructuring efforts, a sourcebook of both poor and excellent qualitative studies, and so forth). A good deal of the work plan, however, would need to be created as the investigation unfolded. The students would contribute much more of the developmental work in this type of revised training program than they do in traditional preparation settings.

CHANGES IN THE DELIVERY SYSTEM[16]

> If creativity is to be fostered, responsibility for much of the learning in preparatory programs will need to be shifted to trainees. (Culbertson & Farquhar, 1971c, p. 14)

Preparation programs designed to prepare tomorrow's leaders will also employ dramatically different instructional strategies. In many ways, these new approaches will be so tightly interwoven with issues of program content that it will be impossible to pull them apart. The following principles appear appropriate for rethinking the current instructional "delivery system" in preparation programs for school leaders:

1. Learning should be student-centered (as opposed to professor-centered).
2. Active learning should be stressed (as opposed to passive consumption).
3. Personalized learning should be emphasized (as opposed to collective consumption).
4. A balance of instructional approaches is needed (as opposed to dominant reliance on the lecture-discussion model).

5. Cooperative approaches to learning and teaching should be underscored (as opposed to individualistic competitive strategies).
6. Outcome-based (or mastery-based) learning should be stressed (as opposed to process-based learning).
7. Delivery structures should be built on developmentally based learning principles (as opposed to universally applicable principles).

At the heart of these principles is a shift that would make instruction increasingly less teacher (professor)-centered and increasingly more student (learner)-centered. Currently, as reported in Chapter 4, instructional methods in preparation programs mirror teaching approaches in elementary and secondary schools. Professors are jugs of knowledge whose job it is to pour information into empty mugs (i.e., students). In the future, professors will need to be seen as managers of learning activities and students will need to be viewed as producers of knowledge: "The instructional program should stress 'doing' rather than passive listening" (Griffiths, 1977, p. 433). The notion of student-as-worker that is at the core of this change (J. Murphy, 1991b) will need to be institutionalized in training programs. The current focus on acquiring information will be replaced by a concern for students' abilities to use knowledge and to learn how to learn. Professors will act less as founts of knowledge and more as facilitators, modelers, and coaches who invest students with responsibility for their own learning and then guide them in a highly personalized process of developing understanding (Bridges & Hallinger, 1991; Prestine & LeGrand, 1990).

The lecture-discussion (teaching is telling) model that dominates instruction in traditional preparation programs gives way to "methodological flexibility" (Culbertson & Farquhar, 1971c, p. 14) and to a greater variety of approaches when teaching for meaningful understanding replaces content coverage as a goal. Since what "the individual learns about *himself* could well be the most important learning that he experiences . . . [and since] the mass-produced graduating class is a crime against human dignity and intelligence" (McIntyre, 1957, p. 21), instruction in restructured programs becomes less generic and more personalized.

There is a dramatic shift in the primary learning mode in these programs. Because "learning and planning together to create change in education is probably the best way for a person to develop as a leader" (Egan, 1990, p. 59), the "process of collaborative inquiry serves as a model" for instruction (Rogers & Polkinghorn, in press). Stable "teams of learners," or cohorts, within the framework of a learning community, systematically engage in "the social construction of knowledge" (Achilles et al., 1990, pp. 8, 9). Cooperative learning activities based on psycho-sociological models of understanding replace many of the individually competitive activities that are grounded upon traditional psychological views of learning. Instruction in restructured training programs becomes more cooperative for students and more collegial for professors. Professors act less like individual discipline-based entrepreneurs and more like colleagues engaged in a cooperative interdisciplinary endeavor (Fullan, 1991). More responsibility for learning will be passed to their colleagues, with whom they plan, and to their students, who play a stronger part in helping to chart their paths, and who have a much more active role in their quest for understanding.[17] Like the curriculum, instruction becomes both more complex and more cohesive.

Revisions in instructional format are designed to underscore the centrality of human relations in training programs, to reduce program segmentation, and to emphasize demonstration of skills and knowledge. At the core of these alterations is a shift away from impersonal, certification-based, calendar-based, and discipline-based arrangements. There is a movement away from the current emphasis on seat time and units completed. Structures in the reformed training programs are based more on learning theory and exhibits or demonstrations of learning than on administrative convenience.

One major change is the enhanced use of outcome-based education. Under this approach, it is the expected outcomes, "not the calendar, that determine credit and, in turn, define what constitute a 'course' and the content needed in that course" (Spady, 1988, p. 5). In restructured preparation programs, different students (and groups of students) will demonstrate mastery at different times depending on the order in which they tackle issues, the paths they select (with professorial guidance) to reach an outcome, and the capacity they bring and the amount of effort they devote to the endeavor. Mastery can be exhibited in a greater variety of ways than is currently the case. For example, assessment of a videotape of a student conducting a small group meeting makes more sense than evaluation of a written exam if one is trying to judge competency in running meetings.

Emphasis on the principles of adult cognition is consistent with a mastery approach to learning, as well as with the instructional strategies noted earlier. Developmentally appropriate strategies for adults are those that allow individuals and small groups to assist in defining problems and charting solution strategies, to work at their own rates, and to bring craft knowledge to the problem-solving process (J. Murphy & Hallinger, 1987). The use of developmentally appropriate strategies helps nurture the formation of a community of student and professor learners who are engaged in active pursuit of a serious academic task.

Central to changes in the core technology of preparation programs is a more serious engagement by students in their learning. The goal here is to break the highly dysfunctional system of bargains, compromises, trade-offs, and treaties discussed in Chapter 4, in which professors, in return for continued enrollment and compliant behavior, ask little of their students. By providing students with meaningful content, while turning them loose on the quest for understanding, by providing direction, by holding students accountable for results, and by creating a learning structure supportive of this type of curriculum and instruction, the restructured preparation program fosters the type of sustained personal engagement that promotes both understanding and learning to learn. It leads to the development of what Culbertson (1964) has labeled "the perceptive generalist" (p. 54)—a leader who is "a sophisticated analyst *and* a vigorous actor" (Culbertson, 1962, p. 154), an administrator who is seen "as a champion of values, as a proponent of change, [and] as a messenger of participation" (Foster, 1988, p. 78).

STRUCTURAL ISSUES[18]

Without belaboring the point further, it is suggested that unless legislatures, professional associations, certifying officers, college administrators, and professors are willing to put more emphasis on quality and less on numbers, the quality of school administration in this country will continue to be a major educational and social problem. (Hall & McIntyre, 1957, p. 398)

Supporters of alternative models believe that until the basic structure of the prevailing model is changed the result will not be appreciably improved. (Cooper & Boyd, 1987, p. 16)

Throughout the history of education in general and of school administration in particular, we have often allowed structural issues to determine our goals and actions. Thus, in many ways, structural matters define our views of schooling and education. It is for that reason that I have deliberately kept discussion of program structure to a minimum and to the end. It is my belief that structural decisions should backward map from—rather than establish—goals and program principles (J. Murphy, 1991b). The specific objectives and design principles discussed earlier may be used to construct programs in a variety of ways; different structures will work best at different times in different places. Consistency and coordination of effort within an institution around an appropriate vision of preparation will go a long way toward ensuring the creation of a strong program.

Starting with goals and principles helps us see persistent questions in new ways. For example, one long-standing issue in preparation programs is the amount of choice students should have in building their individual program of studies—what Farquhar (1977) calls the "freedom-control" issue (p. 348). Under current arrangements, freedom means the ability to select a number of individual courses. Given the part-time nature and well-documented lack of coherence of most programs, choice has produced a situation of "academic drift and curricular debris" (J. Murphy, Hull, & Walker, 1987, p. 341). However, within the alternative framework presented in this chapter, choice means deciding how to work with colleagues and how to proceed in constructing meaning. It is not something that needs to be balanced—some point on a continuum that needs to be established—but, within the context of a situated learning problem, something that is desirable.

Nonetheless, it still appears that the resolution of structural decisions in certain directions is more likely to facilitate the evolution of programs that more easily accommodate the design principles presented earlier. For example, a number of thoughtful scholars have argued recently that the vision of preparation described in this volume will require a movement away from our infatuation with the arts and sciences (Clifford & Guthrie, 1988; Griffiths, 1988b; NPBEA, 1989a), that the "school of education [that] has been cast in the role of the ugly stepsister of arts and sciences instead . . . [must take] its place with the other professional schools housed in the university" (Griffiths et al., 1988b, p. 291). As noted in Chapter 4, some of the most ingrained problems in our field can be traced to programs that distance themselves from the professional dimensions of school leadership. The development of a new structure to house preparation, that is, the movement to a "professional preparation model" (Miklos, in press), will help address two specific problems that hinder our capacity and effort to develop alternative training frameworks. It will provide the context in which reward systems in universities can be restructured (Clifford & Guthrie, 1988; Griffiths et al., 1988b). It will also allow the profession to gain control over the occupation of school administration, thus reversing the current situation. Absent some progress on both of these issues, our best efforts at reform are likely to be ineffectual.

A corollary of the move to a professional model is the need to develop structures that create "greater tie[s] between universities and schools" (Spaedy, 1990, p. 158). To bring the goals and principles of this chapter to life, "[d]epartments of administration need to develop strong cooperative relations with *local school systems*" (Wynn, 1957, p. 474). In the future, "the responsibility for preparing educational administrators should be shared with the profession and the public schools" (Griffiths et al., 1988b, p. 293). Alternative designs that capture a rich mix of ingredients from both arms of the profession are likely to prove necessary to help prospective administrators meet the four program goals discussed earlier (NCEEA, 1987; NPBEA, 1989a). Cooper and Boyd (1987) maintain that one way to break the current model is to establish an alternative structure in which "programs [are] sponsored jointly by school districts, universities, and professional associations" (p. 19; see also NAESP, 1990).

Throughout our history it "has been assumed tacitly that the same program that prepares administrators can prepare professors of administration" (Wynn, 1957, p. 493). That solution to what Miklos (1983) labels one of the profession's "long-standing questions" (p. 168) appears to be less than ideal. The goal framework underlying the alternative perspective proposed above acknowledges that the responsibilities of professors of administration and of practitioners of administration differ and that "the kind of people who are good at one may not be good at the other" (Walton, 1962, p. 92). I concur with Wynn (1957), and others (Clifford & Guthrie, 1988; Culbertson & Farquhar, 1971b; Griffiths, 1977; NPBEA, 1989a; Prestine & LeGrand, 1990), who have argued for 35 years that "the two functions be differentiated and an educational program be designed for each" (p. 468). "The functionally appropriate vehicle for professional educators is the doctor of education degree" (Clifford & Guthrie, 1988, p. 359). Like Griffiths (1977), however, I believe that the development of distinct programs does not require that they be totally separate. As a matter of fact, paths where programs intersect will need to be carefully developed or we will be likely to develop professors who are unable to work effectively in the proposed alternative program design. These points of intersection should be created in many places throughout the two programs.[19]

At the same time, given the importance of educational matters and situated learning in the framework we have developed, it seems reasonable to suggest that a structure be created that allows for considerably more overlap between the education of teachers and that of administrators than has been the case throughout the 20th century.[20] If the future is anything like the picture drawn in Chapter 5, then the notion of a more unified profession becomes a distinct possibility (J. Murphy, 1991b; Sergiovanni, 1991a), both at the macro level of the profession and at the micro level of the individual school. It can be argued that the knowledge work of tomorrow's leaders will have more in common with teachers than with professors of educational administration. The structure of preparation should evolve to reflect these realities.

Finally, a framework for the program that provides sufficient time for students to engage seriously with real problems in a sustained fashion appears necessary. In short, "[r]esidency requirements in preparation programs will also have to undergo important changes" (Culbertson, 1963, p. 58). I agree with both earlier (Callahan, 1962; Culbertson, 1963; Goldhammer, 1963; Gregg, 1969) and more recent (Griffiths et al., 1988b; NPBEA, 1989a) assessments that, if "quality instruction and learning are to be achieved it appears necessary that able, career-committed students should have the opportunity to devote themselves to full-time study for a prolonged period of time" (Gregg, 1969, p. 998). As a matter of fact, the design principles at the heart of the preparation framework discussed in this volume make the need for large blocks of time even more imperative (see McIntyre, 1957; Prestine & LeGrand, 1990; Reed, 1991). Thus I concur with the NPBEA (1989) that, although a number of difficulties are involved, for tomorrow's leaders "the study of educational administration should be a full-time endeavor" and, "if the difficulties are too great, alternatives to full-time study should be developed that will guarantee the benefits available to full-time students" (Griffiths et al., 1988b, pp. 292-293).

In closing, it might be helpful to say a few words about the faculty who will work in these reconstructed programs.[21] What knowledge should they possess? What frames of reference or specializations make most sense? These are complex questions and there are differences of opinion on how to proceed to answer them (see Burlingame, 1990, and Campbell et al., 1960, for views different from the one presented herein). We know that to date faculty interests have concentrated on issues of the field *or* on matters of the university. In the former case, there has been specialization by administrative tasks, functions, and/or roles (Farquhar & Piele, 1972). In the latter case, specialization has occurred on the basis of academic roles (researcher, teacher, developer) or of disciplinary interest.

As we look to the future, it is likely that our infatuation with specialization of any variety may prove counterproductive. The principle of integration through simplification (as opposed to integration through isolation) discussed in our review of program content appears to be applicable here as well.[22] That is, the "ideal professor of educational administration ought to be a competent scholar, teacher, counselor, researcher, field worker, and professional leader" (Wynn, 1957, p. 493). The analog is to the perceptive generalist at the school site. The objective here is not to deny the importance of expertise but to embed it within a more integrative approach to preparing leaders for tomorrow's schools. A fallback position from the ideal is to develop faculty who, although they cannot be all things to all students, do nevertheless define their roles more broadly than many of us do now. Teams of these faculty could then shape preparation programs. What seems clear under this scenario is that a part of the faculty will need to be able to bring recent craft knowledge to the preparation mix (Hills, 1975; Pepper, 1988). For this to work, it is important that these members of the team be full-time professors, not be seen as adjuncts, and "be provided with significant status within the university community" (Muth, 1989, p. 14)—the same types of status afforded to those occupying more traditional professorial roles.

Notes

Notes for Chapter 1

1. Although there was fairly widespread agreement with the analysis of the problems treated in these two reports, there was—and continues to be—a lack of consensus about the reports' solution strategies. Perhaps the major critique is that the reports are not sufficiently forward-looking. As Cunningham (1990) has reported, they were criticized for putting "old wine in new bottles" (p. 3).

2. See J. Murphy (1989b, 1991a) for descriptions of progress made to date in reforming preparation programs.

3. The Danforth Foundation has been a catalyst for nearly all the major activities unfolding in the reform of administrator preparation during this era. For example, it helped fund the work of both the NCEEA and the NPBEA and continues to support the ongoing efforts of the latter organization.

4. North Carolina is the state that has taken the most holistic approach to the reform of preparation programs (see *The Education of North Carolina's Teachers*, 1988; National Policy Board for Educational Administration, 1989b).

5. The activity of the Holmes Group is probably the best example of this phenomenon.

6. "Influential" does not mean "most," however. As McCarthy and her colleagues (1988) have documented, there is a good deal of compla-

cency about preparation programs within the educational administration professoriate.

7. The fact that this link is problematic has been noted by a number of thoughtful analysts, including Clark Kerr (1991), who concludes that "it has not been proven that education has been *the* key to the nation's competitiveness; that there has been too much blame with too little proof." He goes on to note "that seldom in the course of policymaking in the United States have so many firm convictions held by so many been based on so little convincing proof" (p. 30; see also March, 1974). It is also important to emphasize that a number of critics have severely challenged what Mitchell (1990) has labeled the maxim of "economic salvation through educational excellence" (p. 28). See Beck (1991) for a review of the work of analysts who are deeply troubled by the idea of undertaking reform based upon a competitive, economic ethic.

8. See J. Murphy (1990a) for a review of these measures—especially Table 1-1, pp. 11 to 18.

9. There is a pervasive feeling that the efforts to repair the overall educational system have not been terribly successful. For an alternative viewpoint, see J. Murphy (1989a).

10. A number of historical studies have confirmed that views of administration are shaped significantly by the larger social and political context in which schools find themselves. See, for example, Beck and Murphy (in press b); Callahan, (1962); Campbell et al. (1987); Tyack and Hansot (1982).

11. Elsewhere we have devoted considerable space to describing this body of literature. See especially Hallinger and Murphy, 1985, 1986; Hallinger, Leithwood, and Murphy, in press; J. Murphy, 1990d; J. Murphy and Hallinger, 1986, 1988.

Notes for Chapter 2

1. All quotes from Button (1966) are reprinted with permission of the publisher.

2. There are, of course, other useful ways to describe the reform of training programs in education. For example, Zeichner and Tabachnich (1991) employ the term *traditions of reform* (p. 3) to describe reform in teacher education programs during this century. They discuss four traditions: academic, social efficiency, developmental, and social recontructionist. In the case of educational leadership, there is a fairly reasonable match between some of these traditions and the particular eras described herein —the social efficiency tradition and the prescriptive era and academic

and social efficiency traditions and the behavioral science era. In addition, there is a good deal of Zeichner and Tabachnich's social reconstructionist tradition in the dialectic era of administrator preparation.

3. Those studies used the following elements: recruitment of students, selection of students, monitoring/assessing programs, clinical experiences, program content, teaching and learning strategies, degree structure, involvement of practitioners in development, involvement of practitioners in delivery, involvement of faculty in schools, mix of students, services for practicing administrators, selection of faculty, departmental staffing, faculty development opportunities, and departmental mission/agenda.

4. The components of the Culbertson et al. framework are: program content, program structure, recruitment and selection, instructional approaches, field and related experiences, student research, requirements for graduation, program evaluation and development, departmental functions and staffing, and inservice programs.

5. The fact that there is a great deal of similarity in the conclusions of the analysts is worth noting as well.

6. Beck and Murphy (in press-b) note that there is also a lag of a decade or so between the introduction of new ideologies in educational administration and their incorporation into the practice-based literature.

7. As noted throughout this volume, at any point in the history of educational leadership there is a good deal of correspondence between the high-status professions in society and the prevailing doctrine of school administration.

8. There is some discrepancy in reports on the number of preparation programs operating at the close of the prescriptive era. Although Silver lists the number at approximately 125, H. Moore (1964) maintains that "by the end of WWII approximately 300 institutions of higher education claimed programs of preparation for school administrators" (p. 12).

9. At the end of the prescriptive era, accreditation of educational administration programs was not in place, however (H. Moore, 1964).

10. The prevalence of this pattern well into the behavioral science era has been documented (Silver & Spuck, 1978; Valverde & Brown, 1988).

11. Although pragmatists clearly dominated the debate about the most appropriate content for practitioners during this time, other points of view could still be heard. According to Tyack and Cummings (1977), for example:

From 1910 through 1954 professors of educational administration vigorously debated about what sort of curriculum gave the best training for the superintendency. Arguments basically centered around preparing them pragmatically for the job as it was or giving them a broad perspective that would help them to adapt the schools to changing circumstances. (p. 60)

Campbell et al. (1987) also remark on these different views:

It also seems clear that tension existed between two views of preparatory programs. From Dutton and Snedden to Reeder, there was strong concern with the performance of administrative tasks. By contrast, the works of Newlon and Moehlman stressed the importance of helping future leaders develop ethical sensitivity, intellectual acumen, and societal understanding. Cubberley's approach seemed to span the two schools of thought. (p. 180)

12. It is interesting to see how little research in the field of educational administration has progressed since Newlon's time. For his measure of research activity, he selected doctoral dissertations, a criterion that makes good sense during the developmental phase of a new profession. However, nearly 60 years later most of the research in the field continues to be undertaken through doctoral studies (Clark, 1988).

13. The scientific management movement did bring a false sense of scientific respectability to educational administration and to the training of educational leaders (Callahan, 1962).

14. Griffiths (1959) reminds us of the limitations of these types of practice-based testimonials:

Although a certain amount of reporting of practice is useful, the saturation point is reached quickly. One finds that the "authorities" commonly contradict one another; and, when reports of practicing administrators are investigated, it is not unusual to find the event differs from the report. (p. 10)

15. For a reinterpretation of the theme of administrator vulnerability, see Button (1991).

Notes for Chapter 3

1. The NCPEA fell upon hard times after its prominence in the 1950s. The rise of the UCEA in the late 1950s and the fragmentation and balkanization of the field drained a good deal of leadership and energy from

the NCPEA. By the mid-1960s, Griffiths's (1959) observation that the NCPEA annual meeting was "the conference at which pioneer thinking in administration is presented and tested" (p. 3) was no longer true and the locus of the "movement of great significance" (p. 3) that had begun with the NCPEA at Endicott had shifted elsewhere. Recently, the NCPEA has been undergoing a process of renidification. Attempts to pump new vigor into the organization include the appointment of a nonrotating executive secretary, a change in name—to the National Council of Educational Administration—and attempts to attract younger members of the professoriate. In addition, for the first time, a permanent home for the Council has been established at the University of Wisconsin, Madison.

2. CPEA (Cooperative Program in Educational Administration) centers were located at: George Peabody College for Teachers; Harvard University; The Ohio State University; Stanford University; Teachers College, Columbia University; The University of Chicago; the University of Oregon; and the University of Texas.

3. According to Griffiths (1959):

> The field of educational administration serves as a case study of how a great foundation exerts its influence. In the opinion of the author, at least, the influence has been all to the good. Beginning in 1946, the W. K. Kellogg Foundation of Battle Creek, Michigan, became vitally concerned with the administration of public schools. From that date to 1959, grants estimated at some nine million dollars were made, largely to universities, for the study and improvement of educational administration. Prior to 1950, the date of the first substantial grants, and the innovation of the Cooperative Program in Educational Administration (CPEA), there was little interest in the substantive study of educational administration. Since that date there has been a rising tide of interest. The interest created, the funds and facilities provided, and the talent recruited have in the past few years moved the field farther along than it had moved in the preceding half-century. In large measure, the present urgency concerning theory can be traced to the stimulus given by the Kellogg Foundation. (pp. 4-5)

4. The UCEA entered into a period of decline in the mid-to-late 1970s. A combination of declining institutional membership and decreasing external support for new initiatives drastically reduced the UCEA's influence. More recently, under the direction of Patrick Forsyth, the

UCEA has returned to center stage in discussions and activities in the area of school administration. Although unable to reach the pinnacle it occupied in the 1950s and 1960s, by the mid-1980s the UCEA was poised to take the leading role in shaping discussions about a post-behavioral science era of leadership preparation.

5. It is interesting to observe the continuity across the years in suggestions about the minimum number of faculty needed to operate a preparation program. In 1957, Wynn proposed four. In the late 1980s, both the NCEEA (1987) and the NPBEA (1989a) set the figure at five.

6. Part of the explanation for the decline in number of full-time professors per department may be attributable to the substantial increase in the number of institutions operating training programs.

7. For example, at the end of World War II, nearly all professors had administrative experience in the public schools. But, by 1988, McCarthy et al. concluded that "educational administration faculty members seldom bring recent administrative experience to their professorial role. . . . Less than a quarter of the current cohort [of faculty] joined the faculty ranks directly from a superintendency or other K-12 administrative experience" (p. 170).

8. For example, McCarthy and her colleagues (1988) found that the highest number of faculty respondents identified with a discipline (13% with organizational theory), while the second largest group classified themselves in a way that revealed a primary affiliation with a task area or administrative level (12% with the principalship). Other responses cut across a variety of orientations and a multitude of subgroups within each orientation.

All quotes from Farquhar (1977) reprinted from Cunningham, L. L., Hack, W. G., & Nystrand, R. O., *Educational Administration: The Developing Decades*, copyright 1977 by McCutchan Publishing Corporation, Berkeley, CA 94702. Permission granted by the publisher.

9. Lortie (1962) divides the group of professors concerned with problems of practice into two subsets:

> Such men [the researchers] will have colleagues, however, of equal brilliance but of different viewpoint. These will be "scholars of the practical" with special expertness in areas such as facilities, staff organization, public relations, finance, who will bring research abilities and analytic minds to various facets of school administration. Their publications will break new ground in the major problem areas important to chief school officers. They will, of course, be well-informed on what is happening in the schools, but they will not spend any appreciable time giving service on local, idio-

syncratic problems to individual school systems. Such a use of
their time would be wasteful as it would compete with the broader
contribution they have to make to the entire profession. Service
work to schools will be done by men of less genius in creative
research but of high skill in the solution of immediate problems.
(pp. 82-83)

10. Nagle and Nagle (1978) report that black enrollment was considerably lower (a little less than 20%)—a difference that may be attributable to changes in conditions in training programs between the earlier
and later parts of the decade. In either case, it is clear that black enrollment was fueled by fellowships and scholarships that were "reasonably
plentiful" (Campbell et al., 1987, p. 186).
11. Although most of the students in training programs during the
prescriptive era were already practicing administrators, as the behavioral science era unfolded more and more of the students were preparing for their first managerial position.
12. During the 1960s, there was also some movement away from
these traditional criteria. According to Culbertson and Farquhar (1970),
in the mid-1960s:

Almost one-third of the university representatives stated that their
institutions had stopped using such common tests as the Miller
Analogies, had introduced new measures such as the Current
Affairs Test, or had rendered more precise the means by which test
results are assessed. Several others reported that they were employing a greater number and variety of non-test indicators in
screening applicants than they had prior to 1963. The devices specified included interviews and evaluations of non-cognitive personality factors like social commitment. (p. 11)

13. The use of interviews as a screening tool increased significantly
from the late 1950s to the late 1970s. While in the Nagle and Nagle sample, 62% of the schools required an interview, in 1960 only a small percentage of the institutions had done so.
14. Also particularly troubling to some commentators is the fact that
there is considerable overlap in course work at the doctoral level between
the Ed.D. and Ph.D. degrees (see Miskel, 1988; M. Norton & Levan, 1987;
Silver & Spuck, 1978).
15. Formal degree-granting preparation programs to prepare administrators are a uniquely American institution. Through the first

decade of the behavioral science era, the United States was the only nation to emphasize this avenue of administrator training. For example, the first graduate program outside the United States was not initiated until 1956 at the University of Alberta (Miklos & Nixon, 1978). Most nations continue to rely on less formal strategies to develop school leaders. On the other hand, the content and pedagogical strategies developed in the United States have influenced professional preparation abroad—"the pebbles dropped in the U.S. [professional preparation] mill pond have produced ripples—and sometimes rolling waves—all around the world" (Walker, 1991, p. 26).

16. Farquhar and Piele (1972) discuss the justification for full-time study as follows:

> The typical defense of the residency is based on benefits such as those noted by the New York State Regents Advisory Committee on Educational Leadership: "library facilities are discovered and used, dialogue between professors and students is facilitated, interchanges between students occur and the student has adequate time to do the critical thinking and assimilation of material necessary to make it useful". (1967, p. 4)

> To these advantages, the interviewees in a survey by the Committee for the Advancement of School Administration (CASA) added freedom from the distractions of day-to-day operational decisions and opportunity to learn how social scientists view education (AASA, 1963a, pp. 19-20). Neagley's study (1967) of faculty and students in 36 UCEA member universities yielded "opportunity to participate in research" as an additional gain derived from full-time residency. (pp. 39-40; see also Goldhammer, 1963)

17. This requirement was repealed in the early 1970s (Farquhar, 1977).

18. Although almost all institutions have maintained residency requirements on paper, most bear little resemblance to traditional standards designed to ensure full-time study. That is, in most programs residency requirements can be met while pursuing coursework on a part-time basis.

19. At the close of the scientific era, there was considerable disagreement about how extensively and deeply theory and research from the behavioral sciences had penetrated preparation programs. For example, in 1977 Getzels concluded that the social psychological paradigm "was incorporated into the lore, vocabulary, and common sense of the field" (p. 12; see also Griffiths, 1988a). Goldhammer (1983) also reported

that the theory movement exerted considerable influence over the content of training programs. Other seasoned analysts, however, read the situation differently (Campbell et al., 1987; Miklos, 1983; W. G. Walker, personal communication, May 1986). For example, in their historical review of this period, Campbell and his colleagues (1987) conclude that "the theory movement may have been something of a revolution in ideas, but its manifestations in graduate programs were not so dramatic" (p. 180). Whatever its effects on program content, the theory movement did not appear to exert much influence on the *structure* of preparatory programs (Goldhammer, 1983, p. 257, emphasis added).

20. The focus here is on what we call macro-level interdisciplinary activity—what Miklos (1983) has astutely labeled "redefining the substance of administrative study and the redrawing of boundaries" (p. 161). Goldhammer (cited in Farquhar & Piele, 1972) sees the problem in similar terms:

We have been guilty of erroneously thinking that we could apply the social sciences globally to educational administration rather than to the components of tasks, problems, and processes which comprise the content of administrative actions and behaviors. (p. 11)

Under this macro-level approach, students were exposed to the various disciplines and then they were expected to apply the knowledge gained to problems of practice as they arose (Cunningham et al., 1963). This approach stands in contrast to the more microlevel interdisciplinary activity we discuss in the concluding chapter. Under this approach, students begin with problems of practice and then draw on relevant social science content as needed to solve these issues.

21. The increase in residency requirements in the 1960s noted earlier greatly facilitated the ability of departments of educational leadership to require work external to colleges of education.

22. According to Silver (1982), internships were introduced into educational administration training programs in the late 1940s.

23. The list of "questions" raised about the internship in the 1960s— "those pertaining to a guiding conceptual framework, control of the intern's experiences, selection of interns and sponsors, the stage of preparation at which the internship should take place, finance, and evaluation" (Gregg, 1969, p. 999)—do not look considerably different from those plaguing this educational intervention today (see Chapter 4).

24. For a discussion of the issue of specialized versus common learnings, see Leu and Rudman (1963), Miklos (1972), and Miller (n.d.).

25. We do not wish to overstate the extent or depth of this trend. For example, while Miklos (1972) concludes that some programs "had taken seriously the concept that there are common administrative elements and that some form of training-in-common is not only feasible but desirable" (p. 48), he also finds "an almost universal practice of stressing that which is unique to that which is common" (p. 1).

26. About 7 hours; down from the 12 to 15 hours of the 1960s.

27. Earlier (see Note 14) we noted the great similarity between Ed.D. and Ph.D. programs in educational administration. Although the nature of dissertation experience would be expected to be one of the key areas that separate these two programs, Nagle and Nagle (1978) discovered that "the classic distinction drawn between Ph.D. and Ed.D. dissertation research" (p. 127) does not apply to educational administration programs.

28. There is a difference of opinion in the literature on the extent of specialization during the 1970s. Farquhar (1977) and Silver (1974) report on momentum toward greater flexibility and specialization. Nagle and Nagle (1978), on the other hand, conclude that "specialization [did] not appear to fare well" during the 1970s. Although there are elements of accuracy in both perspectives, in retrospect it appears that the Nagles provide a more realistic picture of the activity of this time. The development of standardized methods and content to prepare school leaders —a "One Best" system according to Cooper and Boyd (1987)—was fairly well entrenched by the end of the behavioral science era.

29. Griffiths et al. (1988b) labeled the competency movement, which lasted for about 10 years in the 1960s and 1970s, "a lost decade in the search for a concept of educational administration" (p. 286).

30. The use of different metrics to classify coursetaking over the decades makes it virtually impossible to make comparisons between the studies of scholars working at different points in time. The general problem is that investigators mix criteria in their classification systems in different ways and in ways that allow coders to assign a course to more than one category. Particularly troublesome is the failure to develop a system that clearly defines categories and then combines those categories (i.e., where the course was taken—educational administration department, college of education, university, public school; the general nature of the course—educational administration, elective, cognate, minor, etc.; the particular type of course; and the nature of course presentation—formal or informal) in a useful fashion.

31. Perhaps the most important attempt to use cases in this way is the Advancing Principal Excellence (APEX) program developed by Paula Silver at the University of Illinois in the mid-1980s (Silver, 1985a,

1985b, 1986, 1987). Since Professor Silver's death in 1987, the APEX Center has moved to Hofstra University.

32. In-basket exercises "consist of letters, memoranda, notes, news-clippings, and other printed materials about which administrators must make decisions" (Culbertson, 1964, p. 326).

33. The incorporation of case studies into educational administration training programs occurred in the late 1940s. They were originally introduced at the Harvard Graduate School of Business Administration in 1919 (Culbertson, 1964).

34. In closing, it is curious to note that in an era so preoccupied with research and developing scientific grounds for decisions—and despite clear calls to do so (Culbertson & Farquhar, 1971c; Cunningham, 1969)—virtually no research was conducted on the effects of these various methods of instruction (Silver, 1982).

35. See Sergiovanni (1991a) for a provocative treatment of this aspect of current efforts at reforming training programs.

36. We acknowledge that during this era we are enmeshed in transition activity, while we have enjoyed the benefit of distance and time in reviewing transitions between other training phases. This may account in part for our inability to uncover an emerging vision that is widely accepted.

37. For example, a number of scholars point to the absence of serious theory building work as a contributing cause (Campbell et al., 1987; Griffiths, 1988a). Others note the tendency of the disciplines to be used in furthering the disciplines themselves, rather than in the service of education (Campbell, 1981). Such analysts, although acknowledging weaknesses in the theory movement itself, note that contextual explanations, rather than the impoverished nature of administration as science, are largely responsible for the fact that a dependable knowledge base failed to develop during the era of professionalization (see also Willower, 1987).

38. The development of a philosophy of administration qua administration in school leadership has been nicely portrayed by Culbertson (1965). Of particular interest is the discussion of factors external to the field in the evolution of this perspective.

39. A major theme of the post-behavioral science era can be determined by comparing the titles of the influential 1960 AASA document, *Preparing Administrators for America's Schools*, and, the NCEEA 1987 report, *Leaders for America's Schools* (see also J. Murphy, 1990c).

40. The NPBEA later moved to the campus of George Mason University under the direction of Scott D. Thomson.

41. The 10 groups comprising the NPBEA are: American Association of Colleges for Teacher Education, American Association of School Administrators, Association for Supervision and Curriculum Development, Association of School Business Officials, Council of Chief State School Officers, National Association of Elementary School Principals, National Association of Secondary School Principals, National Council of Professors of Educational Administration, National School Boards Association, and University Council for Educational Administration.

42. Those interested in critical reviews of the NPBEA report are directed to Erlandson (1990) and W. Hawley (1990).

Notes for Chapter 4

1. It is important to note that some of the problems we face are the result of the recency of educational administration as an area of practice and study. Not surprisingly, we would expect a certain amount of groping about and misdirected efforts that would be likely to create new problems and exacerbate old ones. Some of the weaknesses we discuss are also attributable to quite understandable efforts on the part of training programs to adapt to shifts in conceptions about organizations and the role of leaders therein. Given these facts, other analysts reach different —and more sanguine—conclusions about the health of the field in general and about preparation programs in particular (Walker, 1991). Given these caveats, and March's (1974) warning "not to be over-seduced by a recitation of problems" (p. 19), the weight of the evidence causes most analysts to arrive at the conclusion that preparation programs in educational leadership are indeed seriously flawed.

2. The framework and a small amount of the material in this chapter are taken from Murphy, J. J. (1990e). "The Reform of School Administration: Pressures and Calls for Change." In J. J. Murphy (Ed.), *The Educational Reform Movement of the 1980s: Perspectives and Cases*. Berkeley, CA: McCutchan. Copyright © 1990 by McCutchan Publishing Corporation, Berkeley, CA, 94702. Permission granted by the publisher.

3. These concerns gain legitimacy when we recall the large body of literature demonstrating the conservative nature of teaching (Lortie, 1975) and school administration (Achilles, 1984).

4. See Tyack and Cummings (1977) for a discussion of how conservatism in educational administration preparation programs mirrors a similar phenomenon in the larger profession.

5. The fact that approximately half of the students in training programs are now women should not be accepted as evidence that more

appropriate recruitment procedures are finding their way into educational administration programs. Most of these women, as were their male predecessors, are self-selected.

6. Stout (1973), in a delightful essay on selection, reminds us of an important fact—the type of leaders selected for preparation programs using the current procedures are unlikely to reorient a profession (school leadership) and an industry (schooling) in need in fundamental reform. He and other pioneers in this area (see especially McIntyre, 1966) suggest that considerably more attention be given to the topic of selection criteria for prospective administrators.

7. One good piece of evidence for the prevalence of this viewpoint can be seen in the organization of the *Handbook on Research in Educational Administration* (Boyan, 1988b). See especially Culbertson (1988a).

8. The same lack of effect noted in the area of administration appears to hold for the field of teaching (Stigler & Stevenson, 1991) and for schools of education in general. For example, Clifford and Guthrie (1988) report:

> it is not sufficient to say that the greatest strength of schools of education is that they are the only places available to look at fundamental issues from a variety of disciplinary perspectives. They have been doing so for more than a half century without appreciable effect on professional practice. (pp. 349-350)

9. Clifford and Guthrie (1988) and J. Murphy (1987) cast this discussion in terms of the different cultures prevailing in universities and schools. Language is one key aspect of that culture in which there are important differences. Goldhammer (1963) captures the fundamental element of this difference when he remarks that "the language of the practitioner is the language of action, while that of the scientist is academic and abstract" (p. 25; see also Cunningham et al., 1963).

10. This narrow view is characteristic of American history generally which, as Ravitch (1991) reminds us, has "long ignored the historical experiences of minority groups and women" (p. 20).

11. Although many institutions have made some progress on the issue of diversity of representation within their training programs in terms of attracting more women and people of color, considerably less progress has been realized on the much more difficult task of nurturing diversity of thought.

12. For a discussion of this issue at the elementary and secondary school level, see Asante (1991).

13. Interest in having administrators learn more about teaching and learning has an empirical as well as a philosophical foundation. For example, numerous studies over the past 20 years have concluded that technological acumen often distinguishes more effective from less effective administrators (Hallinger & Murphy, 1985; J. Murphy, 1990d): "leadership in high-performance schools is more pedagogical and less managerial than in low-performance ones" (Chubb, 1988, p. 33).

14. Part of separation of administration from teaching can also be traced to the perceived need of an emerging profession to separate itself clearly from the field to which it was previously connected—in this case management from teaching (see Sergiovanni, 1991a; Sergiovanni et al., 1987).

15. Empirical evidence for the absence of attention to educational issues in preparation programs is abundant. Khlief (1979) presents a particularly cogent example of how one elite training program for superintendents socializes prospective administrators away from educational issues and concerns for students and toward management and organizational issues. Sergiovanni and his colleagues (1987) show how these socialization pressures actually de-skill principals in curricular and instructional areas.

After analyzing the content of superintendent training programs, Champagne and his colleagues (1984) reach the following conclusions:

> Our investigation indicates that the training of our most powerful educational leaders, our superintendents, is directed mainly to concerns other than those of the learning of students. In fact, a great many superintendent training programs appear to exclude *any* in-depth study of curriculum, instruction or supervision. (p. 14)

> Thus we are saying that principals do not study any of these areas in any depth either. (p. 16)

Gerritz et al. (1984) conclude that a major problem with university training programs, according to California school administrators, is their failure to provide skills in the technical areas of observation and evaluation of classroom behavior.

16. The failure of school administrators to engage seriously in educational issues has also been well documented, both by scholars approaching the topic from a critical perspective and by those studying the instructional role of educational leaders more directly. Descriptive studies from this latter group that assess how administrators allocate time

to their various job functions disclose a dearth of instructional leadership activities. Hannaway and Sproull (1979) summarize the typical state of affairs when they note that "the technical tasks associated with producing student learning are not supervised, managed, or coordinated in any serious sense across managerial levels in school districts" (p. 4).

Principals have historically spent little time and energy engaged in the educational aspects of their jobs (Morris et al., 1984). In their studies of secondary schools, Little and Bird (1984) and Blank (1986) discover that principals rarely display instructional leadership behaviors. Another study at the secondary level finds that only 17% of principals' time and only 8% of the tasks on which they work deal with academic matters (Martin & Willower, 1981). Similar conclusions are drawn in a fourth study on student course-taking patterns in high schools (California State Department of Education, 1984). The authors report that principals have little direct involvement with the school curriculum and that almost all important decisions in this area are made by departments and department chairpersons. In their comprehensive ethnographic study, Morris and his colleagues (1984) conclude that secondary school principals are "conspicuous by their relative absence from the site of teaching and learning" (p. 57), spending on average only 7% of their time in classrooms. In a similar study, Willis (1980) reports that the secondary principals he observed spend only 2% of their time visiting classrooms.

Research on the instructional leadership role of elementary school principals reinforces the findings from secondary schools. Morris and his colleagues (1984) report that the elementary principals they observed devote 9% of their time to visiting classrooms. Peterson (1978) finds that elementary principals spend less than 7% of their time working with curriculum issues and less than 5% of their time in classrooms.

Congruent results are reported in studies that examine instructional leadership in both elementary and secondary schools. For example, in the schools that he studied, Hanson (1981) finds that almost all the significant decisions in the areas of curriculum and instruction are made by teachers. In their comparative study in elementary and secondary schools, Guzzetti and Martin (1986) discover that instructional leadership on the part of principals is conspicuous by its absence at both levels. In this study, less than 6% of the principals report that they use the following activities to improve instruction in their schools: peer observations (1%); personal delivery of inservice activities (2%); use of school climate improvement process (5%); clinical supervision (4%); and teacher evaluation (5%).

Finally, there is little evidence that teachers view administrators as educational or instructional leaders (Fullan & Newton, 1986; Gersten & Carnine, 1981; Pitner, 1986). Studies of teachers and their work report a virtual absence of administrative instructional leadership. Self-reports from principals also reveal that instructional leadership activities are not heavily underscored in schools (Alvy & Coladarchi, 1985; Blank, 1986; Guzzetti & Martin, 1986).

17. See Twombly and Ebmeier (1989) for a discussion of this phenomenon.

18. Clifford and Guthrie (1988) report that this condition applies to schools and colleges of education in general.

19. For a description of this phenomenon at the secondary school level, see Powell, Farrar, and Cohen (1985), Sedlack et al. (1986), and Sizer (1984).

20. Callahan (1962) reminds us that certification of school administrators was one of the key avenues by "which the business-managerial conception was spread throughout the country" (p. 250).

21. Contreras (1989) and Miklos (in press) remind us that women and people of color tend disproportionately to occupy roles that deny them the chance to experience important career-oriented socialization experiences and to form sponsorships as administrators.

Notes for Chapter 5

1. Banathy (1988) dates the transformation from an industrial age at approximately 1950.

2. It is important to note that these analysts are not working on a blank slate, however. For example, in an especially insightful paper, D. Cohen (1988) reveals how "recent reform ideas resemble early manifestos in a long revolution" (p. 14).

3. For a more thorough analysis of these changes, see J. Murphy (1991b, chaps. 2-5).

4. For a fuller treatment of choice, see Boyd and Kerchner (1988) and Boyd and Walberg (1990).

5. These new efforts have already passed through two phases, a focus on children's policy in the mid-1980s and, more recently, recognizing the connections between the child and the family, a focus on family policy (see Kirst, 1987, 1989; Kirst et al., 1989). For a powerful analysis of the role of school leaders in children's and family policy, see Mitchell and Cunningham (1990).

6. For analyses of the changing role of state agencies in transformed schools, see J. A. David, Cohen, Honetschlager, and Traiman (1990) and J. Murphy (in press).

7. Organizational analysts outside of education have developed a variety of labels for these postindustrial organizations: "The kind of organization which emerges has been variously described as a constellation, as a federation, as atomized, as dispersed, as a 'membership organization,' as a network organization or as the 'shamrock organization' " (Beare, 1989, p. 15).

8. This shift away from a science of teaching parallels the movement in educational administration in general and in leadership training in particular away from a science of administration. See Chapter 3, "The Dialectic Era."

9. There is considerable disagreement on the economic justification for school reform in general and on the importance of leadership in this area in particular. Although the bulk of the reform literature accepts the economic rationale for reform and leadership, there are dissenters. One group of critics includes those who point out that the connections between schooling and educational productivity are problematic. These authors argue that schools have been unfairly blamed for the economic ills of society (Kerr, 1991). A second group of analysts raises serious questions about the ethics of constructing reform initiatives and leadership activities on a platform of economic competitiveness (Beck, 1991; Giroux, 1988; Mitchell, 1990).

10. The logical third corollary is that the training of leaders for tomorrow's schools must change, or, as Mulkeen and Tetenbaum (1990) conclude: "The message is clear: new knowledge and skills are called for on the part of educational administrators and these cannot be developed in existing preparation programmes" (p. 14). We take up this issue in Chapter 6.

11. There are, of course, many other ways to tackle this issue of leadership for the twenty-first century. Metaphorical analysis makes sense to us for a number of reasons, however. First, because metaphors "have the profundity of a concrete immediacy" (Fernandez, 1986, p. 7), they allow us to convey the essence of the envisioned changes in an evocative fashion but in a minimum of space. Second, this strategy is consistent with the larger historical approach stressed throughout this volume (see Beck & Murphy, in press-a). Metaphors dramatically convey the "far reaching repercussions" (Bates, 1984, p. 264) in shifts from one era to the next. Consistent with the transformational character of this chapter, "metaphorical thinking provides a different way of knowing about organizations as an alternative to conventional methods of enquiry"

(Owens & Steinhoff, 1989, p. 13). Finally, the use of metaphors allows us to step back and use a macro-level lens to examine emerging conceptions of leadership, a strategy that is most appropriate for viewing transformational change. For a more complete description of metaphorical approaches to understanding school administration, see Beck and Murphy (in press-a, in press-b).

12. Some thoughtful analysts remain skeptical about society's willingness to respond to the problems of the underclass (Clark, 1990; Natriello et al., 1990).

13. For a particularly thoughtful examination of the place of a caring ethic in educational administration, see Beck (1991).

Notes for Chapter 6

1. It is worth noting that a not-so-subtle shift, from a technical to a normative conception of rationality, appears to be evolving as we move into the dialectic era.

2. In his seminal 1975 article, Hills went so far as to suggest "that those things that can be taught to prospective administrators are *relatively* unimportant, and those things that are critically important to success cannot be taught" (p. 7; see also W. Greenfield, 1988). Looking at the latter links of the chain, March (1974) reaches only a slightly more positive conclusion: "[Administration] is a minor matter; but our prospects for human control over events are built on collections of minor matters" (p. 23).

3. C. Hodgkinson (1975) reminds us that

in both the general area of administration and the special area of educational administration certain dialectics become evident over time. These movements simultaneously reflect prevalent social ideologies and the state of contemporary administrative theory. . . . Although the terms are much too broad and diffuse, it might be helpful for our purposes to characterize these two recycling historical modes as authoritarian and permissive. The rightist authority-oriented mode derived its grounds of justification in the organization, specifically, in the goals of the organization. On the left, the permissivist mode sought its grounds in the membership of the organization. (p. 14)

4. Indeed, as reported in Chapter 4, there is still a lack of consensus —if not outright confusion—about the tenets that will define the dialectic era. For example, at the current time the NPBEA is suggesting orienting training experiences toward specific functional skill areas. The UCEA, on the other hand, is organizing program revisions around seven broadly defined areas of knowledge. Others, this author included, raise questions about both strategies.

5. The dysfunctions of backward mapping the goals of the program from the knowledge base are described in Chapters 2 through 5. Of particular significance has been the dismissal of "the central realities of administration as irrelevant" (T. Greenfield, 1988, p. 131), especially the fact that "administrative man had to disappear as a value-bearer" (p. 138) and educator (Callahan, 1962; Evans, 1991; J. Murphy, 1990d).

6. This reorientation, or "shift away from the traditional focus on knowledge structures" (Iran-Nejad et al., 1990, p. 512), is finding acceptance in more general discussions of learning as well.

7. The primary focus in this volume is on educational programs for practitioners. We touch briefly on preparation programs for professors in the last part of this chapter.

8. As Lortie (1962) and Culbertson (1962) told us more than a quarter of a century ago, this is particularly true when the knowledge base is defined in terms of competencies and solutions. According to Lortie, "nothing wears out faster than specific solutions to specific problems" (p. 75), and Culbertson reminds us that "technical information becomes obsolescent quickly" (p. 165).

9. For an excellent treatment of ways of knowing, see Halpin (1960).

10. I am indebted to Hills (1975) for his insightful analysis of inquiry skills within the context of real school problems.

11. The separation of curriculum from instruction is made here solely for purposes of analysis. As the discussion in this chapter reveals, in the preparation program that we envision for tomorrow's leaders, these are no longer distinct program elements, but rather tightly intertwined strands of learning experiences (Wasley, 1991). It is a central tenet of this volume that achieving this interconnectedness is an essential step in overcoming the deeply ingrained theory-practice problem in school administration.

12. Over the years, I have been a strong supporter of the necessity of teaching technical skills to prospective administrators. In 1963, Culbertson remarked upon the importance of this type of learning:

The importance of technical content should not be minimized since excellence in education cannot be defined in terms of purposes alone; the appropriate technique means to achieve purposes is of equal import. Those who head educational organizations must be able to see that wisely chosen ends are properly joined with appropriate means. If this is not achieved, then there is danger of an increasing gap between those who head educational organizations and those who are responsible for technical functions to improve school learning. (pp. 53-54)

A quarter century later, attention was again drawn to the importance of instruction in the area of technical skills (Griffiths, 1988b; J. Murphy & Hallinger, 1987). The historical problem in this area is similar to the problem of discipline-based preparation. That is, each is often taught as an end in itself without reference to the larger purpose of schooling. In the area of technical skills, the result has been the preparation of "students who function less as scholars and more as clerks" (Giroux, 1988, p. 9). A second problem is that an overemphasis on techni-cal skills often leads to the development of a belief that administrative problems are routine and that they can be solved by referring to the inventory of available technical tools. Because "the most important problems principals face comprise zones of practice that are beyond the reach of technical, rational solutions" (Sergiovanni, 1991b, p. 3; see also Cuban, 1990, 1991), the prevalence of this belief in preparation programs is generally dysfunctional. Nonetheless, there is a need to prepare future leaders with a variety of important technical skills. Griffiths's (1977) notion of an "administrative skills center" (p. 433) in each department may offer one way to deal more effectively with instruction in the area of technical skills.

13. The most important work on the issue of problem-based learning in educational leadership is being done by Professor Bridges at Stanford University and Professor Hallinger at Vanderbilt University (Bridges, 1989, 1990; Bridges & Hallinger, 1991). I acknowledge my debt to these authors.

14. The focus on practice-driven preparation programs conjures up fears among some of a return to a prescriptive era with emphasis on untested principles of practice, war stories, and non-theoretically grounded prescriptions—to the development of a "fragmented collection of recipes and rules of thumb with no understanding of the basis of the rules or sense of when to break them" (Petrie, 1990, p. 25; see also Immegart, 1990). There is also a concern that this approach may lead to situations in which professors "eschew scholarship in the name of practice" (Willower, 1983, p. 194)—a situation that, as Willower correctly notes, is a grave injustice to practice—and pay insufficient attention to

issues of purpose and meaning (Callahan, 1962; Newlon, 1934). Walton (1962) also cautions that, because "intellectual sophistication . . . is not likely to develop under the exigencies of practice" (p. 94), time for reflection must be a critical component of practice-based learning. Willower (1988) in turn reminds us that, although the notion that

> the intellectual content of educational administration should arise from the subject matter of practice . . . has much to recommend it . . . one should not forget that inquiry into the phenomena of practice or anything else must be directed by ideas and concepts. They are what organize and make sense of phenomena. (p. 731)

Tackling the same issue, Ratsoy (1989) reinforces the point that the clinical, problem-based aspects of preparation programs should not come "at the expense of the research and theory component of administrator preparation" (p. 3). Finally, "moves to base preparation in the problems of practice will necessitate major curriculum revisions which may prove difficult to initiate and implement" (Miklos, in press; see also Culbertson, 1988b), especially given the fact that, unlike in other professions, "practical problem solving [in education] has a kind of low-class reputation" (Berliner, 1986, p. 13).

15. The material in the remainder of this subsection and in the subsection on "Changes in the Delivery System" is taken primarily from J. Murphy, "Restructuring the Technical Core of Preparation Programs in Educational Administration," which appeared in the *UCEA Review* in the Fall of 1990 (Vol. 31, No. 3, pp. 4-5, 10-13). It is used with the permission of the University Council for Educational Administration.

16. I would particularly like to acknowledge the path-breaking work of Professor McIntyre (1957) and his colleagues at The University of Texas. His "Learning in a Block-of-Time Program" for preparing school administrators—developed nearly 40 years ago—captures many of the instructional principles we discuss in this section.

17. Good examples of student-planned learning experiences can be found in McIntyre (1957) and J. Murphy and Hallinger (1987).

18. I will be the first to acknowledge that in general the ideas discussed in this section are more speculative than those presented earlier. Also, the list of issues discussed is only an incomplete sample of the wide array of structural matters that will need attention.

19. I am well aware that, as with all the points raised herein, there are other valid perspectives currently being proposed. I also want to reinforce the position raised in the introduction to this subsection:

there are a variety of structural models that can capture the goals and principles outlined in this chapter. It is not at all inconceivable, for example, that a university could develop a strong program that prepared practitioners and professors together. However, such an endeavor would seem to be exceedingly more complex than the already difficult task of creating a program for practitioners that is responsive to the objectives listed earlier.

20. The separation of departments of school administration from departments of teaching and learning continues to have deleterious effects on the preparation of school leaders (J. Murphy, 1990d).

21. For an informative analysis of one faculty's answer to this question, see Fullan (1991).

22. One way some have suggested to help achieve this integration is to ensure that all professors have experience as school administrators. However, given the bifurcated preparation program described above, it appears that this will become an increasingly less viable option.

References

Achilles, C. M. (1984, Fall). Forecast: Stormy weather ahead in educational administration. *Issues in Education, 2*(2), 127-135.

Achilles, C. M. (1990, February). *Research in educational administration: One position.* Paper prepared for a Danforth Foundation meeting, San Francisco.

Achilles, C. M., Brubaker, D., & Snyder, H. (1990, October). *Organizing for leading and learning: The interplay of school reform and restructuring with preparation program reform and restructuring.* Paper presented at the annual meeting of the University Council of Educational Administration, Pittsburgh.

Alkire, G. (1978). Master's programs in educational administration. In P. F. Silver & D. W. Spuck (Eds.), *Preparatory programs for educational administration* (pp. 52-82). Columbus, OH: University Council for Educational Administration.

Alvy, H. B., & Coladarci, T. (1985). Problems of the novice principal. *Research in Rural Education, 3*(1), 39-47.

American Association of Colleges for Teacher Education. (1988). *School leadership preparation: A preface for action.* Washington, DC: Author.

American Association of School Administrators. (1960). *Professional administrators for America's schools* (Thirty-eighth AASA yearbook). Washington, DC: National Educational Administration.

Anderson, G. L. (1990, February). Toward a critical constructionist approach to school administration: Invisibility, legitimation, and the study of non-events. *Educational Administration Quarterly, 26*(1), 38-59.

Anderson, J. R. (1990). *Cognitive psychology and its implications.* New York: W. H. Freeman.

Anderson, W. A., & Lonsdale, R. C. (1957). Learning administrative behavior. In R. F. Campbell & R. T. Gregg (Eds.), *Administrative behavior in education* (pp. 426-463). New York: Harper.

Angus, L. (1988, April). *School leadership and educational reform.* Paper presented at the annual meeting of the American Educational Research Association, New Orleans.

Asante, M. K. (1991, May). Multiculturalism: An exchange. *Network News and Views, 10*(5), 16-20.

Astuto, T. A. (1990, September). *Reinventing school leadership* (pp. 2-5) [Working memo prepared for the Reinventing School Leadership Conference]. Cambridge, MA: National Center for Educational Leadership.

Baltzell, D. C., & Dentler, R. A. (1983, January). *Selecting American school principals: A sourcebook for educators.* Washington, DC: U.S. Department of Education/National Institute of Education.

Banathy, B. H. (1988). An outside-in approach to design inquiry in education. In Far West Laboratory for Educational Research and Development, *The redesign of education: A collection of papers concerned with comprehensive educational reform* (Vol 1., pp. 51-71). San Francisco: Far West Laboratory.

Barth, R. S. (1986, December). On sheep and goats and school reform. *Phi Delta Kappan, 68*(4), 293-296.

Barth, R. S. (1988). School: A community of leaders. In A. Lieberman (Ed.), *Building a professional culture in schools* (pp. 128-147). New York: Teachers College Press.

Bates, R. J. (1984). Toward a critical practice of educational administration. In T. J. Sergiovanni & J. E. Corbally (Eds.), *Leadership and organizational culture: New perspectives on administrative theory and practice* (pp. 260-274). Urbana: University of Illinois Press.

Beare, H. (1989, September). *Educational administration in the 1990s.* Paper presented at the national conference of the Australian Council for Educational Administration, Armidale, New South Wales, Australia.

Beck, L., (1991). *Reclaiming educational administration as a caring profession.* Unpublished doctoral dissertation, Vanderbilt University, Nashville.

Beck, L., & Murphy, J. (in press-a). Searching for a robust understanding of the principalship. *Educational Administration Quarterly.*

Beck, L., & Murphy, J. (in press-b). *Understanding the principalship: A metaphorical analysis from 1920 to 1990*. New York: Teachers College Press.

Belisle, E. L., & Sargent, C. G. (1957). The concept of administration. In R. F. Campbell & R. T. Gregg (Eds.), *Administrative behavior in education* (pp. 82-119). New York: Harper.

Bennett, W. J. (1986). *First lessons: A report on elementary education in America*. Washington, DC: U.S. Department of Education.

Berliner, D. C. (1986, August/September). In pursuit of the expert pedagogue. *Educational Researcher, 15*(7), 5-13.

Blackman, M. C. (1990, September). *Reinventing school leadership* (pp. 8-11) [Working memo prepared for the Reinventing School Leadership Conference]. Cambridge, MA: National Center for Educational Leadership.

Blank, R. K. (1986, April). *Principal leadership in urban high schools: Analysis of variation in leadership characteristics*. Paper presented at the annual meeting of the American Educational Research Association, San Francisco.

Blumberg, A. (1984, Fall). The craft of school administration and some other rambling thoughts. *Educational Administration Quarterly, 20*(4), 24-40.

Bolin, F. S. (1989, Fall). Empowering leadership. *Teachers College Record, 91*(1), 81-96.

Boyan, N. J. (1963). Common and specialized learnings for administrators and supervisors: Some problems and issues. In D. J. Leu & H. C. Rudman (Eds.), *Preparation programs for school administrators: Common and specialized learnings* (pp. 1-23). East Lansing: Michigan State University.

Boyan, N. J. (1981, February). Follow the leader: Commentary on research in educational administration. *Educational Research, 10*(2), 6-13, 21.

Boyan, N. J. (1988a). Describing and explaining administrator behavior. In N. J. Boyan (Ed.), *Handbook of research on educational administration* (pp. 77-97). New York: Longman.

Boyan, N. J. (Ed.). (1988b). *Handbook of research on educational administration*. New York: Longman.

Boyd, W. L. (1990). Balancing control and autonomy in school reform: The politics of "Perestroika." In J. Murphy (Ed.), *The reform of American public education in the 1980s: Perspectives and cases* (pp. 85-96). Berkeley, CA: McCutchan.

Boyd, W. L., & Crowson, R. L. (1981). The changing conception and practice of public school administration. In D. C. Berliner (Ed.), *Review of research in education* (Vol. 9, pp. 311-373). Washington, DC: American Educational Research Association.

188   THE LANDSCAPE OF LEADERSHIP PREPARATION

Boyd, W. L., & Hartman, W. T. (1988). The politics of educational productivity. In D. H. Monk & J. Underwood (Eds.), *Microlevel school
finance: Issues and implications for school policy* (pp. 271-308). Cambridge, MA: Ballinger.

Boyd, W. L., & Kerchner, C. (Eds.). (1988). *The politics of excellence and
choice in education.* New York: Falmer Press.

Boyd, W. L., & Walberg, H. J. (Eds.). (1990). *Choice in education: Potential
and problems.* Berkeley, CA: McCutchan.

Boyer, E. L. (1983). *High school: A report on secondary education in America.*
New York: Harper.

Bradley Commission on History in the Schools. (1988). *Building on a
history curriculum: Guidelines for teaching history in the schools.* Washington, DC: Educational Excellence Network.

Bransford, J. D. (1991, September). *Reflections on a decade of research on
thinking.* Paper presented at the Conference on Cognition and
School Leadership, Vanderbilt University, National Center for Educational Leadership, Nashville.

Bransford, J. D., Franks, J. J., Vye, N. J., & Sherwood, R. D. (1989). New
approaches to instruction: Because wisdom can't be told. In S.
Vosniadon & A. Orton (Eds.), *Similarity and analogical reasoning* (pp.
470-497). New York: Cambridge University Press.

Bredeson, P. V. (1989, March). *Redefining leadership and the roles of school
principals: Responses to changes in the professional worklife of teachers.*
Paper presented at the annual meeting of the American Educational Research Association, San Francisco.

Bridges, E. M. (1977). The nature of leadership. In L. L. Cunningham,
W. G. Hack, & R. O. Nystrand (Eds.), *Educational administration: The
developing decades* (pp. 202-230). Berkeley, CA: McCutchan.

Bridges, E. M. (1982, Summer). Research on the school administrator:
The state of the art, 1967-1980. *Educational Administration Quarterly,
18*(3), 12-33.

Bridges, E. M. (1989, October). *Combining theory, research, and practice:
Problem-based learning.* Paper presented at the annual meeting of the
University Council for Educational Administration, Scottsdale, AZ.

Bridges, E. M. (1990, January). *Problem-based learning in management
education.* Paper presented for the Center for the Advanced Study
of Educational Leadership, Vanderbilt University, Peabody College of Education, Center for the Advanced Study of Educational
Leadership, Nashville.

Bridges, E. M., & Hallinger, P. (1991, Fall). Problem-based learning: A
promising approach for preparing educational administrators. *UCEA
Review, 32*(3), 3-5, 7-8.

Brown, J. S., Collins, A., & Duguid, P. (1989, January/ February). Situated cognition and the culture of learning. *Educational Researcher*, *18*(1), 32-42.
Bryant, M. T. (1988, April). *An inquiry-based orientation for preparation programs in educational administration*. Paper presented at the annual meeting of the American Educational Research Association, New Orleans.
Burlingame, M. (1990, October). *The clinical experience and the clinical professorship in preparation programs for educational administrators: An analysis and a proposal*. Paper presented at the annual meeting of the University Council for Education Administration Convention, Pittsburgh.
Button, H. W. (1966). Doctrines of administration: A brief history. *Educational Administration Quarterly*, *2*(3), 216-224.
Button, H. W. (1991, August). Vulnerability: A concept reconsidered. *Educational Administration Quarterly*, *27*(3), 378-391.
California State Department of Education. (1984, January). *California high school curriculum study: Paths through high school*. Sacramento: Author.
Callahan, R. E. (1962). *Education and the cult of efficiency*. Chicago: University of Chicago Press.
Callahan, R. E., & Button, H. W. (1964). Historical change of the role of the man in the organization: 1865-1950. In D. E. Griffiths (Ed.), *Behavioral science and educational administration* (Sixty-third NSSE yearbook, Part II, pp. 73-92). Chicago: University of Chicago Press.
Campbell, R. F. (1981, Winter). The professorship in educational administration: A personal view. *Educational Administration Quarterly*, *71*(1), 1-24.
Campbell, R. F., Charters, W. W., & Gragg, W. L. (1960). Improving administrative theory and practice. In R. F. Campbell & J. M. Lipham (Eds.), *Administrative theory as a guide to action* (pp. 171-189). Chicago: University of Chicago, Midwest Administration Center.
Campbell, R. F., Fleming, T., Newell, L. J., & Bennion, J. W. (1987). *A history of thought and practice in educational administration*. New York: Teachers College Press.
Campbell, R. F., & Newell, L. J. (1973). *A study of professors of educational administration: Problems and prospects of an applied academic field*. Columbus, OH: University Council for Educational Administration.
Carlson, R. O. (1963). Common learnings for all administrators. In D. J. Leu & H. C. Rudman (Eds.), *Preparation for school administration: Common and specialized learnings* (pp. 24-33). East Lansing: Michigan State University.

Carnegie Council on Adolescent Development. (1989). *Turning points.* Washington, DC: Author.

Carnegie Forum on Education and the Economy. (1986, May). *A Nation prepared: Teachers for the 21st century.* New York: Author.

Carver, F. D. (1988, June). *The evaluation of the study of educational administration.* Paper presented at the EAAA Allerton House Conference, University of Illinois at Urbana-Champaign.

Champagne, D. W., Morgan, J. L., Rawlings, M. B. R., & Swany, D. (1984, April). *Analysis of the content of training programs for chief school administrators in the areas of instructional methodology, curriculum, and instructional supervision.* Paper presented at the annual meeting of the American Educational Research Association, New Orleans.

Chapman, J., & Boyd, W. L. (1986, Fall). Decentralization, devolution, and the school principal: Australian lessons on statewide educational reform. *Educational Administration Quarterly, 22*(4), 28-58.

Chase, F. S. (1960). The administrator as implementor of the goals of education for our time. In R. F. Campbell & J. M. Lipham (Eds.), *Administrative theory as a guide to action* (pp. 191-201). Chicago: University of Chicago, Midwest Administration Center.

Chubb, J. E. (1988, Winter). Why the current wave of school reform will fail. *The Public Interest,* (90), 28-49.

Clark, D. L. (1988, June). *Charge to the study group of the National Policy Board for Educational Administration.* Unpublished manuscript.

Clark, D. L. (1990, September). *Reinventing school leadership* (pp. 25-29) [Working memo prepared for the Reinventing School Leadership Conference]. Cambridge, MA: National Center for Educational Leadership.

Clark, D. L., & Meloy, J. M. (1989). Renouncing bureaucracy: A democratic structure for leadership in schools. In T. J. Sergiovanni & J. A. Moore (Eds.), *Schooling for tomorrow: Directing reform to issues that count* (pp. 272-294). Boston: Allyn & Bacon.

Clifford, G. J., & Guthrie, J. W. (1988). *Ed school.* Chicago: University of Chicago Press.

Clinton, B. (1987, July). *Speaking of leadership.* Denver: Educational Commission of the States.

Cognition and Technology Group at Vanderbilt. (1990, August-September). Anchored instruction and its relationship to situated cognition. *Educational Researcher, 19*(6), 2-10.

Cohen, D. K. (1988, September). *Teaching practice: Plus ca change . . .* (Issue Paper 88-3). East Lansing: Michigan State University, The National Center for Research on Teacher Education.

Cohen, D. K. (1989, May). *Can decentralization or choice improve public education?* Paper presented at the conference on Choice and Control in American Education. Madison: University of Wisconsin-Madison.

Cohen, M. D., March, J. G., & Olsen, J. P. (1972, March). A garbage can model of organizational choice. *Administrative Science Quarterly, 17*(1), 1-26.

Collins, A., Hawkins, J., & Carver, S. M. (1991). A cognitive apprenticeship for disadvantaged students. In United States Department of Education (USDE) (Ed.), *Teaching advanced skills to educationally disadvantaged students* (final report; pp. 173-194). Washington, DC. USDE.

Collins, J. (1990, September). *Reinventing school leadership* (pp. 31-35) [Working memo prepared for the Reinventing School Leadership Conference]. Cambridge, MA: National Center for Educational Leadership.

Conley, S. C. (1989, March). *Who's on first? School reform, teacher participation, and the decision-making process.* Paper presented at the annual meeting of the American Educational Research Association, San Francisco.

Contreras, A. R. (1989, March). *Preliminary exploration of exemplary practices in the preparation of minorities in educational administration.* Paper presented at the annual meeting of the American Educational Research Association, San Francisco.

Conway, J. A., & Jacobson, S. L. (1990). An epilogue: Where is educational leadership going? In S. L. Jacobson & J. A. Conway (Eds.), *Educational leadership in an age of reform* (pp. 181-195). New York: Longman.

Cooper, B. S., & Boyd, W. L. (1987). The evolution of training for school administrators. In J. Murphy & P. Hallinger (Eds.), *Approaches to administrative training* (pp. 3-27). Albany: SUNY Press.

Copeland, W. D. (1989, July/August). Technology-mediated laboratory experiences and the development of clinical reasoning in novice teachers. *Journal of Teacher Education, 40*(4), 10-18.

Corcoran, T. B. (1989). Restructuring education: A new vision at Hope Essential High School. In J. M. Rosow & R. Zager (Eds.), *Allies in educational reform* (pp. 243-274). San Francisco: Jossey-Bass.

Cronin, J., & Horoschak, P. O. (1973). *Innovative strategies in field experiences for preparing educational administrators.* (ERIC/CEM state-of-the-knowledge series, number 21; UCEA monograph series, number 8). Danville, IL: Interstate.

Crowson, R. L., & McPherson, R. B. (1987). The legacy of the theory movement: Learning from the new tradition. In J. Murphy & P. Hallinger (Eds.), *Approaches to administrative training in education* (pp. 45-64). Albany: SUNY Press.

Cuban, L. (1984). *How teachers taught*. New York: Longman.

Cuban, L. (1988, January). A fundamental puzzle of school reform. *Phi Delta Kappan, 69*(5), 341-344.

Cuban, L. (1989, June). The "at-risk" label and the problem of urban school reform. *Phi Delta Kappan, 70*(10), 780-784, 799.

Cuban, L. (1990, October). *Reforming school administration: Theory and practice*. Paper presented at the annual meeting of the University Council for Educational Administration, Pittsburgh.

Cuban, L. (1991, April). *Managing the dilemmas of practitioners, researchers, and reformers*. Paper presented at the annual meeting of the American Educational Research Association, Chicago.

Culbertson, J. A. (1962). New perspectives: Implications for program change. In J. A. Culbertson & S. P. Hencley (Eds.), *Preparing administrators: New perspectives* (pp. 151-173). Columbus, OH: University Council for Educational Administration.

Culbertson, J. A. (1963). Common and specialized content in the preparation of administrators. In D. J. Leu & H. C. Rudman (Eds.), *Preparation programs for administrators: Common and specialized learnings* (pp. 34-60). East Lansing: Michigan State University.

Culbertson, J. A. (1964). The preparation of administrators. In D. E. Griffiths (Ed.), *Behavioral science in educational administration* (Sixtythird NSSE yearbook, Part II, pp. 303-330). Chicago: University of Chicago Press.

Culbertson, J. A. (1965). Trends and issues in the development of a science of administration. In Center for the Advanced Study of Educational Administration, *Perspectives on Educational Administration and the Behavioral Sciences* (pp. 3-22). Eugene: University of Oregon, Center for the Advanced Study of Educational Administration.

Culbertson, J. A. (1966). Preface. In K. E. McIntyre, *Selection of educational administrators* (pp. iii-iv). Columbus, OH: University Council for Educational Administration.

Culbertson, J. A. (1981, Winter). Antecedents of the theory movement. *Educational Administration Quarterly, 17*(1), 25-47.

Culbertson, J. A. (1988a). A century's quest for a knowledge base. In N. J. Boyan (Ed.), *Handbook of research on educational administration* (pp. 3-26). New York: Longman.

Culbertson, J. A. (1988b, August). *Tomorrow's challenges to today's professors of educational administration*. The 1988 Walter Hoching lecture presented to the National Council of Professors of Educational Administration, Kalamazoo, Michigan.

Culbertson, J. A., & Farquhar, R. H. (1970, October). Preparing educational leaders: Recruiting and selecting candidates for administrative preparation. *UCEA Newsletter, 12*(1), 10-13.

Culbertson, J. A., & Farquhar, R. H. (1971a, January). Preparing educational leaders: Structure of administrative preparation programs. *UCEA Newsletter, 12*(2), 11-15.

Culbertson, J. A., & Farquhar, R. H. (1971b, April). Preparing educational leaders: Content in administration preparation. *UCEA Newsletter, 12*(3), 8-11.

Culbertson, J. A., & Farquhar, R. H. (1971c, July). Preparing educational leaders: Methods employed in administrative preparation. *UCEA Newsletter, 12*(4), 11-14.

Culbertson, J., Farquhar, R. H., Gaynor, A. K., & Shibles, M. R. (1969). *Preparing educational leaders for the seventies.* Columbus, OH: University Council for Educational Administration.

Culbertson, J. A., & Silver, P. F. (1978). Purpose and structure of the study. In P. F. Silver & D. W. Spuck (Eds.), *Preparatory programs for educational administrators in the United States* (pp. 6-14). Columbus, OH: University Council for Educational Administration.

Cunningham, L. L. (1969). Simulation and the preparation of educational administrators. In G. Baron, D. H. Cooper, & W. G. Walker (Eds.), *Educational administration: International perspectives* (pp. 187-206). New York: Rand-McNally.

Cunningham, L. L. (1990a). Educational leadership and administration: Retrospective and prospective views. In B. Mitchell & L. L. Cunningham (Eds.), *Educational leadership and changing contexts of families, communities, and schools* (Eighty-ninth NSSE Yearbook, Part II, pp. 1-18). Chicago: University of Chicago Press.

Cunningham, L. L. (1990b, September). *Reinventing school leadership* (pp. 42-47) [Working memo prepared for the Reinventing School Leadership Conference]. Cambridge, MA: National Center for Educational Leadership.

Cunningham, L. L., Downey, L. W., & Goldhammer, K. (1963). The social sciences and the preparation of school administrators. In L. W. Downey & F. Enns (Eds.), *The sound sciences and educational administration* (pp. 97-109). Edmonton, Alberta: University of Alberta.

Daresh, J. C. (1987, February). *The practicum in preparing educational administrators: A status report.* Paper presented at the Eastern Educational Research Association meeting, Boston.

Daresh, J. C., & LaPlant, J. C. (1984, April). *Inservice for school administrators: A status report.* Paper presented at the annual meeting of the American Educational Research Association, New Orleans.

David, J. (1989). *Restructuring in progress: Lessons from pioneering districts.* Washington, DC: National Governors' Association.

David, J. A., Cohen, M., Honetschlager, D., & Traiman, S. (1990). *State actions to restructure schools: First steps.* Washington, DC: National Governors' Association.

Davis, W. (1978). Departments of educational administration. In P. F. Silver & D. W. Spuck (Eds.), *Preparatory programs for educational administrators in the United States* (pp. 23-51). Columbus, OH: University Council for Educational Administration.

Davis, W. & Spuck, D. W. (1978). A comparative analysis of masters, certification, specialist and doctoral programs. In P. F. Silver & D. W. Spuck (Eds.), *Preparatory programs for educational administration* (pp. 150-177). Columbus, OH: University Council for Educational Administration.

Deck, L. (1990, September). *Reinventing school leadership* (pp. 48-51) [Working memo prepared for the Reinventing School Leadership Conference]. Cambridge, MA: National Center for Educational Leadership.

Donmoyer, R. (1985, Spring). Cognitive anthropology and research on effective principals. *Educational Administration Quarterly, 21*(2), 31-57.

Driscoll, M. E. (1990). The formation of community in public schools: Findings and hypotheses. *Administrator's Notebook, 34*(4), 1-4.

Eaton, W. (1986). From ideology to conventional wisdom: School administration texts from 1915-1933. In T. E. Glass (Ed.), *An analysis of texts on school administration 1820-1985* (pp. 23-38). Danville, IL: Interstate.

Education Commission of the States. (1983). *Action for excellence.* Denver: Education Commission of the States.

The education of North Carolina's teachers: A doctoral program for senior school administrators. (1988). A report to the president of the University of North Carolina, Chapel Hill.

Egan, K. (1990, September). *Reinventing school leadership* (pp. 58-60) [Working memo prepared for the Reinventing School Leadership Conference]. Cambridge, MA: National Center for Educational Leadership.

Elmore, R. F. (1987, November). Reform and the culture of authority in schools. *Educational Administration Quarterly, 23*(4), 60-78.

Elmore, R. F. (1988). *Early experience in restructuring schools: Voices from the field.* Washington, DC: National Governors' Association.

Elmore, R. F. (1990, September). *Reinventing school leadership* (pp. 62-65) [Working memo prepared for the Reinventing School Leadership Conference]. Cambridge, MA: National Center for Educational Leadership.

Elmore, R. F. (1991, April). *Teaching, learning and organization: School restructuring and the recurring dilemmas of reform.* Paper presented at the annual meeting of the American Educational Research Association, Chicago.

Erickson, D. A. (1964, November). Forces for change in the principalship. *The Elementary School Journal, 65*(2), 57-64.

Erickson, D. A. (1977). An overdue paradigm shift in educational administration, or how can we get that idiot off the freeway. In L. L. Cunningham, W. G. Hack, & R. O. Nystrand (Eds.), *Educational administration: The developing decades* (pp. 114-143). Berkeley, CA: McCutchan.

Erickson, D. A. (1979, March). Research on educational administration: The state-of-the-art. *Educational Researcher, 8*, 9-14.

Erlandson, D. A. (1979, Fall). Language, experience, and administrator preparation. *Planning and Changing, 10*(3), 150-156.

Erlandson, D. (1990, April-June). Agenda for reform: A critical appraisal. *Journal of Educational Policy, 5*(2), 187-191.

Erlandson, D. A., & Witters-Churchill, L. (1988, March). *Design of the Texas NASSP study.* Paper presented at the annual convention of the National Association of Secondary School Principals.

Evans, R. (1991, April). *Ministrative insight: Educational administration as pedagogic practice.* Paper presented at the annual meeting of the American Educational Research Association, Chicago.

Evertson, C., & Murphy, J. (in press). Beginning with classrooms: Implications for restructuring schools. In H. H. Marshall (Ed.), *Redefining student learning.* Norwood, NJ: Ablex.

Farquhar, R. H. (1968, October). The humanities and educational administration: Rationales and recommendations. *Journal of Educational Administration, 6*(2), 97-115.

Farquhar, R. H. (1977). Preparatory programs in educational administration. In L. L. Cunningham, W. G. Hack, & R. O. Nystrand (Eds.), *Educational administration: The developing decades* (pp. 329-357). Berkeley, CA: McCutchan.

Farquhar, R. H. (1981, June). Preparing educational administrators for ethical practice. *The Alberta Journal of Educational Research, 27*(2), 192-204.

Farquhar, R. H., & Piele, P. K. (1972). *Preparing educational leaders: A review of recent literature.* (ERIC/CEM state-of-the-knowledge series, number 14; UCEA monograph series, number 1). Danville, IL: Interstate.

Fernandez, D. W. (1986). *Persuasions and performance: The play of tropes in culture.* Bloomington: Indiana University Press.

Fisher, C. W. (1990, January). The research agenda project as prologue. *Journal for Research in Mathematics Education, 21*(1), 81-89.

Foster, W. P. (1984). Toward a critical theory of educational administration. In T. J. Sergiovanni & J. E. Corbally (Eds.), *Leadership and organizational culture: New perspective on administrative theory and practice* (pp. 240-259). Urbana: University of Illinois Press.

Foster, W. (1988). Educational administration: A critical appraisal. In D. E. Griffiths, R. T. Stout, & R. B. Forsyth (Eds.), *Leaders for America's schools* (pp. 68-81). Berkeley, CA: McCutchan.

Foster, W. (1989, March). *School leaders as transformational intellectuals: A theoretical argument.* Paper presented at the annual meeting of the American Educational Association, San Francisco.

Frank, L. (1990, September). *Reinventing school leadership* (pp. 67-71) [Working memo prepared for the Reinventing School Leadership Conference]. Cambridge, MA: National Center for Educational Leadership.

Frymier, J. (1987, September). Bureaucracy and the neutering of teachers. *Phi Delta Kappan, 69*(1), 9-14.

Fullan, M. (1991, July). *The best faculty of education in the country* [Unpublished report]. University of Toronto, Faculty of Education.

Fullan, M., & Newton, E. (1986, April). *Principals as leaders of instructional change in large high schools: The perspective of external researchers.* Paper presented at the annual meeting of the American Educational Research Association, San Francisco.

Gerritz, W., Koppich, J., & Guthrie, J. (1984, November). *Preparing California school leaders: An analysis of supply, demand, and training.* Berkeley: University of California, Policy Analysis for California Education.

Gersten, R., & Carnine, D. (1981, September). *Administrative and supervisory support functions for the implementation of effective educational programs for low income students.* Eugene: University of Oregon, Center for Educational Policy and Management.

Getzels, J. W. (1977). Educational administration twenty years later, 1954-1974. In L. L. Cunningham, W. G. Hack, & R. O. Nystrand (Eds.), *Educational administration: The developing decades* (pp. 3-24). Berkeley, CA: McCutchan.

Giroux, H. A. (1988). *Teachers as intellectuals: Toward a critical pedagogy of learning.* Granby, MA: Bergin & Garvey.

Glass, T. E. (Ed.). (1986a). *An analysis of texts on school administration 1820-1985*. Danville, IL: Interstate.

Glass, T. E. (1986b). An overview: School administration texts 1820-1985. In T. E. Glass (Ed.), *An analysis of texts on school administration 1820-1985* (pp. 115-133). Danville, IL: Interstate.

Goldhammer, K. (1963). *The social sciences and the preparation of educational administrators*. Columbus, OH: University Council for Educational Administration.

Goldhammer, K. (1983, Summer). Evolution in the profession. *Educational Administration Quarterly, 19*(3), 249-272.

Good, T. L., & Marshall, S. (1984). Do students learn more in heterogeneous or homogeneous groups? In P. L. Peterson, L. C. Wilkinson, & M. Hallinon (Eds.), *The social context of instruction: Group organization and group processes* (pp. 15-38). Orlando, FL: Academic Press.

Goodlad, J. I. (1984). *A place called school: Prospects for the future*. New York: McGraw-Hill.

Grace, A. G. (1946). The professional preparation of school personnel. In N. B. Henry (Ed.), *Changing conceptions in educational administration* (Forty-fifth NSSE yearbook, Part II, pp. 176-182). Chicago: University of Chicago Press.

Graff, O. B., & Street, C. M. (1957). Developing a value framework for educational administration. In R. F. Campbell & R. T. Gregg (Eds.), *Administrative behavior in education* (pp. 120-152). New York: Harper.

Greenfield, T. B. (1975). Theory about organization: A new perspective and its implications for schools. In M. G. Hughes (Ed.), *Administering education: International challenge* (pp. 71-99). London: Athlone.

Greenfield, T. B. (1988). The decline and fall of science in educational administration. In D. E. Griffith, R. T. Stout, & P. B. Forsyth (Eds.), *Leaders for America's schools* (pp. 131-159). Berkeley, CA: McCutchan.

Greenfield, W. D. (1988). Moral imagination, interpersonal competence, and the work of school administrators. In D. E. Griffiths, R. T. Stout, & P. B. Forsyth (Eds.), *Leaders for America's schools* (pp. 207-232). Berkeley, CA: McCutchan.

Greenfield, W. D. (1990, September). *Reinventing school leadership* (pp. 73-74) [Working memo prepared for the Reinventing School Leadership Conference]. Cambridge, MA: National Center for Educational Leadership.

Greenfield, W. D., Marshall, C., & Reed, D. B. (1986, Winter). Experience in the vice-principalship: Preparation for leading schools? *Journal of Educational Administration, 22*(1), 107-121.

Gregg, R. T. (1960). Administration. In C. W. Harris (Ed.), *Encyclopedia of educational research* (3rd ed., pp. 19-24). New York: MacMillan.

Gregg, R. T. (1969). Preparation of administrators. In R. L. Ebel (Ed.), *Encyclopedia of educational research* (4th ed., pp. 993-1004). London: MacMillan.

Griffiths, D. E. (1957). Toward a theory of administrative behavior. In R. F. Campbell & R. T. Gregg (Eds.), *Administrative behavior in education* (pp. 354-390). New York: Harper.

Griffiths, D. E. (1959). *Administrative theory.* New York: Appleton-Century-Crofts.

Griffiths, D. E. (1965). Research and theory in educational administration. In CASEA, *Perspectives on educational administration and the behavioral sciences* (pp. 25-48). Eugene: University of Oregon, Center for the Advanced Study of Educational Administration.

Griffiths, D. E. (1977). Preparation programs for administrators. In L. L. Cunningham, W. G. Hack, & R. O. Nystrand (Eds.), *Educational administration: The developing decades* (pp. 401-437). Berkeley, CA: McCutchan.

Griffiths, D. E. (1979, Fall). Intellectual turnout in educational administration. *Educational Administration Quarterly, 15*(3), 43-65.

Griffiths, D. E. (1988a). Administrative theory. In N. J. Boyan (Ed.), *Handbook of research on educational administration* (pp. 27-51). New York: Longman.

Griffiths, D. E. (1988b). *Educational administration: Reform PDQ or RIP* (Occasional paper, no. 8312). Tempe, AZ: University Council for Educational Administration.

Griffiths, D. E., Stout, R. T., & Forsyth, P. B. (1988a). *Leaders for America's schools: The report and papers of the National Commission on Excellence in Educational Administration.* Berkeley, CA: McCutchan.

Griffiths, D. E., Stout, R. T., & Forsyth, P. B. (1988b). The preparation of educational administrators. In D. E. Griffith, R. T. Stout, & P. B. Forsyth (Eds.), *Leaders for America's schools: The report and papers of the National Commission on Excellence in Educational Administration* (pp. 284-304). Berkeley, CA: McCutchan.

Guba, E. G. (1960). Research in internal administration—What do we know? In R. F. Campbell & J. M. Lipham (Eds.), *Administrative theory as a guide to action* (pp. 113-141). Chicago: University of Chicago, Midwest Administration Center.

Guthrie, J. W. (1986, December). School-based management: The next needed education reform. *Phi Delta Kappan, 68*(4), 305-309.

Guzzetti, B., & Martin, M. (1986, April). *A comparative analysis of elementary and secondary principals' instructional leadership behavior.* Paper presented at the annual meeting of the American Educational Research Association, San Francisco.

Hall, R. M., & McIntyre, K. E. (1957). The student personnel program. In R. F. Campbell & R. T. Gregg (Eds.), *Administrative behavior in education* (pp. 393-425). New York: Harper.

Hallinger, P. (1990). *Reinventing school leadership* (pp. 75-78) [Working memo prepared for the Reinventing School Leadership Conference]. Cambridge, MA: National Center for Educational Leadership.

Hallinger, P., Leithwood, K., & Murphy, J. (Eds.). (in press). *A cognitive perspective on educational administration*. New York: Teachers College Press.

Hallinger, P., & Murphy, J. (1985, November). Assessing the instructional management behavior of principals. *Elementary School Journal, 86*(2), 217-247.

Hallinger, P., & Murphy, J. (1986, May). The social context of effective schools. *American Journal of Education, 94*(3), 328-355.

Hallinger, P., & Murphy, J. (1991, March). Developing leaders for tomorrow's schools. *Phi Delta Kappan, 72*(7), 514-520.

Hallinger, P., Murphy, J., & Hausman, C. (in press-a). Restructuring schools: Principals' perceptions of fundamental educational reform. *Educational Administration Quarterly*.

Hallinger, P., Murphy, J., & Hausman, C. (in press-b). Restructuring schools: Teachers' and principals' views. *Educational Research and Perspectives*.

Halpin, A. W. (1957). A paradigm for research on administrative behavior. In R. F. Campbell & R. T. Gregg (Eds.), *Administrative behavior in education* (pp. 155-199). New York: Harper.

Halpin, A. W. (1960). Ways of knowing. In R. F. Campbell & J. M. Lipham (Eds.), *Administrative theory as a guide to action* (pp. 3-20). Chicago: University of Chicago, Midwest Administration Center.

Hannaway, J., & Sproull, L. S. (1979). Who's running the show? Coordination and control in educational organizations. *Administrator's Notebook, 27*(9), 1-4.

Hanson, H. M. (1981). Organizational control in educational systems: A case study of governance in schools. In S. B. Bacharach (Ed.), *Organizational behavior in schools and school districts* (pp. 245-276). New York: Praeger.

Harbaugh, G. L., Casto, R. M., & Burgess-Ellison, J. A. (1987, Spring). Becoming a professional: How interprofessional training helps. *Theory Into Practice, 26*(2), 141-145.

Harlow, J. G. (1962). Purpose-defining: The central function of the school administrator. In J. A. Culbertson & S. P. Hencley (Eds.),

Preparing administrators: New perspectives (pp. 61-71). Columbus, OH: University Council for Educational Administration.

Harvey, G., & Crandall, D. P. (1988). A beginning look at the what and how of restructuring. In C. Jenks (Ed.), *The redesign of education: A collection of papers concerned with comprehensive educational reform* (pp. 1-37). San Francisco: Far West Laboratory.

Hawley, W. D. (1988). Universities and the improvement of school management. In D. E. Griffiths, R. T. Stout, & P. B. Forsyth (Eds.), *Leaders for America's schools* (pp. 82-88). Berkeley, CA: McCutchan.

Hawley, W. D. (1989). Looking backward at educational reform. *Education Week, 9*(9), 32-35.

Hawley, W. (1990). Policy board proposals ignore real problems. *School Administrator, 46*(10), 8-11, 14-15.

Hencley, S. P. (1962). Forces shaping the new perspective. In J. A. Culbertson & S. P. Hencley (Eds.), *Preparing administrators: New perspectives* (pp. 1-8). Columbus, OH: University Council for Educational Administration.

Hills, J. (1975, Autumn). The preparation of administrators: Some observations from the "firing line." *Educational Administration Quarterly, 11*(3), 1-20.

Hinojosa, D. (1990, September). *Reinventing school leadership* (pp. 80-84) [Working memo prepared for the Reinventing School Leadership Conference]. Cambridge, MA: National Center for Educational Leadership.

Hodgkinson, C. (1975, Winter). Philosophy, politics, and planning: An extended rationale for synthesis. *Educational Administration Quarterly, 11*(1), 11-20.

Hodgkinson, H. L. (1991). Educational reform versus reality. In American Association of School Administrators (AASA)/National School Boards Association (NSBA) (Eds.), *Beyond the schools: How schools and communities must collaborate to solve the problems facing America's youth.* Washington, DC: AASA/NSBA.

Holmes Group. (1986, April). *Tomorrow's teachers.* East Lansing, MI: Author.

Honig, B. (1990, February 28). "Comprehensive" strategy can improve schools. *Education Week, 9*(23), 56, 31.

Houston, H. M. (1989, March). *Professional development for restructuring: Analyses and recommendations.* Paper presented at the annual meeting of the American Educational Research Association, San Francisco.

Hoyle, J. R. (1987). The AASA model for preparing school leaders. In J. Murphy & P. Hallinger (Eds.), *Approaches to administrative training* (pp. 83-95). Albany: SUNY Press.

Hutchins, C. L. (1988a). Design as the missing piece in education. In Far West Laboratory for Educational Research and Development, *The redesign of education: A collection of papers concerned with comprehensive educational reform* (Vol. 1., pp. 47-49). San Francisco: Far West Laboratory.

Hutchins, C. L. (1988b). Redesigning education. In Far West Laboratory for Educational Research and Development, *The redesign of education: A collection of papers concerned with comprehensive educational reform* (Vol. 1., pp. 73-78). San Francisco: Far West Laboratory.

Iannaccone, L. (1977). Three views of change in educational politics. In J. D. Scribner (Ed.), *The politics of education* (Seventy-sixth NSSE yearbook, Part II, pp. 255-286). Chicago: University of Chicago Press.

Immegart, G. L. (1977). The study of educational administration, 1954-1974. In L. L. Cunningham, W. G. Hack, & R. O. Nystrand (Eds.), *Educational administration: The developing decades* (pp. 298-328). Berkeley, CA: McCutchan.

Immegart, G. L. (1990). What is truly missing in advanced preparation in educational administration? *Journal of Educational Administration, 28*(3), 5-13.

Iran-Nejad, A., McKeachie, W. J., & Berliner, D. C. (1990, Winter). The multicourse nature of learning: An introduction. *Review of Educational Research, 60*(4), 509-515.

Jackson, B. L. (1988). Education from a black perspective with implications for administrator preparation programs. In D. E. Griffiths, R. T. Stout, & P. B. Forsyth (Eds.), *Leaders for America's schools* (pp. 305-316). Berkeley, CA: McCutchan.

Jacobson, S. L. (1990). Reflections on the third wave of reform: Rethinking administrator preparation. In S. L. Jacobson & J. A. Conway (Eds.), *Educational leadership in an age of reform* (pp. 30-44). New York: Longman.

Johnson, F. W. (1925). *The administration and supervision of the high school.* New York: Ginn.

Johnston, C. H., Newlon, D. H., & Pickell, F. G. (1922). *Junior-senior high school administration.* Atlanta: Scribner.

Kanter, R. M. (1983). *The change masters.* New York: Simon & Schuster.

Kearnes, D. L. (1988, April). An education recovery plan for America. *Phi Delta Kappan, 69*(8), 565-570.

Kennedy, M. M. (1987). Inexact sciences: Professional education and the development of expertise. In E. Z. Rothkoph (Ed.), *Review of Research in Education* (Vol. 14, pp. 133-167). Washington, DC: American Educational Research Association.

Kerchner, C. T. (1988, November). Bureaucratic entrepreneurship: The implications of choice for school administration. *Educational Administration Quarterly, 24*(4), 381-391.

Kerr, C. (1991, February 27). Is education really all that guilty? *Education Week, 10*(23), 30.

Khleif, B. B. (1979). Professionalization of school superintendents: A sociological study of an elite program. In R. Barnhordt, J. Chilcott, & H. Wolcott (Eds.), *Anthropology and educational administration* (pp. 52-67). Tuscon, AZ: Impresora Sahuaro.

Kirst, M. W. (1987, October). PEER: An interview with Michael Kirst. *Phi Delta Kappan, 60*(2), 161-164.

Kirst, M. W. (Ed.). (1989). *Conditions of children in California.* Berkeley: Policy Analysis for California Education.

Kirst, M. W., McLaughlin, M., & Massell, D. (1989). *Rethinking children's policy: Implications for educational administration.* Center for Educational Research at Stanford, College of Education, Stanford University, Stanford, CA.

Lam, D. (1990, September). *Reinventing school leadership* (pp. 85-87). [Working memo prepared for the Reinventing School Leadership Conference]. Cambridge, MA: National Center for Educational Leadership.

Leu, D. J., & Rudman, H. C. (1963). *Preparation programs for school administrators: Common and specialized learnings.* East Lansing: Michigan State University.

Levine, S. L., Barth, R. S., & Haskins, K. W. (1987). The Harvard principals' center: School leaders as adult learners. In J. Murphy & P. Hallinger (Eds.), *Approaches to administrative training* (pp. 150-163). Albany: SUNY Press.

Lieberson, S., & O'Conner, J. F. (1972). Leadership and organizational performance: A study of large corporations. *American Sociological Review, 37,* 117-130.

Little, J. W., & Bird, T. D. (1984, April). *Is there instructional leadership in high schools? First findings from a study of secondary school administrators and their influence on teachers' professional norms.* Paper presented at the annual meeting of the American Educational Research Association, New Orleans.

Lortie, D. C. (1962). Complexity, specialization, and professional knowledge: Overall strategies in the preparation of school administrators. In J. A. Culbertson & S. P. Hencley (Eds.), *Preparing administrators: New perspectives* (pp. 73-88). Columbus, OH: University Council for Educational Administration.

Lortie, D. C. (1975). *Schoolteacher.* Chicago: University of Chicago Press.

Lotto, L. S. (1983, Winter). Believing is seeing. *Organizational Theory Dialogue, 3*(1), 6-26.

Lotto, L. S., & Murphy, J. (1990). Making sense of schools as organizations: Cognition and sensemaking in schools. In P. W. Thurston and L. S. Lotto (Eds.), *Advances in educational administration: Changing perspectives on the school* (Vol. 1, Part B; pp. 201-240). Greenwich, CT: JAI Press.

Louis, K. S., & Miles, M. B. (1990). *Improving the urban high school: What works and why.* New York: Teachers College Press.

Maccoby, M. (1989, December). *Looking for leadership now.* Paper presented at the National Center for Educational Leadership Conference, Harvard University, Cambridge, MA.

Maehr, M. L., & Midgley, C. (in press). Enhancing student motivation: A school-wide approach. *Educational Psychologist.*

Mann, D. (1975, May). What peculiarities in educational administration make it difficult to profess: An essay. *Journal of Educational Administration, 13*(1), 139-147.

March, J. G. (1974, May). Analytical skills and the university training of educational administrators. *Journal of Educational Administration, 12*(1), 17-44.

March, J. G. (1978, February). American public school administration: A short analysis. *School Review, 86,* 217-250.

Marland, S. P. (1960). Superintendents' concerns about research applications in educational administration. In R. F. Campbell & J. M. Lipham (Eds.), *Administrative theory as a guide to action* (pp. 21-36). Chicago: University of Chicago, Midwest Administration Center.

Marshall, H. H. (Ed.). (in press-a). *Redefining student learning.* Norwood, NJ: Ablex.

Marshall, H. H. (in press-b). Supporting student learning: Raising questions and identifying critical factors. In H. H. Marshall (Ed.), *Redefining student learning.* Norwood, NJ: Ablex.

Martin, W. J., & Willower, D. J. (1981, Winter). The managerial behavior of high school principals. *Educational Administration Quarterly, 17*(1), 69-90.

Mason, R. (1986). From idea to ideology: School administration texts 1820-1914. In T. E. Glass (Ed.), *An analysis of texts on school administration 1820-1985* (pp. 1-21). Danville, IL: Interstate.

McCall, M. W. (1976, January). *Leaders and leadership: Of substance and shadow.* Paper presented at the annual meeting of the British Psychological Society, Occupational Psychology Section, Keefe, Staffordshire, England.

McCarthey, S. J., & Peterson, P. L. (1989, March). *Teacher roles: Weaving new patterns in classroom practice and school organization.* Paper presented at the annual meeting of the American Educational Research Association, San Francisco.

McCarthy, M. M., Kuh, G. D., Newell, L. J., & Iacona, C. M. (1988). *Under scrutiny: The educational administration professoriate.* Tempe, AZ: University Council for Educational Administration.

McCartney, C., & Schrag, F. (1990, November-December). Departmental and school leadership in promoting higher-order thinking. *Journal of Curricular Studies, 22*(6), 529-543.

McDonald, J. P. (1988, Summer). The emergence of the teacher's voice: Implications for the new reform. *Teachers College Record, 89*(4), 1-15.

McIntyre, K. E. (1957). *Learning in a block-of-time program.* Austin, TX: Southwest School Administration Center.

McIntyre, K. E. (1966). *Selection of educational administrators.* Columbus, OH: University Council for Educational Administration.

McNeil, L. M. (1988, January). Contradictions of control, part 1: Administrators and teachers. *Phi Delta Kappan, 69*(5), 333-339.

McPherson, R. B. (1990, September). *Reinventing school leadership* (pp. 94-96) [Working memo prepared for the Reinventing School Leadership Conference]. Cambridge, MA: National Center for Educational Leadership.

Means, B., & Knapp, M. S. (1991). Models for teaching advanced skills to educationally disadvantaged children. In United States Department of Education (Ed.), *Teaching advanced skills to educationally disadvantaged students.* Washington, DC: United States Department of Education.

Meindl, J. R., Ehrlich, S. B., & Dukerich, J. M. (1985, March). The romance of leadership. *Administrative Science Quarterly, 30,* 78-102.

Meyer, J. W., & Rowan, B. (1975). *Notes on the structure of educational organizations: Revised version.* Paper presented at the annual meeting of the American Sociological Association, San Francisco.

Miklos, E. (1972). *Training-in-common for educational, public, and business administrators.* (ERIC/CEM state-of-the-knowledge series, number 17; UCEA monograph series, number 4). Danville, IL: Interstate.

Miklos, E. (1983, Summer). Evolution in administrator preparation programs. *Educational Administration Quarterly, 19*(3), 153-177.

Miklos, E. (1987, October). *Reforming the educational administration curriculum.* Paper presented at the annual convention of the University Council for Educational Administration, Charlottesville, VA.

Miklos, E. (1988). Administrator selection, career patterns, succession, and socialization. In N. J. Boyan (Ed.), *Handbook of research on educational administration* (pp. 53-76). New York: Longman.

Miklos, E. (1990). Review of *Ministrative insight: Educational administration as pedagogic practice* by P. R. Evans. *Phenomenology + Pedagogy, 8*, 337-342.

Miklos, E. (in press). Administrator preparation, educational [first draft]. *Encyclopedia of Educational Research.*

Miklos, E., & Nixon, M. (1978). *Educational administration programs in Canadian universities.* Edmonton, Alberta: University of Alberta, Department of Educational Administration.

Miller, V. (1957). Assessment and projection. In R. F. Campbell & R. T. Gregg (Eds.), *Administrative behavior in education* (pp. 513-527). New York: Harper.

Miller, V. (n.d.). *Common and specialized learnings for educational administrators.* Columbus, OH: University Council for Educational Administration.

Milstein, M. M. (1990). Rethinking the clinical aspects of preparation programs: From theory to practice. In S. L. Jacobson & J. A. Conway (Eds.), *Educational leadership in an age of reform* (pp. 119-130). New York: Longman.

Milstein, M. M., Bobroff, B. M., & Restine, L. N. (1991). *Internship programs in educational administration: A guide to preparing educational leaders.* New York: Teachers College Press.

Miskel, C. (1988, October). *Research and the preparation of educational administrators.* Paper presented at the annual meeting of the University Council for Educational Administration, Cincinnati.

Mitchell, B. (1990). Children, youth, and educational leadership. In B. Mitchell & L. L. Cunningham (Eds.), *Educational leadership and changing contexts of families, communities, and schools* (Eighty-ninth NSSE yearbook, Part II, pp. 19-51). Chicago: University of Chicago Press.

Mitchell, B., & Cunningham, L. L. (Eds.). (1990). *Educational leadership and changing contexts of families, communities, and schools* (Eighty-ninth NSSE yearbook, Part II). Chicago: University of Chicago Press.

Mojkowski, C., & Fleming, D. (1988, May). *School-site management: Concepts and approaches.* Andover, MA: Regional Laboratory for Educational Improvement of the Northeast and Islands.

Moore, C. C. (1937). The educational administrator and his opportunities. *Educational Administration and Supervision, 23*, 622-632.

Moore, H. A. (1964). The ferment in school administration. In D. E. Griffiths (Ed.), *Behavioral science and educational administration* (Sixtythird NSSE yearbook, Part II, pp. 11-32). Chicago: University of Chicago Press.

Moorman, H. (1990, September). *Reinventing school leadership* (pp. 98-103) [Working memo prepared for the Reinventing School Leadership Conference]. Cambridge, MA: National Center for Educational Leadership.

Morris, V. C., Crowson, R. L., Porter-Gehrie, C., & Hurwitz, E., Jr. (1984). *Principals in action: The reality of managing schools.* Columbus, OH: Charles E. Merrill.

Mulkeen, T. A. (1990, September). *Reinventing school leadership* (pp. 105-105) [Working memo prepared for the Reinventing School Leadership Conference]. Cambridge, MA: National Center for Educational Leadership.

Mulkeen, T. A., & Cooper, B. S. (1989, March). *Implications of preparing school administrators for knowledge-work organizations.* Paper presented at the annual meeting of the American Educational Research Association, San Francisco.

Mulkeen, T. A., & Tetenbaum, T. J. (1990). Teaching and learning in knowledge organizations: Implications for the preparation of school administrators. *Journal of Educational Administration, 28*(3), 14-22.

Murphy, J. (1987, Spring). Notes from a beginning professor of educational administration. *UCEA Review, 28*(3), 14-16.

Murphy, J. (1988, Summer). Methodological, measurement, and conceptual problems in the study of administrator instructional leadership. *Educational Evaluation and Policy Analysis, 10*(2), 117-139.

Murphy, J. (1989a, Fall). Educational reform in the 1980s: Explaining some surprising success. *Educational Evaluation and Policy Analysis, 11*(3), 209-223.

Murphy, J. (1989b). Effects of educational reform on programs of school administration in Illinois. *Administrator's Notebook, 33*(3), 1-4.

Murphy, J. (1989c, October). *The place of the dissertation in professional programs of study in educational administration.* Panel presentation at the Annual Conference of the University Council for Educational Administration, Scottsdale, AZ.

Murphy, J. (1990a). The educational reform movement of the 1980s: A comprehensive analysis. In J. Murphy (Ed.), *The reform of American public education in the 1980s: Perspectives and cases* (pp. 3-55). Berkeley, CA: McCutchan.

Murphy, J. (1990b, April-June). Improving the preparation of school administrators: The National Policy Board's story. *The Journal of Educational Policy, 5*(2), 181-186.

Murphy, J. (1990c). Preparing school administrators for the twenty-first century: The reform agenda. In B. Mitchell & L. L. Cunningham (Eds.), *Educational leadership and changing contexts of families, communities, and schools* (Eighty-ninth NSSE yearbook, Part II, pp. 232-251). Chicago: University of Chicago Press.

Murphy, J. (1990d). Principal instructional leadership. In L. S. Lotto & P. W. Thurston (Eds.), *Advances in educational administration: Changing perspectives on the school* (Vol. 1, Part B, pp. 163-200). Greenwich, CT: JAI Press.

Murphy, J. (1990e). The reform of school administration: Pressures and calls for change. In J. Murphy (Ed.), *The reform of American public education in the 1980s: Perspectives and cases* (pp. 277-303). Berkeley, CA: McCutchan.

Murphy, J. (1990f, September). *Reinventing school leadership.* Working memo prepared for the Reinventing School Leadership Conference (pp. 108-113). Cambridge, MA: National Center for Educational Leadership.

Murphy, J. (1990g, April-June). A response to "Agenda for Reform: A Critical Appraisal." *The Journal of Educational Policy, 5*(2), 193.

Murphy, J. (1990h, Fall). Restructuring the technical core of preparation programs in educational administration. *UCEA Review, 31*(3), 4-5, 10-13.

Murphy, J. (1991a, Spring). The effects of the educational reform movement on departments of educational leadership. *Educational Evaluation and Policy Analysis, 13*(1), 49-65.

Murphy, J. (1991b). *Restructuring schools: Capturing and assessing the phenomena.* New York: Teachers College Press.

Murphy, J. (1991c, February). The superintendent: The "Maytag man" of school reform. *The School Administrator, 2*(48), 32-33.

Murphy, J. (in press). Restructuring America's schools: An overview. In C. E. Finn & T. Rebarber (Eds.), *Educational reform in the 1990s.* New York: Macmillan.

Murphy, J., & Hallinger, P. (1986, Summer). The superintendent as instructional leader: Findings from effective school districts. *Journal of Educational Administration, 24*(2), 213-236.

Murphy, J., & Hallinger, P. (1987). Emerging views of the professional development of school administrators: A synthesis with suggestions for improvement. In J. Murphy & P. Hallinger (Eds.), *Approaches to administrative training* (pp. 245-281). Albany: SUNY Press.

Murphy, J., & Hallinger, P. (1988, February). The characteristics of instructionally effective school districts. *Journal of Educational Research, 81*(3), 175-181.

Murphy, J., & Hallinger, P. (1989, March-April). Equity as access to learning: Curricular and instructional treatment differences. *Journal of Curriculum Studies, 21*(2), 129-149.

Murphy, J., Hallinger, P., Lotto, L. S., & Miller, S. K. (1987, December). Barriers to implementing the instructional leadership role. *Canadian Administrator, 27*(3), 1-9.

Murphy, J., Hallinger, P., Weil, M., & Mitman, A. (1983, Fall). Problems with research on educational leadership: Issues to be addressed. *Educational Evaluational and Policy Analysis, 5*(3), 297-305.

Murphy, J., Hull, T., & Walker, A. (1987, July-August). Academic drift and curricular debris: An analysis of high school course-taking patterns with implications for local policy makers. *Journal of Curriculum Studies, 19*(4), 341-360.

Murphy, J. T. (1989, June). The paradox of decentralizing schools: Lessons from business, government, and the Catholic church. *Phi Delta Kappan, 70*(10), 808-812.

Murphy, J. T. (1991, March). Superintendents as saviors: From the Terminator to Pogo. *Phi Delta Kappan, 72*(7), 507-513.

Murphy, M. J., & Hart, A. W. (1988, October). *Preparing principals to lead in restructured schools.* Paper presented at the annual meeting of the University Council for Educational Administration, Cincinnati.

Muth, R. (1989, October). *Reconceptualizing training for educational administrators and leaders: Focus on inquiry* (Notes on Reform, no. 2). Charlottesville, VA: National Policy Board for Educational Administration.

Nagle, J., & Nagle, E. (1978). Doctoral programs in educational administration. In P. F. Silver & D. W. Spuck (Eds.), *Preparatory programs for educational administrators in the United States* (pp. 114-149). Columbus, OH: University Council for Educational Administration.

National Association of Elementary School Principals. (1990). *Principals for 21st century schools.* Alexandria, VA: Author.

National Association of Secondary School Principals. (1985). *Performance-based preparation of principals: A framework for improvement.* Reston, VA: Author.

National Commission for the Principalship. (1990). *Principals for our changing schools: Preparation and certification.* Fairfax, VA: Author.

National Commission on Excellence in Education. (1983, April). *A nation at risk: The imperative of educational reform.* Washington, DC: Government Printing Office.

National Commission on Excellence in Educational Administration. (1987). *Leaders for America's schools.* Tempe, AZ: University Council for Educational Administration.

National Commission on Social Studies in the Schools. (1989). *Charting a course: Social studies for the 21st century.* Washington, DC: Author.

National Governors' Association. (1986). *Time for results.* Washington, DC: Author.

National Policy Board for Educational Administration. (1989a, May). *Improving the preparation of school administrators: The reform agenda.* Charlottesville, VA: Author.

National Policy Board for Educational Administration. (1989b, August). *The North Carolina story* (Notes on Reform, no. 1). Charlottesville, VA: Author.

Natriello, G., McDill, E. L., & Pallas, A. M. (1990). *Schooling disadvantaged children: Racing against catastrophe.* New York: Teachers College Press.

Newlon, J. H. (1934). *Educational administration as social policy.* New York: Scribner.

Newmann, F. M. (1988, January). Can depth replace coverage in the high school curriculum? *Phi Delta Kappan, 69*(5), 345-348.

Newmann, F. M. (1991, February). Linking restructuring to authentic student achievement. *Phi Delta Kappan, 72*(6), 458-463.

Norton, J. (1957). The contemporary scene. In R. F. Campbell & R. T. Gregg (Eds.), *Administrative Behavior in Education* (pp. 41-81). New York: Harper.

Norton, M. S. (1991, Spring). UCEA center on patterns of professional preparation: A center close up. *UCEA Review, 32*(2), 10-11.

Norton, M. S., & Levan, F. D. (1987, Winter). Doctoral studies of students in educational administration programs in UCEA member institutions. *Educational Considerations, 14*(1), 21-24.

Notar, E. E. (1988-1989). What do new principals say about their university training and its relationship to their jobs? *National Forum of Applied Educational Research Journal, 1*(2), 14-18.

Nunnery, M. Y. (1982). Reform of K-12 educational administrator preparation: Some basic questions. *Journal of Research and Development in Education, 15*(2), 44-51.

Oakes, J. (1985). *Keeping track: How schools structure inequality.* New Haven, CT: Yale University Press.

Ohde, K., & Murphy, J. (in press). The acquisition of expertise. In P. Hallinger, K. Leithwood, & J. Murphy (Eds.), *Cognition and educational leadership.* New York: Teachers College Press.

O'Neil, J. (1989, November). Social studies: Charting a course for a field adrift. *ASCD Curriculum Update, 31*(7).

Ortiz, F. I. (1990, September). *Reinventing school leadership* (pp. 115-118) [Working memo prepared for the Reinventing School Leadership

Conference]. Cambridge, MA: National Center for Educational Leadership.

Owens, R. G., & Steinhoff, C. R. (1989). Toward a theory of organizational culture. *Journal of Educational Administration, 27*(3), 6-16.

Page, R. N. (1984, April). *Lower-track classes at a college-preparatory high school: A caricature of educational encounters.* Paper presented at the annual meeting of the American Educational Research Association, New Orleans.

Parker, D. C. (1986). From conventional wisdom to concept: School administration texts 1934-1945. In T. E. Glass (Ed.), *An Analysis of texts on school administration 1820-1985* (pp. 39-75). Danville, IL: Interstate.

Pepper, J. B. (1988). Clinical education for school superintendents and principals: The missing link. In D. E. Griffiths, R. T. Stout, & P. R. Forsyth (Eds.), *Leaders for America's Schools* (pp. 360-366). Berkeley, CA: McCutchan.

Perkins, D. N. (1991, October). Educating for insight. *Educational Leadership, 49*(2), 4-8.

Peterson, K. D. (1978). The principal's task. *Administrator's Notebook, 26*(8), 1-4.

Peterson, K. D., & Finn, C. E. (1985, Spring). Principals, superintendents and the administrator's art. *The Public Interest, 79,* 42-62.

Petrie, H. G. (1990). Reflecting on the second wave of reform: Restructuring the teaching profession. In S. L. Jacobson & J. A. Conway (Eds.), *Educational leadership in an age of reform* (pp. 14-29). New York: Longman.

Pfeffer, J. (1978). The ambiguity of leadership. In M. W. McCall & M. M. Lombardo (Eds.), *Leadership: Where else can we go?* (pp. 13-34). Durham, NC: Duke University Press.

Pitner, N. J. (1986, Spring). Substitutes for principal leader behavior: An exploratory study. *Educational Administration Quarterly, 22*(2), 23-42.

Pitner, N. J. (1987). Principles of quality staff development: Lessons for administrator training. In J. Murphy & P. Hallinger (Eds.), *Approaches to administrative training in education* (pp. 28-43). Albany: SUNY Press.

Pitner, N. J. (1990, September). *Reinventing school leadership* (pp. 129-131) [Working memo prepared for the Reinventing School Leadership Conference]. Cambridge, MA: National Center for Educational Leadership.

Popper, S. H. (1982, Winter). An advocate's case for the humanities in preparation programs for school administration. *Journal of Educational Administration, 20*(1), 12-22.

Popper, S. H. (1987). *Pathways to the humanities in educational administration.* Tempe, AZ: University Council for Educational Administration.

Powell, A. G., Farrar, E., & Cohen, D. K. (1985). *The shopping mall high school: Winners and losers in the educational marketplace.* Boston: Houghton-Mifflin.

Prestine, N. A., & LeGrand, B. (1990, April). *Cognitive learning theory and the preparation of educational administrators: Implications for practice and policy.* Paper presented at the annual meeting of the American Educational Research Association, Boston.

Purpel, D. E. (1989). *The moral and spiritual crises in education: A curriculum for justice and compassion in education.* Granby, MA: Bergin & Garvey.

Quality Education for Minorities Project. (1990). *Education that works: An action plan for the education of minorities.* Cambridge: MIT Press.

Rallis, S. F. (1990). Professional teachers and restructured schools: Leadership challenges. In B. Mitchell & L. L. Cunningham (Eds.), *Educational leadership and changing contexts of families, communities, and schools* (Eighty-ninth NSSE yearbook, Part II, pp. 184-209). Chicago: University of Chicago Press.

Ratsoy, E. W. (1989, March). *Research on administrative behavior: Implications for the academic education of administrators.* Paper presented at the annual meeting of the American Educational Research Association, San Francisco.

Ravitch, D. (1991, May). Multiculturalism: An exchange. *Network News and Views, 10*(5), 20-24.

Reed, D. B. (1991, April). *An invitation to share craft knowledge: Students as case researchers and writers.* Paper presented at the annual meeting of the American Educational Research Association, Chicago.

Reyes, P., & Capper, C. A. (1991, November). Urban principals: A critical perspective on the context of minority student dropout. *Educational Administration Quarterly, 27*(4), 530-557.

Roberts, L. (1990, September). *Reinventing school leadership* (pp. 132-136) [Working memo prepared for the Reinventing School Leadership Conference]. Cambridge, MA: National Center for Educational Leadership.

Rogers, J. S., & Polkinghorn, R. (in press). The inquiry process in the accelerated school: A Deweyan approach to school renewal. In H.

Levin (Ed.), *Accelerating the education of at-risk students*. New York: Falmer Press.

Rossmiller, R.A. (1985, Winter). Some contemporary trends and their implications for the preparation of educational administrators. *UCEA Review, 27*(1), 2-3.

Sanford, R. A. L. H. (1990, September). *Reinventing school leadership* (pp. 144-145) [Working memo prepared for the Reinventing School Leadership Conference]. Cambridge, MA: National Center for Educational Leadership.

Schlechty, P. C. (1990). *Schools for the 21st century: Leadership imperatives for educational reform*. San Francisco: Jossey-Bass.

Scribner, J. D. (1991, Winter). Liberating educational administration from hedgehog thinking: A planning proposal for the new millenium. *UCEA Review, 32*(1), 4-7, 12.

Sedlack, M. W., Wheeler, C. W., Pullin, D. C., & Cusick, P. A. (1986). *Selling students short: Classroom bargains and academic reform in the American high school*. New York: Teachers College Press.

Seeley, D. S. (1980, February). *The bankruptcy of service delivery*. Paper presented at the Foundation Lunch Group: Panel on Children, at the Edwin Gould Foundation for Children, New York City.

Seeley, D. S. (1988, February). A new vision for public education. *Youth Policy, 10*(2), 34-36.

Sergiovanni, T. J. (1984). Developing a relevant theory of administration. In T. J. Sergiovanni & J. E. Corbally (Eds.), *Leadership and organizational culture: New perspectives on administrative theory and practice* (pp. 275-291). Urbana: University of Illinois Press.

Sergiovanni, T. J. (1989a). Mystics, neats, and scruffies: Informing professional practice in educational administration. *The Journal of Educational Administration, 27*(2), 7-21.

Sergiovanni, T. J. (1989b). Value-driven schools: The amoeba theory. In H. J. Walberg & J. J. Lane (Eds.), *Organizing for learning: Toward the 21st century* (pp. 31-40). Reston, VA: National Association of Secondary School Principals.

Sergiovanni, T. J. (1991a, March). The dark side of professionalism in educational administration. *Phi Delta Kappan, 72*(7), 521-526.

Sergiovanni, T. J. (1991b). *The principalship: A reflective practice perspective* (2nd ed.). Boston: Allyn & Bacon.

Sergiovanni, T. J., Burlingame, M., Coombs, F. D., & Thurston, P. W. (1987). *Educational governance and administration* (2nd ed.). Englewood Cliffs, NJ: Prentice-Hall.

Shakeshaft, C. (1988). Women in educational administration: Implications for training. In D. E. Griffiths, R. T. Stout, & P. R. Forsyth

(Eds.), *Leaders for America's schools* (pp. 403-416). Berkeley, CA: McCutchan.

Shakeshaft, C. (1990, September). *Reinventing school leadership* (pp. 147-150) [Working memo prepared for the Reinventing School Leadership Conference]. Cambridge, MA: National Center for Educational Leadership.

Shattuck, R. (1960). What is pataphysics? *Evergreen Review* (13), 1-4.

Silver, P. F. (1974, June). Some apparent trends in preparatory programs for educational administrators. *UCEA Newsletter, 15*(5), 20-25.

Silver, P. F. (1978a). Some areas of concern in administrator preparation. In P. F. Silver & D. W. Spuck (Eds.), *Preparatory programs for educational administrators in the United States* (pp. 202-215). Columbus, OH: University Council for Educational Administration.

Silver, P. F. (1978b). Trends in program development. In P. F. Silver & D. W. Spuck (Eds.), *Preparatory programs for educational administrators in the United States* (pp. 178-201). Columbus: University Council for Educational Administration.

Silver, P. F. (1982). Administrator preparation. In H. E. Mitzel (Ed.), *Encyclopedia of educational research* (5th ed., Vol. 1, pp. 49-59). New York: Free Press.

Silver, P. F. (1985a, January). *The case for case records in school administration.* Unpublished manuscript. Urbana-Champaign: University of Illinois.

Silver, P. F. (1985b, September). Problems in school administration: A preliminary typology. *APEX Case Report, 2*(1), 1-6.

Silver, P. F. (1986, Summer). Case records: A reflective practice approach to administrator development. *Theory Into Practice, 25*(3), 161-167.

Silver, P. F. (1987). The center for advancing principal excellence (APEX): An approach to professionalizing educational administration. In J. Murphy & P. Hallinger (Eds.), *Approaches to administrative training* (pp. 67-82). Albany: SUNY Press.

Silver, P. F., & Spuck, D. W. (1978). *Preparatory programs for educational administrators in the United States.* Columbus, OH: University Council for Educational Administration.

Sirotnik, K. A. (1989). The schools as the center of change. In T. J. Sergiovanni & J. H. Moore (Eds.), *Schooling for tomorrow: Directing reforms to issues that count* (pp. 89-113). Boston: Allyn & Bacon.

Sizer, T. R. (1984). *Horace's compromise: The dilemma of the American high school.* Boston: Houghton-Mifflin.

Soder, R. (1988, December). Standardizing the education of educators: What we can learn from other professors. *Phi Delta Kappan, 70*(4), 299-305.

Spady, W. G. (1988, October). Organizing for results: The basis of authentic restructuring and reform. *Educational Leadership, 46*(2), 4-8.

Spaedy, M. (1990, September). *Reinventing school leadership* (pp. 156-159) [Working memo prepared for the Reinventing School Leadership Conference]. Cambridge, MA: National Center for Educational Leadership.

Starratt, R. J. (1991, May). Building an ethical school: A theory for practice in educational leadership. *Educational Administration Quarterly, 27*(2), 185-202.

Stigler, J. W., & Stevenson, H. W. (1991, Spring). How Asian teachers polish each lesson. *American Educator, 15*(1), 12-20, 43-47.

Stout, R. T. (1973). *New approaches to recruitment and selection of educational administrators.* (ERIC/CEM state-of-the-knowledge series, number 18; UCEA monograph series, number 5). Danville, IL: Interstate.

Sykes, G., & Elmore, R. F. (1989). Making schools more manageable. In J. Hannaway & R. L. Crowson (Eds.), *The politics of reforming school administrations* (pp. 77-94). New York: Falmer Press.

Thompson, T. E. (1990, September). *Reinventing school leadership* (pp. 161-165) [Working memo prepared for the Reinventing School Leadership Conference]. Cambridge, MA: National Center for Educational Leadership.

Tonnsen, S. (1990). *Reinventing school leadership* (pp. 167-170) [Working memo prepared for the Reinventing School Leadership Conference]. Cambridge, MA: National Center for Educational Leadership.

Twentieth Century Fund. (1983). *Making the grade.* New York: Author.

Twombly, S., & Ebmeier, H. (1989, December). *Educational administration programs: The cash cow of the university?* (Notes on Reform, No. 4). Charlottesville, VA: National Policy Board for Educational Administration.

Tyack, D. B. (1974). *One best system.* Cambridge, MA: Harvard University Press.

Tyack, D. B., & Cummings, R. (1977). Leadership in American public schools before 1954: Historical configurations and conjectures. In L. L. Cunningham, W. G. Hack, & R. O. Nystrand (Eds.), *Educational administration: The developing decades* (pp. 46-66). Berkeley, CA: McCutchan.

Tyack, D. B., & Hansot, E. (1982). *Managers of virtue: Public school leadership in America, 1920-1980.* New York: Basic Books.

U.S. Department of Education. (1987). *Principal selection guide.* Washington, DC: U.S. Department of Education.

Valverde, L. A., & Brown, F. (1988). Influences on leadership development among racial and ethnic minorities. In N. J. Boyan (Ed.), *Handbook of research on educational administration* (pp. 143-157). New
York: Longman.
Vazquez, A. (1990, September). *Reinventing school leadership* (pp. 172-
174) [Working memo prepared for the Reinventing School Leadership Conference]. Cambridge, MA: National Center for Educational
Leadership.
Wagstaff, L. H., & Gallagher, K. S. (1990). Schools, families, and communities: Idealized images and new realities. In B. Mitchell & L. L.
Cunningham (Eds.), *Educational leadership and changing contexts of
families, communities, and schools* (pp. 91-117). Chicago: University
of Chicago Press.
Walker, W. G. (1984, Fall). Administrative narcissism and the tyranny
of isolation: Its decline and fall, 1954-1984. *Educational Administration Quarterly, 20*(4), 6-23.
Walker, W. G. (1991, April). *Tight ship to tight flotilla: The first century of
scholarship in educational administration.* Paper presented at the
annual meeting of the American Educational Research Association, Chicago.
Waller, W. (1932). *The sociology of teaching.* New York: John Wiley.
Walton, J. (1962). The education of educational administrators. In J.
Culbertson & S. Hencley (Eds.), *Preparing administrators: New perspectives* (pp. 89-101). Columbus, OH: University Council for Educational Administration.
Wasley, P. A. (1991, Fall). Stirring the chalkdust: Changing practices in
essential schools. *Teachers College Record, 93*(1), 28-58.
Watkins, J. M., & Lusi, S. F. (1989). *Facing the essential tensions: Restruc-
turing from where you are.* Paper presented at the annual meeting of
the American Educational Research Association, San Francisco.
Watson, B. C. (1977). Issues confronting educational administrators,
1954-1974. In L. L. Cunningham, W. G. Hack, & R. O. Nystrand
(Eds.), *Educational administration: The developing decades* (pp. 67-94).
Berkeley, CA: McCutchan.
Weick, K. E., & McDaniel, R. R. (1989). How professional organizations
work: Implications for school organization and management. In T.
J. Sergiovanni & J. H. Moore (Eds.), *Schooling for tomorrow: Directing
reforms to issues that count* (pp. 330-355). Boston: Allyn & Bacon.
Weindling, D., & Earley, P. (1987, November). The first years of head-
ship—toward better practice. *Educational Research, 29*(3), 202-212.
Wengert, E. S. (1962). Preparing school administrators: Some problems and issues. In J. Culbertson & S. Hencley (Eds.), *Preparing*

administrators: New perspectives (pp. 35-59). Columbus, OH: University Council for Educational Administration.

Wiggins, G. (1989, April). Teaching to the (authentic) test. *Educational Leadership, 46*(7), 41-47.

Willis, Q. (1980, July). The work activity of school principals: An observational study. *Journal of Educational Administration, 18*(1), 27-54.

Willower, D. J. (1983, Summer). Evolutions in the professorship: Past philosophy, future. *Educational Administration Quarterly, 19*(3), 179-200.

Willower, D. J. (1987, Winter). Inquiry into educational administration: The last twenty-five years and the next. *The Journal of Education Administration, 25*(1), 12-28.

Willower, D. J. (1988). Synthesis and projection. In N. J. Boyan (Ed.), *Handbook of research on educational administration* (pp. 729-747). New York: Longman.

Wimpelberg, R. K. (1990, September). *Reinventing school leadership* (pp. 176-178) [Working memo prepared for the Reinventing School Leadership Conference]. Cambridge, MA: National Center for Educational Leadership.

Wise, A. E. (1989). Professional teaching: A new paradigm for the management of education. In T. J. Sergiovanni & J. H. Moore (Eds.), *Schooling for tomorrow: Directing reforms to issues that count* (pp. 301-310). Boston: Allyn & Bacon.

Wolf, D., Bixby, J., Glenn, J., & Gardner, H. (1991). To use their minds well: Investigating new forms of student assessment. In G. G. Grant (Ed.), *Review of Research in Education* (Vol. 17, pp. 31-74). Washington, DC: American Educational Research Association.

Wright, L. V. (1990, September). *Reinventing school leadership* (pp. 185-186) [Working memo prepared for the Reinventing School Leadership Conference]. Cambridge, MA: National Center for Educational Leadership.

Wynn, R. (1957). Organization and administration of the professional program. In R. F. Campbell & R. T. Gregg (Eds.), *Administrative behavior in education* (pp. 464-509). New York: Harper.

Wynn, R. (1972). *Unconventional methods and materials for preparing educational administrators.* (ERIC/CEM state-of-the-knowledge series, number 15; UCEA monograph series, number 2). Danville, IL: Interstate.

Zeichner, K. M., & Tabachnich, B. R. (1991). Reflections on reflective teaching. In B. R. Tabachnich & K. M. Zeichner (Eds.), *Issues and practices in inquiry-oriented teacher education.* London: Falmer Press.

Index